MW01015067

A MASTER GUIDE TO INCOME PROPERTY BROKERAGE

Boost Your Income By Selling Commercial and Income Properties

Fourth Edition

JOHN M. PECKHAM III, CCIM, CIPS, RECS

WILEY

John Wiley & Sons, Inc.

ISBN-13: 978-0-471-74915-8 (cloth)
ISBN-10: 0-471-74915-x (cloth)

10 9 8 7 6 5 4 3 2 1

CONTENTS

CONTENTS

Contents

CONTENTS

It is tough to acknowledge all those who have contributed to my real estate education. I guess I would have to start with my many friends from the CCIM Institute, the Greater Boston Real Estate Board, the Massachusetts Association of Realtors, the National Association of Realtors, and the many members of the Real Estate Cyberspace Society, who have exchanged ideas and shared their expertise with me over the years.

Real estate people are unique that way. And if there is anything I enjoy more than selling real estate, it is reciprocating the kindness of those who have shared ideas with me—by speaking to groups and conducting seminars around the country on the subject of income property brokerage and using the tools contained in this Guide.

This fourth edition is particularly meaningful because it brings together the updated time proven basics of the previous editions with all the new and powerful tools that cyberspace has brought to this specialty. The two together will give you a strong competitive advantage in the field. Once you have finished Chapter 14 (How to Sell Like a Giant Using Cyberspace Tools), I would suggest that you go to http://www.REcyber.com and consider joining with over 10,000 other real estate pros who use these powerful tools to put them way out in front of the pack!

I want to convey my special thanks to Ryan Barney and Christopher Davis, my valued "virtual assistants" and to Gene Osborne and Tom Feeley, certified public accountants, for their constant guidance over the years and for their specific help with this new edition of the Guide. Also to my valued legal guru Harris Baseman who has sometimes rightfully managed to curb my enthusiasm and even while doing so has inspired me to close many unique transactions. In addition my thanks to the editorial gurus Laurie Harding and Brian Neill at John Wiley & Sons, Inc. and Susan Dodson at Graphic Composition, Inc. for their guidance and help in producing this fourth edition.

And of course, my love to my wonderful wife Ann and my daughter Holly for their patience and love during this update.

And finally to each of the earlier readers of this Guide who often let me know how it has changed their life.

1. This new edition is particularly important to you because it provides you with the new cyberspace tools that will give you an immediate edge on those who have been practicing this specialty for years. Combine these with the practical and tested methods in this guide and you are sure to multiply your income many fold—and have fun doing it!

2. It gives you a detailed rundown on the *various types of income property;* shows the type that is most sought after, and why; and gives you the guidelines to follow in every case for the greatest profit.

3. It details everything you must look for in the property itself to make it pay off for you. (Unlike residential property, an income property can be run-down, ugly, located in a deteriorating neighborhood, but still profitable for the shrewd investor—and easily salable for the astute broker.)

4. It shows you how to maximize the impact of special *tax advantages* uniquely available through income property. It includes an eye-opening tax analysis chart, a real sales clincher—especially since tax savings and tax benefits mean important new sources of available income.

5. It demonstrates how to calculate quickly if a property has been *priced* at the right level—and shows you what to do if it hasn't. You get proven rules of thumb, surefire guidelines to action pricing, and, most important, the *Action Price Level*—a pricing technique that's as simple and revolutionary as the point-count system Goren gave to bridge.

6. It explains the special *financing* techniques that can boost your sales and profits—but that require no more than simple arithmetic to work out. Sources of financing, leverage, mortgages, depreciation, tax-savings—and much more—are all covered in simple, easy-to-follow everyday terms. Financing know-how is very often the key to large profits in real estate. The Guide shows how to understand and use it the *easy* way.

7. It illustrates the most vital single *sales aid* to income property sales—the operating statement—and gives actual examples to show you how to use it.

8. It highlights the dramatic income property *advertising* techniques that really pay off: the three basic rules for sales-building ads, the big "money words" that work like magic, the dynamic eye-catchers that make your ads stand out wherever they appear.

9. It shows you how to find the *action buyers* for your properties. It gives 13 immediate sources of buyers, and tells about the 10 classic buyer types, and how to deal with each.

10. It tells how to *qualify prospects,* how to handle interviews, and how to cash in on the three concerns that motivate *all* prospects.

11. It explains exactly how to *show income property* to make the prospect want it. Here are six strong selling points you can apply to *any* property, five dynamic showing strategies, and nine possible trouble spots that you not only neutralize, but use to your advantage.

12. It demonstrates how to handle the tricky questions that prospects often ask, and tells how to turn client *objections* into positive selling points.

13. It goes into the latest techniques for making profitable *condominium conversions,* and tells how to succeed in this expanding field. It shows how to evaluate a property's suitability for conversion, how to set up a conversion "team," how to advertise your services, and how to handle *commercial* condominiums.

14. It gives you a method of *closing sales* that's virtually foolproof, a proven-in-action technique that turns prospects into buyers on the spot. This is where theory is converted into cash, and this master closing method puts the cash in *your* pocket.

15. It provides a systematic yet flexible *20-week timetable* you can use for successfully entering the income-brokerage field—and making the most of its spectacular profit opportunities.

In short, *A Master Guide to Income Property Brokerage* shows how to make a fortune in an exciting and growing field!

Your Golden Opportunity for Big New Commissions and Profits in Income Property Brokerage

Why This Guide Is So Important to You

The average income property sales price runs well into six figures—and often into seven or eight figures. This is one of the very few fields where you can leave home in the morning with no sales in sight, and return in the evening with a possible $800,000 sale well launched.

Income property salespeople, however, are a realistic lot. They recognize, just as the residential salesperson does, that the bread-and-butter sales, by themselves, will earn them a very respectable income. When they work steadily on these sales, they will gain the experience and skill needed to give greater and quicker assurance of success on the $5,000,000 to $20 million sales.

If you are already engaged in income property brokerage, this Guide will give you proven techniques that will beef up your income and your success. Or if you are now engaged in residential sales, commercial-industrial leasing, or even an avocation outside of real estate, you can read here how to use the simple secrets of income property brokerage. Don't ever let anyone tell you that selling income property, such as apartment houses or stores, shopping centers or office buildings, is difficult. It isn't. The figures sometimes sound a little overwhelming to some people; but don't let these frighten you one bit. Simply move the decimal point a place or two to the right on the figures you're using today, and it will all look familiar. Get ready to move that decimal point on the commissions, too!

A Word about Big Commissions

Commission rates on income property sales are negotiable and can range from one to ten percent or more, depending on individual circumstances. Using five percent, for example, the commission on a sale of $800,000 is $40,000 . . . on $1,800,000 it is $90,000 . . . on $9,800,000 it is $490,000.

In some areas, the commission rates scale down somewhat on sales over a set level, but the foregoing will give you some indication of the commission amounts we are discussing. Some income property salespeople earn as much on one sale as the average residential salesperson earns in ten years!

If it's not all that difficult to earn these commissions, is it worth a try? *You bet it is!*

I hope you will look upon this Guide as a personal visit to my office to discuss the practical methods involved in successful income property brokerage. I have prepared the contents as though I were writing it for my own brother or best friend. I have tried to keep the contents practical and usable, and have avoided theory and conjecture.

For the sake of clear, simple explanation, I have concentrated on the most common, understandable, and profitable form of income property: the apartment building. But the techniques described apply equally to office buildings, hotels, store blocks, and all other major types of income-producing real estate.

Combine the information between these covers with your native ability and you should profit immensely. When you do, that will also be my reward.

Residential Sales—A Fine Background for Income Brokerage

An understanding of residential sales will help you in selling income property; the two procedures are similar in many ways. The residential salesperson is charged with matching prospective homeowners with a house that satisfies their needs, at a price they can afford. The income broker is also charged with a matching chore. His job is to match an investor with the property that best accomplishes his or her financial goals, within an acceptable price range.

A residential salesperson would not feel strange walking into a moderate sized income property office. Many times the physical layout is much the same as what he or she is used to. Each salesperson is located at a desk with a phone and, usually, a side chair. Each has a listing book, prospect cards, an appointment book, and a computer. The salesperson may be busy on the phone answering calls on yesterday's ads. He or she may be interviewing a prospect, or may be filling out a listing sheet, or might be putting on a coat to leave with a prospect to inspect a property. In short, the scene could look much like the residential salesperson's own office. These people are involved in the same basic chores as residential salespeople. But of course there are some differences.

The Unique Benefits of Income Property Brokerage

The Hours are Better. There are certainly some areas where the income property salesperson's job and routine differ from other kinds of brokerage. He or she normally works a five-day, Monday-to-Friday work week, and is usually not involved in night-time or weekend selling chores. The salesperson's prospects are normally available for appointments during normal working hours.

Keep in mind that residential buyers and sellers are often forced by circumstances to make a move. That is seldom the case with an investor. His motivation is usually more optional and less urgent: He will buy if he sees the right opportunity, and he will sell if he can put his equity to better use. Remember too, that normally, the income property buyer does not intend to live in the property he acquires. He does not have to concern himself with amenities needed to please him and his family. This fact opens the door for him to acquire property in almost any reasonable location, provided the building makes dollars and sense!

You'll Be Dealing with Affluent and Business-Like Buyers. One of the very pleasant differences in our specialty lies in the type of clientele you will be dealing with. Residential salespeople must quite frequently deal with buyers of limited means—buyers with only a modest amount of cash available to buy a house. Many times they have marginal credit ratings and low incomes. This at times can make selling houses a nerve-wracking business.

Income property investors, however, are generally people with substantial cash assets. They also are generally accustomed to conducting their affairs in a business-like manner. They understand the economic realities, and how one must often change to be successful. There are exceptions, of course, and occasionally you must deal with a buyer of limited means; but he is usually willing to speculate and, as you will find later in this Guide, he can become a very valuable client.

The fact that income brokerage does not involve "user" or "occupancy" requirements means that this specialty involves many different techniques and approaches from those in commercial, industrial, and land sales.

Matching Properties and Prospects the IPB Way. In residential sales, the objective is to match a prospective buyer's requirements with one (or more) of the many listings the broker has on file. That is the residential broker's most pressing task: to *select* from the many available listings, the house which best fills the buyer's stated or unstated requirements—and to do it fast, before another office does!

The residential broker's principal—and most challenging—task is to *find a buyer.* The income broker's main job, on the other hand, is to *find a seller.* This difference of emphasis, of course, is determined by supply and demand. In any business, you must spend most of your time looking for what you have least of. Expressed in arbitrary percentages, when a residential broker lines up a good *buyer,* a sale is 75 percent made. When an investment broker lines up a good *property,* the sale is 75 percent made.

Understanding this, it is obvious that the selecting function of the income property broker is concerned with the buyer. The broker searches for the listing (the seller), and then selects from a large file of investors those he or she thinks will most likely buy it.

This use of terms can serve as well: we search for what we lack—and we select from what we have. This is not to imply that when a new prospect contacts the office we do not review our listing files and "select" possible investments for him. We do. But sales are rarely made this way. More often than not, it is just a qualifying step preliminary to putting his objectives in our file of buyers, to be contacted later when the right property turns up. Most of our sales take place when we call the prospect back in a few days, a week, or even months later and say, "Mr. Jones, we have just located an investment that meets your requirements. I would suggest that we get together this afternoon to go over the details."

You Can Work GRADUALLY Into this Lucrative Field. In Chapter 16 you will find a 20-week timetable showing exactly how to get started in this field without interfering with your present schedule. Combine the fact that you can ease into the field and increase activity according to your own chosen pace with the practical contents of this Guide, and there can be no reason to delay the start of a most rewarding adventure!

Who Are the Most Successful Income Property Salespeople?

Income property brokerage is so lucrative that residential brokers in all parts of the country are expanding their operations to include this money-making specialty. In a little suburb of Boston, for example, two of the leading residential firms have both eased several of their salespeople into this specialty. Both have reported substantial increases in their sales volumes only months after taking this progressive step. Income property brokerage will help residential brokers not only to survive, but to prosper.

Many residential salespeople have also made a fast, easy and profitable switch to income brokerage by joining a firm specializing in this field. Over the years, our best salespeople generally have come to us from successful careers in residential selling. And about half of our "big producers" originally came to us from the residential sales field. None of them had any previous experience with income property sales.

Other successful income property salespeople have come from almost every profession imaginable. The most common immediate background, of course, is residential sales; but those from other previous fields have included lawyers, engineers, property owners, builders, stockbrokers, insurance brokers, businesspeople who have sold or liquidated their own business—the list is limitless!

Throughout this guide you will find that in most hypothetical examples and anecdotes I refer to the male gender. This is for no other reason than ease of reading. I freely admit that there are many salespeople—men and women—who can sell circles around me given the tools in this Guide.

You will find, as you continue on in this Guide, that the opportunities for you in the next ten years are staggering. We are entering into an era of specialization, and by building a knowledge of successful income brokerage now and applying these practical and tested techniques in the field, you will launch yourself into a long and increasingly rewarding career.

CHAPTER 1

How to Profit Most from Different Types of Income Property

Take a few minutes to look at what you will have to sell. Just what types of properties do we classify as income property?

Income property brokerage is a specialty within a specialty. First, you must understand the difference between real estate investments and income property.

How an Income Property Differs from a Real Estate Investment

Income property is to real estate investments as an apple is to fruit. Income properties (apples) are a kind of real estate investment (fruit); however, not all real estate investments (fruits) are income properties (apples). What makes the difference? Let's look at each in order.

- *Real Estate Investments (in general).* Any form of real estate can be bought for investment purposes. This includes raw land, houses, apartment houses, condominiums, vacant warehouses; in short, any real estate, anywhere, can be bought for investment. Ten thousand acres of swamp in Brazil—vast acres of desert land—a house lot in ski country—a 40-story skyscraper—all real estate investments!

- *Income Property (a real estate investment that generates rental income).* The name itself includes the element of *income.* In short, income property includes a real estate improvement which generates *rental income* out of which must be paid the regularly recurring operating expenses (i.e., real estate taxes, insurance, heat, payroll, etc.). All financing costs (principal and interest payments) must also be paid from the rental income. What is left over is the "cash flow" or "net return" on the owner's invested capital.

Why Income Property Is So Attractive to Investors

A vacant industrial building can be bought for investment, but not for current income. The same industrial building with rent-paying tenants can be bought for *income.* Vacant land can be bought for investment, but unless leased, cannot be bought for income. The main reason that income property makes such an attractive brokerage commodity is that the investor can often purchase it with relatively low cash down, finance 60 to 90 percent (sometimes more), and obtain enough income from the tenants to pay the operating expenses, the cost of financing, and give him a *current* return on his invested capital. We will discover that even when there is insufficient income to cover all of these costs, it is quite possible, because of our tax laws, to enjoy a positive *after-tax* cash flow.

Potential investors for *non-income*-producing real estate (such as land) are in much shorter supply, because they must not only have 50 to 100 percent cash available for the initial purchase, but must also have sufficient capital to carry the year-to-year expenses—such as taxes—until the time comes to develop or sell their investment. For every such investor there are several thousand investors who are ready, willing, and able to buy income-producing properties.

With this understanding, let's look at some specific types of income property.

Types of Income Property

Apartments

The most common and best understood form of income property is the apartment house. The apartment house can run from the frame two-family house up to the 500-unit apartment complex. Newer apartment houses are generally of brick construction, and range from the suburban *garden type* apartment house to the urban high-rise apartment building.

Older apartment houses of brick construction are usually located in urban areas (although there are a few in older suburban areas). They are often referred to as elevatored buildings or *walk-ups* (without elevators).

Smaller apartment houses of frame construction are scattered throughout both urban and suburban areas. These are generally considered less desirable than brick apartment house investments, but may be just right for certain types of investors who want higher cash flow.

Many larger older homes have been converted into apartment houses. This type of conversion gains momentum as zoning laws are changed to reflect increasing housing demands. If well located, these can make excellent investments. The illustration above shows a suburban stucco mansion that was converted into luxury apartments. It will probably still be standing when some of today's new apartment buildings are long plowed under. This building was purchased in the mid-1960s for $68,000 with no cash down. It sold in the 1970s for $272,000, and was converted into condominiums in the 1980s. Some individual units today sell for over a half a million dollars.

3

Office Buildings

In time, you may want to add office buildings to your inventory of income properties. They are not so easily managed or understood by the unsophisticated investor; however, they comprise an integral segment of income property offerings. The most common type of office building is the older urban multistory building. In most urban areas, there is a great upsurge in demolition of older structures and construction of new ultra-modern office buildings. Suburban areas are now dotted with smaller office buildings often called *professional buildings.* They are relatively easy to manage and make prime candidates for income property listings.

Retail Blocks

A *store block* may be located in heavily populated urban areas, or may comprise the entire downtown of a small suburban locality. They are made up of anywhere from one to a dozen or so retail stores, usually abutting each other and under one roof. Each store usually has its own heating system. Some of the strip store blocks in marginal locations are suffering from the heavyweight competition of the shopping centers. However, store blocks in low-vacancy areas, in prestige towns, or in high foot-traffic areas make sound acquisitions for the investor who doesn't want to be bothered with apartment-house-type complaints, providing the investor is aware that a vacant store takes considerably longer to fill than a vacant apartment and is willing to take the risk inherent to this situation.

Shopping Centers

Shopping centers are a glorified form of retail block, usually located on a large parcel of land with self-contained parking facilities, and usually leased in part to highly rated retail concerns. Shopping center investors are a sophisticated lot and must, by the nature of the investment, be well versed in the intricacies of complicated lease negotiations.

Industrial Buildings

Industrial buildings leased to one or more tenants make excellent investments; however, this is a specialized type of acquisition, and owners of industrial buildings are well versed in negotiating with large business concerns and in the pitfalls of improper lease protection in various areas. Usually an older industrial building will provide a higher-than-average return, and will additionally allow the owner to control strategic land for future development.

New industrial parks now dot the suburban landscape. Many times the developer of an industrial park will sell individual buildings or, on completion, the entire complex of leased buildings. These newer industrial buildings on long-term leases make excellent investments.

Other Special Situations

The income property broker may be called upon to market other special types of income property, including special purpose properties such as post office buildings on lease to the United States Government, gas station sites on lease to major oil companies, ground leases, parking lots—in short, any specialized form of real estate, including single-family homes and condos, which is leased and producing income.

The average income property broker will avoid excessive involvement in properties that require a high degree of business management. Included in this category, for example, are hotels, motels, nursing homes, marinas—and even cemeteries. Also, generally included in this category are restaurants, taverns, and any other form of business where the major portion of the income is produced not by the real estate itself, but by time-consuming management.

Single Tenant Net Leased Properties

Properties that are leased on a relatively long-term basis (10 to 20 years or longer) offer a special opportunity to income property brokers. Usually some good solid experience with other more common property types will provide an agent with a background to deal successfully with this type of product. Single tenant net leased properties are often quite attractive for certain specialized tax situations, are generally management free, can be relatively risk free, and lend themselves to online marketing as discussed later in this guide.

Types of Income Property That Comprise the Bulk of Sales

The average income property broker finds that his time is spent primarily on the sale of apartment houses because, as we have seen, the average investor understands them better and manages them more capably without a high degree of specialized knowledge.

Over the years our sales breakdown is roughly as follows:

Apartment houses	70%
Retail blocks and shopping centers	15%
Office buildings	10%
Other	5%

Should You "Draw a Line" in Taking Listings?

Many brokers who want to enter the income brokerage field ask, "Just where do you draw the line when it comes to listing?"

To answer this properly I should say that, if you are going to augment your residential brokerage business with income property brokerage, then you would not draw any lower limit. A two-family dwelling would certainly be within your selling domain.

In larger offices specializing in income property brokerage, a line must be drawn, however, or the brokers would be swamped with listings that are outside their specialty. Many never accept a listing on a single-family house—no matter how big or desirable and no matter how high-priced. There is a great temptation, on the part of new brokers who have come into this specialty from residential sales, to take listings on expensive homes they run across in the course of normal business. Eventually they learn that, with their specialized knowledge and administrative support, they are much better off in terms of income and satisfaction when they stick to their specialty.

Time Consumers

You may want to consider avoiding listings on going businesses—such as restaurants—or any other type of real estate that does not generate income in and of itself. Occasionally, we will accept a listing on a motel, hotel, or on land explaining to the owner that we can quarterback a contemplated sale of these types of property working with a broker who specializes in them.

Aside from apartments, which will be discussed shortly, the other types of income property—such as store blocks, shopping centers, office buildings, and industrial buildings—are all priced high enough so that we need not set a lower limit.

The important thing to remember, whatever your specialty, is to concentrate on *profitable* properties—and to be careful of time consumers!

Why Size and Distance of the Property Is So Important

Small apartment buildings pose a problem to the income property specialist. We do not usually consider a two-, three-, or four-family dwelling as income property, but more as a private residence for an owner-occupant who wants additional income to offset his living expenses. We will accept a listing on a three- or four-family dwelling if it is very close to our office and in a high-demand area; however, because of the nature of our business, geographical considerations mean a lot. The farther from our office a property is located, the more difficult it is for us to inspire our agents to travel to it—unless it is a very substantial property.

There is one exception to our general rule of not accepting listings on two-, three-, and four-family properties. This occurs when a seller comes to us with several three-families in a package, and wants to sell. Even a small block of rented one-family units could bring a gross consideration that would make it well worth our efforts.

As a rule of thumb, the farther away a property is located, the larger it must be for us to accept the listing. The following illustration will give you some guidelines.

Distance	Minimum Price
4 blocks	$200,000
2 miles	$400,000
5 miles	$500,000
10 miles	$1,000,000
20 miles	$2,000,000
50 miles	$4,000,000
over 50 miles	$6,000,000+

The limitations are arbitrary, but are based on how much money a selling broker can earn in relation to time expended. Exceptions may occur when an unusually prime investment becomes available; then the area will expand. I know, however, that the limits will not expand much beyond the limits indicated above. I owned an exceptional waterview apartment building which today would be listed at around $800,000 and was located twenty miles from our office. If this property had been a two-to-five-mile drive from our office, it would have sold in four weeks after about ten showings. As it happened, though, my agents didn't show it twice in four months!

How to Use Your Efforts Most Profitably

Agents entering the income field often ask, "Where should I direct my efforts? What general type of property is easiest to deal with?"

Apartment buildings are the most productive in terms of total sales from time expended. As noted earlier, there are many more investors for apartments than for the other types of income properties. The average man or woman can understand renting an apartment to another individual, and can understand the relative simplicity of apartment-house leases. The average investor with the assistance of a qualified broker can easily analyze the income potential and operating expenses. On the other hand, they will often shy away from the complex operating procedures of large office buildings, shopping centers, and industrial buildings.

As you continue on in this Guide, you will find that generally we have used the apartment house in examples of how to apply most of the practical techniques given to you from chapter to chapter. This procedure is intentional, as apartment houses are so easily understood. Wherever a technique differs in its application to office buildings, store blocks, shopping centers, or any of the other various forms of income property, this difference is spelled out.

Keep in mind, however, that each of the methods you will learn generally applies to all types of income property. The methods of finding owners who will sell and of obtaining the listings are essentially the same. Pricing at the action level, financing, and setting up the operating statement involve the same basic procedures. The special benefits of ownership apply equally to all income property types. The techniques you will use in dealing with prospects while qualifying, showing the property, and closing the sale are all the same, whatever the type of property involved.

If there is an abundance of non-apartment income property in your area, simply apply the practical procedures in each chapter to that type of property. In most areas you will find that there is a greater abundance of apartment-house listings, and that the turnover in ownership is much greater than in other types. In any event, start with smaller buildings but, after some experience, be prepared to move on to big complexes. The brokerage procedures are exactly the same—the figures are just larger (and so are the commissions).

Cyberspace Marketing Tips

As you begin to use the special cyberspace marketing techniques contained in this Guide you will begin to appreciate the effect your ability to easily reach out across geographic boundaries and market areas will have on your selection of the types of properties you will list and sell.

You can use the Internet to see what properties are for sale by type. Just go to any search engine (Google is in vogue at this writing but others may come into vogue). Type in "apartments for sale." Today that search brought 623,000 results.

Narrow your search by typing "apartments for sale" + "Florida." That narrows your search to 36,500. Narrow your search again by typing "apartments for sale" + "Orlando." That narrows your search to 10,900. By zeroing in on the Internet you can identify the various types of income properties available and very quickly gather significant insights into the availability and characteristics of your potential inventory.

There are also several databases available online that provide specialty specific information. Current examples are those located at www.loopnet.com and www .ccimnet.com. The Real Estate CyberSpace Society maintains very thorough links to just about all industry for sale databases not only in the United States but also in many countries outside the United States. Because companies and links often change your best starting point is usually at: http://www.REcyber.com/ciproperties .html.

CHAPTER 2

Five Quick Ways to Find Property Owners Who Will Sell

As in any form of brokerage, we must have a product to sell. We need listings. We must know how to smoke out sellers—whether they know they fall into this category or not!

In income brokerage, there are two kinds of sellers: (1) those who want to sell and know it; and (2) those who want to sell but don't know it—*yet.*

In the next ten years over 50 percent of all the income property in my area (and probably in yours) will change hands. The broker who doesn't smoke out listings is the broker who will be envious when he sees that his competitor is making all the big sales.

Keep in mind that, *almost without exception,* every income property is for sale. This is because the investor has purchased for profit, and if the profit from a sale is sufficient, the owner will sell.

How to Begin

Let's assume for now that you have just decided to try selling income property, and you have no listings. Where do you start?

Well, if this is your first day at it, no one is likely to ring your telephone and ask: "Please help me sell my ten-unit apartment building on Main Street." Certainly no one will walk in and say: "Charley Jones tells me you did a wonderful job of selling his sixteen units on Elm Street. Would you be interested in helping me?"

So, without unsolicited calls based on your reputation, and referrals, you must roll up your sleeves and dig for owners who will sell.

Where to Find Prospective Sellers

It's really not difficult at all. Look quickly at the following twelve sources of listings. In the case of publications and lists you can access these in paper versions or online.

1. Newspapers	7. Tax rolls
2. Local trade journals	8. Advertisements
3. Local financial reporting papers	9. Blabbermouths
4. Membership in organizations	10. Blitzing
5. Owner lists	11. Newsletters
6. Telephone books	12. Newspaper columns

What Does It Cost?

The total annual cost for these sources, which can open the door to big commissions, is only about $700 in my Boston area. (It might be even less in yours.) This includes two Sunday papers each week, a fine trade journal, a comprehensive financial reporting paper, membership in an 800-member owner organization, and a list of all the owners in the downtown area. Items 6 through 10 are free!

Use these sources and your shelves will soon be flowing with merchandise to sell.

Open Listings—A Problem and a Challenge

Unfortunately, in many areas, open listings on income property are the rule rather than the exception. As professional real estate brokers, we owe it to ourselves and to the public to use every effort to obtain the protection of an exclusive right to sell. Any of the following listing sources can and should be converted to exclusive listing if at all possible.

Some time ago, I received the following letter from a stranger asking why he should give an exclusive listing. My answer to him is also shown. Use this as a guide to convert your open listings and listing sources, and you'll stand above the crowd.

QUESTION: I am moving to Vermont and wish to sell the apartment house I inherited in 1974. It is a 23-unit building in the Copley Square area of Boston. It looks as if there are several firms in Boston that do a good job selling this type of property. A broker from one of these firms is trying to talk me into letting his firm be the only one that can sell it. He says that under this arrangement I couldn't even sell it myself if I have a buyer, but would have to use him as a broker. Wouldn't it make more sense for me to hire several brokers? Why should I sign away my rights?

ANSWER: The broker is requesting an exclusive right to sell your property for several reasons, but primarily because he can represent you better with this protection. Many owners initially feel the way you do, but these people overlook the fact that with adequate protection the broker can roll up his sleeves and conduct a first-rate marketing job for you. He can spend money advertising your property. He can expend time, effort, and money in preparing a top-notch brochure. He is in a position, through his thorough knowledge of marketing income property, to work quickly and effectively on your behalf.

Make sure that the broker you select is willing to cooperate with all other brokers in order to obtain the best possible price for you. Ask him point-blank if he will cooperate. By selecting a broker on an exclusive basis who will cooperate, you have enlisted the aid of a specialist who will see that hundreds of other brokers are made aware of your offering, thus giving you a better chance to sell quickly at market value.

The dangers of not granting the request are manifold. Let me put it this way: doesn't it make more sense to enlist one firm to represent you and act on your behalf (including cooperating with any broker who can help achieve your price), than to hire several brokers who may engage in a tug of war to make the sale?

By granting the exclusive, you get one representative who can do an outstanding marketing job for you. By hiring several, you have no real representative—just a bunch of brokers working at odds with your purpose to sell at the best possible price.

A Broker's Alchemy—How to Turn Newspaper Pulp into Gold

Source 1: Newspapers. Invest a dollar or so every Sunday for your local newspaper. Read the real estate section from beginning to end. What do you look for? Right now, look at the reproduction on page 13 from a typical real estate page.

Competitors will assist you. See the picture with the explanatory caption? This was originally sent out as a news release by the broker who negotiated the sale. The published account of the transaction includes the names of the buyer, the seller, and the sales price. But what does this information mean to you in your search for listings?

From the newspaper account you know that the buyer, John Webster, now owns the property. We even have a picture of the building. It may come as a complete surprise to the residential broker that such a recent owner would even consider selling

Buron & Ross of Peckham Boston Sell
Lynn Apartment to Webster for $960,000

The Peckham Boston Company of Boston has announced the sale of this 24-unit brick apartment building located at 123 West Ocean Street, Lynn, Mass. The estate of Owen Morris sold the property to John Webster for $960,000. The sale was negotiated by Harry Buron and Leonard Ross.

his proud new acquisition. Remember, however, that in income brokerage we are dealing with profit as our prime motivation to action, and because of this, many a proud new owner will consider an immediate resale if it results in a profit to him.

Look again at the news account. The Morris Estate may well be selling off several parcels. This situation also requires some adjustment in the thought patterns of the residential broker. He sells a home for Mr. Smith, and it may be another five to seven years before he can serve Smith again. In the income property field, our relationship with a client is often continuing.

A Strategy That Can Earn Many Tens of Thousands in Commissions. I used the foregoing example for the purpose of driving this point home emphatically. The illustrated release was issued by my office one year in January. It happened that the seller was liquidating several parcels. An alert broker using the newspaper profitably could easily have contacted the seller; and because our listing was an open one, and because the owner was most anxious to sell the remaining six buildings, the broker would have had a real stack of merchandise to work on.

As it turned out, no one used Source 1 effectively, and from January to May, a period of five months, we sold the remaining buildings as well, and earned many tens of thousands of dollars in commissions.

How to Turn Buyers into Sellers, and Sellers into Buyers. I am sure that by now it has occurred to many residential brokers that in income property brokerage most prospective buyers are prospective sellers, and the same is true in reverse. Adjust your thinking immediately to this truth. After you have taken a listing from a seller, always find out what you can sell to him. While showing a property to a prospective buyer, always ask, "What can I sell for you, Mr. Buyer?" We will see later how this simple question can add tens of thousands of dollars to your income. The important point is that a good 50 percent of your time will and should be spent with prospects who are capable of both buying and selling in the same day!

Idea in Action: A broker in my firm had one client who in 12 months accounted for over $2,800,000 in sales—arranging both buying and selling. A second broker from our office accounted for over 80 percent of his annual sales volume with one client who bought and sold over $3 million in properties through our office.

Reminder: Use your newspapers effectively and you will be dealing with these active investors. Use them effectively and, ironically enough, the very brokers with whom you are competing will provide you with at least two or three good leads each week.

How to Find Hot Information about New Projects

Source 2: Local Trade Journals. Most metropolitan areas have a real estate journal. The *New England Real Estate Journal* is the one we subscribe to, advertise in, and read each week from cover to cover. There are several quite similar published throughout the country.

Your trade journal is extremely valuable not only because it is an excellent source for trends in income property activity, but because you can add another half-dozen possible sellers to your list each week. How? By reading published accounts of recent sales as pictured (which again are often provided by your competitor) and by studying accounts of construction projects under way. Many builders will consider a sale upon completion of their apartment or other income project, and will sometimes list even before the foundation is completed.

For example, a while back, we drew contracts to sell a 150-unit apartment building four months before its completion date. Don't overlook this excellent source of listings in your local trade journals.

Look for the Big Sales

Source 3: Local Financial Reporting Papers. Most metropolitan areas have a financial reporting paper which appears weekly and summarizes official reports of all real estate sales recorded in that area. The manner in which these transactions are reported is fairly standard across the country.

In the Boston area, our reporting paper is the excellent *Banker and Tradesman*. You can get the title and publishing source of the paper in your area by calling your local Board of Realtors, or by checking with your local bankers.

Of course, in reading the accounts of sales which occurred during the previous week, you will see many single-family sales and many land sales. The sales you are looking for are the big ones. When you spot a sale *over* $500,000, this will indicate the possibility that it's an income-producing property. From this report (and you will find many such reports in each week's paper), you have two listing leads—a new owner who might sell, and a seller who might have more to sell.

Be a Joiner—Your Colleagues Will Be Your Clients

Source 4: Membership in Organizations. In any metropolitan area there are several organizations in which membership will automatically give you direct access to many potential sellers.

Three examples of these organizations are:

1. Local and regional Boards of Realtors®.
2. Apartment owner organizations.
3. Fraternal organizations and women's leagues.

Membership in your local Board of Realtors should be considered a must. The benefits of membership are numerous, not the least of which is the fact that many of your fellow members can be future clients in selling their income property. I would estimate that over 60 percent of our active clients are licensed real estate brokers, and many of the active sellers have brokerage staffs themselves. You should try to achieve membership on committees of your local and state Realtor organizations. The rewards of such activity go far beyond the many listings you will uncover.

Apartment owners in most metropolitan areas band together in an organization or association. All of the members of these various regional associations of apartment house owners are potential sellers (or buyers). In Boston, the Rental Housing Association (R.H.A.) is the organization to which the great majority of apartment house owners in the area belong. Let us look at the R.H.A. as an example of these organizations. Membership in Boston's R.H.A. numbers around 800. This means that by belonging to an organization similar to this you automatically have common goals with and easy access to 800 potential sellers.

Look at it this way—if a sidewalk vendor approached you on the street and whispered, "I'll sell you a list of the names, addresses, and telephone numbers of the 800 most active investors in this area for peanuts," wouldn't you scramble for your checkbook?

Case in Point: By belonging to the Boston R.H.A. you receive, among many other things, a membership roster containing the names, addresses, and telephone numbers of the 800 most active investors in the area! And this is just a starter. Our owners' organization, as those in other areas do, distributes analyzed reports on pertinent legislation and how such legislation may affect the interests of the apartment house owner. Most important, though, is the fact that the R.H.A. sponsors periodic management clinics and social events where you, the broker, can come to know on a *personal* basis men and women who will sometime be interested in selling their apartment houses. By attending these functions and becoming active on R.H.A. committees, you will not only be advancing the cause of the real estate industry, but you will be gathering listings by the dozens!

Some fraternal organizations are founded along trade lines. In the Boston area, for example, there are two realty lodges. Let me say that membership in these organizations is considered an honor, and their primary function is not to provide business leads. However, I will add that it never hurts your chances of obtaining a listing when you are talking with a man whom you meet in brotherhood each month!

How to Find Out the Owners' Names

Source 5: Owner Lists. In many urban areas, a non-governmental organization publishes, street by street, a list of the owners of each property. For example, in Boston, the Greater Boston Real Estate Board each year publishes the *Book of Assessed Values* (BOAV).

The BOAV shows the total evaluation, then breaks it down into separate figures for land valuation and valuation of the building. The land area of the property is given also. This information is derived from records in the city tax office. Thousands of leads can be found in the BOAV alone. I have known brokers to take certain streets from the book where all buildings are known to be apartments and spend weeks contacting the owners.

You can find out from your local Board of Realtors whether there is such a non-government-published list of owners for your area. It is an extremely useful tool and worth whatever small cash outlay is required.

Don't Overlook the Yellow Pages

Source 6: Telephone Book, Yellow Pages. Don't overlook obvious sources. The Yellow Pages of the telephone book *do* "let your fingers do the walking." The Yellow Pages can put you in immediate contact with real estate people in your area. It lists not only brokers, but also real estate trusts and private owners.

Look under the classified heading *Apartments*. There you will find several hundred listings. Separate the obvious brokers and contact the people who indicate that they are owners. For example:

FROST REALTY TRUST
Owners-Managers
Modern furnished and unfurnished apartments

Back Bay–Beacon Hill
10 Northrodge Street
617-555-8161

In addition, many listings appear under the headings *Office Buildings* and *Shopping Centers.* A few well-selected calls from the Yellow Pages' listings will reap you great rewards in finding properties to sell now, or leads on potential sellers for later.

Look for Personal Contacts and Large Assessments

Source 7: Tax Rolls. Each city, town, or county publishes tax records. These records indicate to whom the tax bill on each property is sent, what kind of property is located at each address, and how much the assessment is.

You can take two approaches, the first of which is as easy as rolling off a log, namely, get to know the clerical help in the towns and cities within your operating area. A friendly chat with a secretary who is familiar with the tax records will many times reveal, for example, that "There are exactly 19 apartment houses in Springvale. Five of them are owned by Tom Smith, and I have a separate list of the rest that you can go over. By the way, Tom Smith wants to sell three of his!"

The second approach is merely to ask to look over the property tax rolls (which are public records and available to anyone). Once you have these records in front of you, look for the properties with the larger assessments, and note the type and the owner.

Don't Write Ads, Read Them

Source 8: Advertisements. As hard as it may be to believe this, the use of ads as a source of listings won't cost you a penny! I have found that buying ads to find people who are selling income property is a waste of money. It may be a useful approach in some forms of brokerage, but certainly not in our field. With this limitation in mind, how can ads help us find listings?

Study other people's ads. There are three types of advertisements important as sources of sellers:

- Ads from other brokers
- For Rent ads
- For-Sale-by-Owner ads

You will find them in all the publications we've mentioned, but the most important of these will be the real estate section of your newspaper.

Ads from Other Brokers. In our business of income property, we have seen that in many areas there are comparatively few exclusive listings. This is a present-day fact of life which is unfortunate. In the meantime, however, if you operate in an open listing market, advertising presents special problems and—as you will see here—special opportunities. Many times when a broker advertises a property for sale, he is only one of several brokers who are trying to sell it. Because of this *open listing market,* you must try to disguise your ads so that your competitors will not pinpoint the property, call the owner, and be competing with you for the sale!

With this in mind concerning your own ads, remember that if another broker does not carefully disguise his ad, you may be able to recognize the property he's advertising. He has actually assisted you in more ways than one. He has given you a listing lead and, before you contact the owner, you already know his selling price and something about the terms he will sell on, as well as the return the building will generate.

Let's say you spot an ad that reads as follows:

Commonwealth Avenue
17 Apartments
2 Stores

A rare find. Priced to sell at $1,460,000. Only $280,000 down. This well located five-story building has a new passenger elevator and central air conditioning. Restaurant and barber shop on first floor. Call today for complete details.
XYZ Realty

You remember that last year the same property was sold by Joe Jones to Ralph Smith. You spotted the building because the broker gave too much information in his ad. He could well have disguised his ad as follows:

**Back Bay
Investment**

Five-story elevatored apartment building priced to sell! Beautifully maintained and modernized income producer. Top-notch location. Call today for all details.
XYZ Realty

Locating the owner, once you know the property is for sale, is actually quite simple, and we will explore several time-saving techniques later in this chapter.

A Word of Caution: Although an open listing that another broker has advertised, or a building that a client has pointed out as being for sale (after seeing it through another broker), is "up for grabs," don't forget professional courtesy. Any subterfuge used by you to extract this information, either from the broker or your client, is considered highly unethical. It would eventually lead to the downfall of your reputation among your fellow brokers and your clients as well. It is not considered ethical practice for you or your associates to call another broker to solicit more information, nor is it considered ethical to ask a client, "What have you seen recently?"—although it's another matter if a client volunteers this information. Remember, too, that if another broker has an exclusive listing, you must respect his exclusive; in this case the property is *not* "up for grabs."

For Rent = Vacancies = Interest in Selling. Remember this formula. Follow up on the For Rent ads, too. They sometimes indicate the owner is having some degree of trouble with vacancies. If his vacancy problem is severe, such an owner is *always* interested in the possibility of selling his property.

This is true of builders, too. Whenever a builder advertises in the For Rent columns, he is doing what does not come naturally to him. Quite often, he is interested in building, not managing. The builder-owner will many times welcome your approach to assist him in selling his property—particularly if his new project is slow in filling up, or if his buildings are suffering from vacancies.

For-Sale-by-Owner Ads Present a Special Problem and a Special Opportunity. This particular sales situation offers a special opportunity to the broker seeking property for a listing. It should be remembered, however, that it is usually for one of two reasons a property will be advertised as "for sale by owner": (1) The seller might be acting under the impression that he can save money by avoiding brokerage fees; or (2) The seller might be trying to impress all prospective buyers with the notion that the sales price will *naturally* be lower than it would be if negotiated through a broker. In *both* instances, the skilled broker should make it known that his professional competence will work to the advantage of the seller.

Whenever I come up against a reluctant attitude on the part of a do-it-himself seller, I begin the educative process with some examples of how disastrous such an attitude can be. Here is one taken from my personal experience.

A For-Sale-By-Owner's $300,000 Mistake

Having run down an individual who placed a for-sale-by-owner ad on a property, the location of which was interesting, I tried to convince him that the resources of my office could work to his advantage in negotiating a sale. Unfortunately, my efforts were in vain.

The property in question was a five-story apartment building in a high-status location in historic Boston. It was owned by a charitable, non-profit corporation. The person who was trying to effect a sale was one of the officials of the institution. A dignified old gentleman, probably last of one of the blueblood families, he was gracious, but firm in his refusal to have my company list the property.

Well, he sold the building all right—for little more than half of what it was worth. To be precise, he sold the property for $600,000 to a speculator who knew the real market value. I hope to this day that the old gentleman, who so wanted to fulfill his official responsibility to the institution by saving brokerage fees, never learned what happened.

The speculator was receptive to my professional proposal. Only two months after he bought the building for $600,000, he sold it through my office for $950,000! To save the fractional brokerage fee, the original seller had lost his institution $300,000 net.

Newspaper advertisements of property for sale by owner are an important source of listings; these prospects can be realized, however, only after a convincing argument as to the benefits of placing the listing in the hands of somebody who knows what he's doing in the brokerage business.

Keeping your Ear to the Ground

Source 9: Blabbermouths. We have said that both problems and opportunities are created by the open listing market. Later, we will discuss how to cope with the problems, and in some cases solve them. Now, however, let us consider the opportunities created.

Bear in mind that if you choose to work on open listings, one of your main problems will be keeping secrecy in dealing with your listings. When a prospect mentions to a competitor, "100 Main Street is on the market; I saw it through XYZ Realty," your listing is compromised and handed to your competitor on a silver platter.

You owe it to yourself to keep alert to leads that clients volunteer. You should not try to solicit this information from a client; but when a buyer who is riding in your car says, "I saw that building with John Doe yesterday," he has handed you a lead. Do not, however, ask your buyer, "What have you seen recently?" This is not considered ethical conduct.

Amazingly enough, our blabbermouth sources of listings encompass the broker himself. If you are in an area of heavily concentrated brokerage offices, a noon visit to one of the real estate fraternity's favorite restaurants will usually produce at least two or three listing leads, particularly if you keep your ears open to conversations such as:

"Our deal on 200 Commonwealth Avenue just fell through."

or

"48 apartments in Smalltown. Sounds great!"

or

"How much does John Jones want for Parkview Towers?"

Surprisingly, many brokers do not guard their conversations regarding open listings, and by this lack of caution will often provide enough listing leads to keep you busy for days.

The Most Aggressive Technique of All: Blitzing

Source 10: Blitzing. In the business of income property brokerage, unlike most other businesses, there is no dearth of customers. In recent years, as an interest in property investment has grown, the number of prospective buyers for every good listing has increased accordingly—enormously! Today, for every good listing available, there are hundreds of possible purchasers.

But good listings don't just come into your office. They have to be sought out.

Tap sources 1 through 9, but remember that earlier in this chapter we said every recorded sale should be examined and evaluated for its future possibilities; every buyer can be interested in selling, and many sellers may have more to sell. Also, as you recall, we said that every property—no matter who owns it—is a potential listing. Simply assume that all income properties are for sale.

This established market is readily analyzed and exploited by utilizing sources 1 to 9: the real estate section of your local newspapers, the trade journals, the financial reporting journals, organization membership, the telephone book, owner lists, tax rolls, advertisements, and blabbermouths. Now, assuming you are a truly aggressive salesperson, you will go one step further. You will create your own market! I call it blitzing. This means going out cold to get a listing. Yes, you "go out," literally!

Leads 1 to 9 will open the door to both types of sellers mentioned earlier. Those who want to sell and know it, and those who want to sell but don't know it—yet! Blitzing really opens the door to those who have not given any thought to selling.

Where and How to Blitz. A good place to blitz is a suburban area where most of the *city brokers* don't generally operate unless an owner calls and asks for the service. When you contact the owner of an apartment building in the suburbs, he is surprised that any one is interested in his area. He is usually more receptive to discussing the possibilities of a sale than his urban counterpart, who is continually besieged by the "big city" brokers. Often the owner is pleased that a broker from Bigtown feels his holding is important enough to discuss.

The technique of blitzing can be utilized in the city or suburbs. To blitz, you must get into your car and go! Go cruising through *any* area—and let your imagination take the wheel.

"There! Stop! Pull over—that building looks salable!"

Where are you? Note the address. Take further notes describing the building. Describe the whole property, as well as you can at first sight.

What caught your eye and caused you to stop? It could be evidence of new construction; it could be a "now renting" or "see our model apartment" sign out front. If it's an older building, keep in mind what it was that attracted your attention. This feature of the building will also serve later, perhaps, to attract the interest of your buyer.

Even though you have no map or floor plan of the property to direct and guide you in a detailed examination of the physical structure, there is still much salient information available on the spot, at first sight.

In the course of one day, you may "case" as many as 30 properties. But to make a case for your listing, you have to know what to look for. Obviously, to make your blitzing day pay off (and you should actually designate periodic blitzing days in your monthly schedule), you should see as many properties as possible, and know precisely what to do in each situation.

What to Do When You Spot a Likely Building. First, try to describe the first impression you had—that which caused you to stop the car in the first place. It must have been some outstanding feature of the property. Put it down!

Next, make concise notes on the most obvious physical features of the building: Size. Type of construction. Number of apartments. Neighborhood surroundings.

The size (number of stories), the type of construction (brick, frame, stucco), and the descriptions of the environs (physical attributes of the immediate neighborhood)—these all are features that can be seen at a glance. But take complete notes! Don't rely on your memory.

Go into the lobby and count the mailboxes. And while doing so, take down the names of some of the tenants—and also make note of any blank name plates, because these might (not necessarily, however) indicate vacancies. Having the names of the tenants, as we will see later, will be very helpful in your campaign to find the owner.

The normal steps in blitzing are to (1) accumulate 20 to 30 leads of possible listings; (2) find out who the owners are; and (3) convince them to sell. You must play percentages.

Of every 30 blitzing leads, you will easily locate 25 owners. You will reach 20 by phone, 10 will give you appointments, 5 will give you a listing. And one listing will be a real fine salable investment. Blitzing, then, boils down to plugging away, and using the old law of averages.

Sources 1 to 7 and 11 and 12 generally lead you directly to an owner. However, when you uncover a specific building that may be for sale from advertisements, blabbermouths, or blitzing, then you are faced with two new problems: How to find out who owns the building, and how to reach the owner.

Source 11: Newsletters. One of the best ways to find both sellers and buyers is to distribute an informative newsletter. I have written such a newsletter, called *Investing in Real Estate,* and have found that it generates hundreds of thousands of dollars worth of commissions each year. A free electronic e-newsletter is available through the Real Estate CyberSpace Society at www.REcyber.com.

Source 12: Newspaper Columns. Such columns are also a very productive source of leads, and are often provided to subscribing brokers and salespeople for publication in their own local papers under their own names. The following article I wrote several years ago discusses this kind of newspaper column, and tells how to get the most from it.

THERE GOES THE EXPERT—<u>YOU</u>!

By John M. Peckham III

Contrary to popular belief, the origins of fame and recognition are not entirely subject to the whims of fate.

Quite frequently real estate brokers and salespeople devote a lifetime of effort based on the premise that success depends on who you know. They generally miss the fact that it is far more important <u>who knows you</u>.

Several years ago I had a visit from Charlie Akerson (who recently served as president of the American Institute of Real

Estate Appraisers). He stopped by the office to gather some comparable sales data in connection with an appraisal report he was preparing. Over a light lunch in my office, I suggested that perhaps we might write a newspaper column together with both of us sharing a byline and with Charlie covering the aspects of real estate valuation while I proposed to discuss the income tax and ownership advantages. I suggested that perhaps we might be able to find a spot for it in one of the Boston area papers.

Two weeks later our column started its weekly appearance in the Boston Herald Traveler.

In less than a year Charlie's travels and other commitments prevented him from continuing with the weekly column, and at that point I continued on and the column appeared each week for approximately ten years.

Because of this experience and the effects I could measure on my brokerage business, which resulted directly from the appearance of that column, it became apparent to me that the column had a far greater impact than any of our regular advertising.

The economics of newspaper advertising

Many real estate marketing experts have observed that the appearance of press releases in local newspapers is worth at least ten times the equivalent cost of a paid ad. This being the case, if the equivalent space costs, for example, $100 for paid advertising, the value of a press release which appeared in a paper with an equivalent circulation would be $1,000.

Cost of paid ad	$ 100
Press release value multiplier	× 10
Estimated value of press release	$1,000

If this is a reasonable approximation of the value of a prepared press release, then, based on over ten years of "on the firing line" experience, I must estimate that the value of a regularly appearing newspaper column is fifty times that of a normal institutional ad, and we shall see that there are many reasons for this.

Picture yourself walking down a side street and being approached by a shifty character with his collar turned up and with dark glasses covering his eyes. He says, "Psst—Hey buddy (or lady), how'd you like to get over $250,000 worth of free advertising next year?"

This analogy may seem a bit far fetched at first. However, when we compare the magnitude of economic benefits gained through the use of a newspaper column for image building with its minimal cost, we will find that perhaps the use of a "far out" analogy may be warranted.

I would estimate the impact value of a regularly appearing column in a local newspaper to be worth somewhere in the vicinity of 50 times its actual cost. If this is the case, using the above example of a column which occupies space that costs $100 the value from an impact standpoint on the public could be calculated as follows:

$ 100	×	cost of paid ad
× 50		impact value of column
$5,000		Estimated total value of column

The shady character we just met was showing us an increment increase in value of $4,900 a week, which expanded for a period of the next 52 weeks amounts to an annual increment in value of $254,800.

Strange things happened once my column had appeared for a few weeks, and they continued to occur in the many years following the initial appearance of the column. At social events, people would introduce me as "the real estate columnist from the Boston Herald" (sometimes it became a little embarrassing when the real estate editor received mail addressed to John M. Peckham III, Real Estate Editor, Boston Herald Traveler). And at one point the real estate editor sent along some of my "fan mail" with a note indicating that he was concerned that I was trying to take over his job! On many other occasions upon meeting people socially, they would indicate that they were sure we had met someplace before. Generally, I would respond by indicating that many people had expressed this feeling but that it usually turned out they had seen my column on one or many occasions. As soon as the mention of the column was made, I had established my reputation as "the real estate expert in the crowd."

Now that the secret is out it should be apparent that my reputation in the community has been "ballooned out of proportion" because of the use of the newspaper column. Without judging whether this is good or bad, there certainly is a message. The obvious message is that people want to deal with the "expert" in the field whether it be in buying or selling a house, in investing in real estate, or in buying or leasing commercial real estate.

Write your own or hire a "ghost writer."

Once you have made the decision to use a newspaper column to magnify the effectiveness of your marketing efforts, whether they be investment, commercial, or residential, there are basically two ways to proceed:

1. You can write the material yourself; or
2. You can hire a ghost writer to prepare that material for you and publish it in your local paper using your own byline by attaching your name and photograph to the column. Don't let the phrase "ghost writer" frighten you off. Most of the successful and powerful individuals in this country use a ghost writer on a regular or frequent basis.

There are advantages and disadvantages to preparing your own column. In preparing your own column you will obviously control the content of the material and the timing of its preparation. A professionally prepared column, however, generally contains material which is applicable to all sections of the country and is delivered in a timely manner. In addition, it is not difficult to effect minor modifications to the material you receive to suit your own need and style. The advantages of hiring a professional ghost writer are many, and for the average real estate practitioner they generally outweigh any disadvantages

- The cost is generally low—less than the equivalent of one hour's earnings for the average broker or salesperson;
- Professionally prepared columns are written to produce results and to produce inquiries;
- Professionally prepared columns are usually more effective image builders. And most important
- By obtaining a professionally prepared column, the real estate practitioner is free to concentrate his or her efforts on the real estate business. Often, a real estate broker will start a program, such as a planned program of press releases or, in this case, a newspaper column, and a few weeks into the program, will drop it due to time pressures or the inability to generate interesting and continuing copy for the column. The use of a ghost writer eliminates the problems of time and procrastination.

How do column services work?

Most ghost-written columns are created and written by professionals who analyze the market and surround themselves with staffs able to produce business-building materials for appearance in local papers. Some of the following are the salient features of subscribing to a ghost-written newspaper column:

- You pay a fee to the publisher of the column, usually on a quarterly basis, and generally, the publisher will mail you a complete set of columns covering that quarter. They are sent directly to you so that you may read them first and, if you desire, modify them before forwarding them to your newspaper.
- Generally, the columns are run each week in a local paper (often a weekly) in the immediate market area of the subscribing Realtor. Even a widely circulated free "shopper" type

approach is effective. The local approach has generally proven more worthwhile because the column is an institutional type of advertising and generally has much more impact where the readership is concentrated within the broker's market area. Additionally, local concentration will give you the ability to take a "gunshot" approach to local exposure and obtain greater readership intensity in the area of your market effectiveness. This saves money and space cost and avoids wasted geographic circulation which may not necessarily be helpful to your operation.

- Normally, newspaper column services will grant you an exclusive right which applies to the use of a specific paper within an area.

- Once you have established your contact with the paper or papers in which you wish to place a column and have agreed upon the format and cost, you will provide the newspaper with your photograph, with your name as you wish it to appear in the byline, and finally, with your action message at the end of the column.

Note the format in Illustration 1 (see page 31) which indicates where your photograph, byline, and action message would appear. Also note the same column in a modified format indicating the flexibility available to the "columnist."

How to expand the effectiveness of your column

If you decide to subscribe to a newspaper column service, there are several things that you can do to increase the effectiveness of your use of the column. Although you will find that the column by itself should enhance and expand your image within the community, you will find that the following ideas can make your column even more effective:

✓ Be sure that you have a good, clear photo to send to the newspaper along with your byline.

Illustration 1

your photo

your byline

Real Estate Investing

→ John M. Peckham III, Realtor

STARTING IN REAL ESTATE

QUESTION: I am tired of reading all about the great benefits of buying apartment houses. I am not rich, and although I own my home free and clear, I can never save a substantial amount of money to invest. To top it off, I'm not one of those fancy fifty percent taxpayers. Is there still a big deal for a guy like me?

ANSWER: The benefits of income property ownership are readily available to you. It is not just the affluent who enjoy these advantages. It has been estimated that over fifty percent of America's homeowners are free and clear of mortgage indebtedness. I am not advocating that you should sell your home to invest in income property, I am only pointing out that the equity you have in your home is just as good as cash for the acquisition of your first prop-

erty. Your stocks, the cash value of your life insurance, and your business property equity are also as good as cash that you could borrow.

You should also keep in mind that many investors start out with less than $20,000. You need not be a reckless speculator to start a tax-saving investment program, and you certainly don't have to be loaded with cash. Perhaps I can show you a few of the many ways to get started. I would be happy to chat with you soon.

Let's discuss your investment program. Email us at BostonRE investing@data.com or call us at 617/555-1212 or stop by The Peckham Boston Company at 123 Chestnut Hill Ave., Boston, MA. We look forward to meeting with you and answering your personal real estate questions.

your action message goes here

✓ Be sure that you have an effective action message to close your column (one of the disadvantages of a normal press release is that you are not able to make a direct appeal for the client's business). In a column, you are able to devote space at the end to deliver a specific message which is a call for action.

✓ Be sure that if your byline differs from your firm name and your name appears both in the white and yellow pages of the telephone directory. In the yellow pages your name should appear under Real Estate or Real Estate Consultants.

✓ From time to time, be sure to offer a special report or article on a timely subject so that readers will contact you promptly. Articles such as those concerning pricing a home for sale, tax tips, or moving checklists will often flush out those homeowners who are in need of your services and cause them to call you.

✓ Be sure to make copies of your column and have them available each week in the waiting area of your office or in community areas with a lot of foot traffic. Be sure to mention the name of the paper and indicate that the copy of the column is reprinted from that newspaper. This will not only enhance your image within the community but it will also build your readership and following.

✓ In addition to the above, it has proven effective to enclose copies of the column similarly reproduced with selected—or all—correspondence and mailings leaving your office.

✓ Provide reprints of your column to local service clubs and organizations and, if you have any desire to speak, be sure to bring reprints when you visit such organizations.

✓ If you are a principal you might consider rotating the photographs of your agents and allowing them to use the byline. This has the obvious advantage of giving them exposure and, in addition, provides them with an added incentive or image, increasing their prestige and the morale within the office.

✓ Similarly, if you have one or more principals in your office, there is no reason that the recognition for the column cannot be twofold or threefold, either on a rotating or regular basis. The same effect can be accomplished by placing the column in two or more papers.

✓ When your column first appears, it may pay great dividends to mail a reprinted copy to the basic mailing list which you have developed for general office mailings. This can be your holiday greeting card list or a much larger expanded list. The list should, in any event, include the former buyers and sellers who are in your area and who can be beneficial by forwarding along referrals. The list should also include all "centers of influence," such as bankers, lawyers, CPAs, and trust officers—in short, any individual who is capable of referring potential buyers and sellers to you. See Illustration 2 for an example of such a letter.

✓ You may also consider enclosing a return post card with the announcement letter or with copies of future columns or special reports sent out in response to the column.

Illustration 3 gives an example of such a return post card used in investment brokerage. Illustration 4 is a suggested format for encouraging residential responses.

Note that neither of the post cards contains a line for the respondent's telephone number. This omission is deliberate because we have found that post card returns will at least triple if we omit a request for the phone number. This is most likely due to the fact that many people are concerned that they will be disturbed by a solicitation. Because over 95% of the respondents' phone numbers are listed, we have found it worthwhile to spend the few minutes it takes to look up the phone number. This little extra effort is minimal when compared to the potential for increased response.

✓ Don't forget to "farm." The appearance of your column triggers a natural and comfortable opening for a "farming contract." You or your salespeople now have a natural opening when calling within a pre-designated area. "I don't know if you noticed Bill

Illustration 2

THE PECKHAM BOSTON COMPANY

Four Longfellow Place
Boston, Massachusetts 02114
617-555-1212

Good Morning!

We are enclosing a copy of the column which is now appearing in the (insert named newspaper) each week.

We are pleased to be providing this as a service to our friends and to the community and to address interesting questions regarding the ownership of real estate.

I hope that we may be of service to you or to your friends or clients in the future. If we may be of any assistance in the area of real estate, please feel free to give us a call. Let me assure you of our prompt attention to your needs.

Sincerely,

John M. Peckham III

Illustration 3

IIIII

NO POSTAGE
NECESSARY
IF MAILED
IN THE
UNITED STATES

BUSINESS REPLY CARD
FIRST CLASS   PERMIT NO. 44021   BOSTON, MA
POSTAGE WILL BE PAID BY ADDRESSEE

Peckham Boston Company
Four Longfellow Place
Boston, Massachusetts 02114

Illustration 4

Hey Jack--

    I'd like some information on all of those investment properties you have for sale.

    My main interest lies in:

    Buying ☐   Selling ☐

☐ Apartments   ☐ Office Buildings
☐ Shopping Centers ☐ Net Leases
☐ Land   ☐ Other_____
☐ Property Management
☐ Other_____   ☐ Consulting

Name_____
Street_____
City/Town_____
State/Zip_____

Broker's (or "my") article in the weekly tribune last week. He suggested that I call you to see if we may be of assistance in any matter relating to real estate or whether I might send you a copy of the article. . . . " Any opening which is comfortable is effective. The label of "expert" or the affiliation with "the expert" can <u>put you miles ahead of the competition when properly used</u>.

Conclusions

The methods of promoting your expertise to the public are changing as rapidly as technology itself. The use of a newspaper column can be one of the most dramatic business-building promotions available if used effectively. You must be patient with the use of a column because its effectiveness builds in proportion to its exposure to the public. This is because the impact upon the public is cumulative.

You will find that the use of a column will both impress the public with your good sense and knowledge and additionally stimulate your sales associates, since it provides them with a continuing source of buyers and sellers. Your associates will also find that being affiliated with the broker who publishes "the column on real estate" will be an excellent door opener for them as they work their farming area and as they come face to face with the general public.

Perhaps as important as all considerations are the end results, which have proven dramatic when compared with the nominal cost involved in using this effective form of image advertising.

After a few months of appearing as "the expert" on real estate in your local newspaper, I'm sure that the result which you experience will reaffirm my contention that it is not nearly as important who you know in our business as <u>who knows you!</u> Good luck!

How to Find Out Who Owns the Building

Unlike residential brokerage where you are generally certain that the owner lives in the house in question, in income brokerage finding the identity of the owner is usually a problem. The problem can be solved, however, if you are aware of a few simple expedients. Without these your task can be laborious and even fruitless. Remember, your time is extremely valuable. To get the listing you've got to reach the owner, and you don't want to expend any more time than is absolutely necessary for this first step. Saving time now will mean more time available later for the main job of obtaining the listing.

There is a positive way to find the owner's name and address, and that is to visit the town hall or county assessor's office and view the tax rolls. This is a direct method, though a personal visit will often take a lot of time. If you have several leads in one town and do not have an owner list for that town in your office, then certainly this is a logical place to start.

If, however, you have only a few listing leads that are scattered in different towns, or if you have one listing lead, this does not warrant a special trip. A visit to town hall would not only be too time consuming, but also your search might be to no avail. After spending hours in search of the public records, you might come up with the answer—but one that is no help at all. Many of the buildings recorded in official documents are listed under the names of real estate trusts! And these faceless entities are very difficult to contact; the only way to locate the trustee is through a further search of the records at the Registry of Deeds or County Clerk's office in your area.

Yes, you could do all this, but there are easier ways. Here are the shortcuts for gathering the information you need:

Five Time-Saving Shortcuts

Shortcut 1: Telephone the Town Assessor. The tax departments of many cities and towns will give you the owner's name and address over the telephone. You can save many steps by finding out which cities and towns will cooperate in this manner.

Shortcut 2: Published Owner Lists. As we noted earlier in this chapter, most urban communities are pretty well described in terms of property ownership. There are the public records already cited here; and private research organizations publish, in most areas, works similar to the one used by income brokers in the Greater Boston area, namely, the *Book of Assessed Values* (BOAV), which is a compilation of information from the public records. In these lists you can find the listed owners of most of the properties in your area.

You should maintain copies of the privately published owner lists such as our BOAV. Keep these publications close at hand and you will be able to find out the owner's name in this easy, time-saving manner.

Shortcut 3: Call a Tenant. A very easy way to find the owner's name and usually his telephone number is to call a tenant and ask him. To find out who lives in the building under question and his or her phone number, simply use an online *cross-reference telephone directory.* By using this, you can find the names and telephone numbers of all the telephone subscribers who are tenants in the building. Your directory search will be listed by street and number, rather than alphabetically by name.

You can also use the list of tenant names you assembled while you visited the property.

Now, let's assume the property that you're interested in is located at 41 Main Street, Your Town, U.S.A. (Remember, you've already carefully noted the exact address during your blitzing campaign.) All you have to do now is look up the address and jot down the telephone numbers of a few of the tenants who occupy the building.

Since it's an apartment building, all the listed telephones at that address will be itemized along with the names of the occupants. Call one of these people and ask if he knows who the owner is. For example: "Hello, Mr. Smith, my name is John Jones. I'm trying to contact the owner of your apartment building. Could you give me his name and address?"

Most tenants are usually very cooperative and will volunteer any information they have. Make sure, however, that it is the owner's name and not that of the superintendent or rental agent. You are certainly not interested in stating your case to the rental agent or superintendent of the building because these are probably the last people in the world who want to see the building sold.

Occasionally a tenant will ask who you are. In income brokerage, it is considered poor policy to let a tenant know or even incorrectly deduce that the property is for sale. This is due to the understandable apprehension about the possibility of the building being sold to a new owner who will mismanage the property or, even worse, raise the rents—or convert the building to condominiums. Because of this policy of hiding the possibility of a future sale from the tenants, it is considered proper simply to explain that you want to reach the owner "concerning a private business matter."

Shortcut 4: Ask a Tenant. Many times when you are blitzing in a new area you will spot a situation where you are, or easily could be, face-to-face with a tenant. You may be checking the parking area of an apartment house when a tenant drives in, or in blitzing a store block area you may see a barber reading a magazine. If you do, you can save yourself time by casually inquiring who owns the property. You might walk into the barber shop and casually ask, "Pardon me, sir, but could you tell me who owns this block of stores?" Most times this simple approach is effective.

Shortcut 5: For Rent Signs. In your blitz on an area, or in the course of ordinary travel, you may see a very salable-looking property with a big sign that says "Apartment (Store, Office, or what have you) For Rent—call Owner at 555-1212." Be sure to jot this information down. The owner has just saved you a lot of work. Here's an important way to separate yourself from the average caller on his sign, or from other brokers who merely call and say, "Saw your sign at 10 Main Street. Could I ask your name, sir?" Before contacting the owner, do a phone number reverse search on the Internet. Unless the number is unpublished, the web directory will show you that the number is listed to John Q. Owner. With this information you can start your call with Mr. Owner's name, and by doing this raise yourself above the crowd.

Finding Sellers at Cyberspace Speed

The Cyber Age has magnified many of the techniques described in this chapter tenfold by adding: (1) Speed, (2) Accessibility to information, and (3) Ease of image promotion to our arsenal. Let's take a look at each of these.

Speed

Remember when we discussed blabbermouths earlier in this chapter? Well let me tell you that blabbermouthing in the Cyber Age can have momentous consequences and can provide momentous opportunities to the recipient of this information at e-speed! Here's an example:

> I was sitting quietly at my computer when an e-mail with a not too protectively de-scribed property hit my screen. It was from a broker in the Midwest. If I were a "prin-cipal only" I could have the good fortune to "buy this 30 million dollar 160,000 square foot office building in Massachusetts occupied by Verizon on a long-term lease." Then another similar e-mail from a broker in the South.
>
> As it happened, there was probably only one building in the world that fit this de-scription and it was owned by a lovely woman—let's call her Laurie—from whom I had earlier purchased an 80-unit apartment building! Shame on her for not calling me when she decided to sell this large property!
>
> Obviously I resisted the temptation to let loose on this nice lady with a barrage ex-pressing my indignance at finding her property being trumpeted all over the country. I simply got on the phone and explained to her that I had an investor for whom her prop-erty would be a perfect fit for a 1031 replacement property (more on that subject later).
>
> She had two passions in life: First, to get the best price imaginable (in her mind) for her property and second, to avoid giving an exclusive listing to anyone at all costs!
>
> Within 30 minutes I had an open listing on this 30 million dollar net leased property—thanks to the information provided by my competitors! Remember "loose lips sink ships!"

For now it is enough to see the speed with which we can obtain information in this day and age. A little further on when we discuss finding buyers I'll show how I took this listing and turned it into a significant commission—a "send three kids through college and graduate school" commission!

Accessibility to Information

There are literally dozens of cross reference phone and address directories on the web. You can always find the latest resources including these at the Real Estate CyberSpace Society Resource Center: www.REcyber.com/cybertools.html.

You can also use the rapid search capabilities of Google (or similar online search services) to locate people and properties for sale. Although the following example may need to be further refined it will give you an example of the power of the re-sources we have available today. Using the following Google search today "Apartment building" + "For sale by owner" we found 1,960,000 results. That should keep us busy for the rest of the week! You might want to narrow this search as follows: "Apartment building for sale by owner" + "Chicago" yielded 48 results.

Ease of Image Promotion

We saw earlier that promoting your expertise and staying in touch with potential buyers and sellers and centers of influence will pay big dividends when it comes time to contact potential sellers (and buyers) or their advisors.

Successful income property brokers are using the power of the Internet and e-mail to reach a much wider pool of potential customers and to build customer recognition. Electronic newsletters and columns are augmenting (or replacing) print versions of this marketing technique.

E-letters and columns help to broaden brokers' reach and to solidify and strengthen their image as Cyber-progressive real estate professionals. As pointed out earlier you can either produce your columns or newsletters yourself or use the services of a professional. Using the latter is often easier and more efficient for the busy broker.

A professionally prepared online image promotion program allows you to send a professionally prepared promotional e-letter by e-mail to your clients and centers of influence (lawyers, bankers, press, accountants, title companies, etc.)—and they are generally easily customizable in minutes. By using such programs you can let the professional writers do the work—and you get the fame!

Once you set up your newsletter (usually a quick one time process) it will be sent to you each month automatically. All you will need to do is send your e-list a short note (usually pre-prepared by the editors for you) letting them know that your newsletter is ready for them to enjoy!

You can get started easily with such a program if you are a member of the Real Estate CyberSpace Society. The Society produces and delivers "Real Estate Cyber Tips" to their members monthly and it appears as your own individual newsletter. Cyber Tips is short, punchy, and very professional and contains Cyber information of interest for your clients, press, and centers of influence. You can also easily and effectively use an e-newsletter or column as a special traffic-building feature on your web site.

As with all Society services, there is no cost to Society members for these business-building services.

CHAPTER 3

Turning Your Leads Into Listings That Sell

With all these potential leads in hand, you're ready to follow them up. To use your time effectively, you must understand which leads are most productive and which leads will yield the most salable listings with the smallest expenditure of time.

Look at the following illustration. This checklist is designed to help you when you are on a "listing binge," replenishing your supply of available investments. Your desk is cluttered with work and you want to know at a glance what you should take care of next, which calls will be most productive, and which calls to put off in favor of these.

Priority Checklist for Listing Efficiency

Itemized in the following are various potential listing situations. By following these according to the priority suggested, you will use your listing time most effectively.

SITUATION PRIORITY	WHAT TO DO
1. An owner has called to list his property.	1. Drop everything—gather the information now.
2. You have a verified lead that an owner has his property on the market.	2. Jump—contact the owner and convince him to use your services.

SITUATION PRIORITY	*WHAT TO DO*

3. You spot a situation that gives the owner strong motivation to sell. In productive order, these are:
  a. problem situation
  b. profit situation
  c. growth situation
	3. A problem situation (whether with the specific building or with a person) will produce more listings than profits or growth situations. Attack your leads in the order listed.

4. You have assembled a list of buildings and owners without any knowledge of the owners' situations.	4. Follow up on these leads after you have exhausted your supply of situations 1 to 3 above.

Note: Remember that any checklist must be flexible. Situations will arise that do not fall neatly into any of these categories, and a situation #4 can quickly become situation #2. When this occurs, you must give it all the attention due its new priority position. In line with remaining flexible, remember also that a potential $5 million listing in priority situation #4 may logically take precedence over a $200,000 listing in a higher category. Use good old common sense and always ask yourself, "How much time will it take, and how much money can this time invested earn me?"

Normally your three steps to listing a property are:

Step 1. Convince the owner to sell.
Step 2. Convince the owner to use your services.
Step 3. Gather the necessary information.

As indicated by the priority checklist, there is a way to save one-third of your time, and that is to first go after the owner who has already decided to sell. Because you don't have to assist him in making his decision to sell, your job is one-third complete. Owners who have decided to sell may contact you directly (once your reputation is made), or you may uncover this fact by using some of the leads in Chapter 2 such as blabbermouths and for-sale-by-owner ads. Other leads may drop in your lap unexpectedly. For example, you may see a competitor touring a known investor through a property!

How to Handle the Owner Who Has Already Decided to Sell

Your approach to an owner who you know has made the decision to sell is quite different from your approach to the owner who has not. First of all, address him by name—and ask point-blank, "Have you sold 100 Main Street yet?" You will see that there is a very important distinction between this approach and the approach that should be used where the decision to sell has not been made.

When the owner answers, "No, I haven't sold 100 Main Street yet," he has immediately confirmed that he will sell. This confirmation puts you in a position to move immediately to Step 2—to convince the owner to use your services. As Step 2 and Step 3 are the same for all situations, we will cover those a bit later in this chapter.

There will be times when you will need to revise your approach. Occasionally, an owner will not admit that 100 Main Street is for sale. Every once in a while your information will be in error. If by chance, the property is not on the market, or the owner will not admit that it is for sale, there's no harm done. In this instance, he'll probably want to know about the possibilities of a sale (he'll realize you must know something that he doesn't, otherwise you wouldn't have called).

In both cases, treat this owner as you would any other owner. Back up and start at Step 1. Treat him just as you would the owner who has not yet decided to sell.

The broker's job is to make things happen. It is generally true that eight out of ten buildings sold were not on the market a few months before the sale was consummated. Income brokers plant the thought-seed regarding a possible sale, and quite frequently, this seed germinates into a handsome commission.

This is one fact of life about income property brokerage that makes our specialty so different from residential brokerage. If you asked ten homeowners whether they wanted to sell their cherished hearth and home, nine of them would react with an offended "NO!"

A universal truism about income property brokerage is that brokers are prime movers, "catalysts." Through our imagination and skill, we create a large portion of the market. And our crucible of creation is the listing.

What is the psychological principle of listing? Motivation. You must use every means to understand what motivates an owner to sell a property, even in cases where he or she had never even dreamed of putting it on the market before your call.

Step 1: Persuading the Owner to Sell

There is no one pat approach that will best convince an owner to sell; however, by understanding owner motivation you can guarantee yourself a high degree of success in obtaining good salable listings.

Based on super-serious brainstorming sessions by our income brokers at Peckham Boston, we have placed our prospective sellers in three main motivational categories:

- Problem-motivated sellers ·
- Profit-motivated sellers
- Growth-motivated sellers

Here are ways to approach each of these:

The Problem-Motivated Seller

Often, there are owners who are experiencing difficulties that fall into two basic categories:

1. Problems with the building such as:
   - Tenant problems
   - Repair problems
   - Financial problems
2. Personal problems such as:
   - Financial problems
   - Inadequate time
   - Family or partnership problems

Owners who are experiencing specific difficulties with a building are prime candidates for a listing. As a broker, you don't have to supply any motivation—it already exists. All you must do is uncover it! The solution to the problem is generally to sell the building to someone who is better able to solve that problem than the present owner—and you are in a position to serve that owner by negotiating a sale.

Many times owners may solve pressing personal problems by selling one or more of their investment properties. The owner who needs cash, or who finds that other interests leave little or no time for his apartment house, or who is suffering from family or partnership disagreement over management policy—all of these owners are potential sellers, and their motivation is strong.

One of the secrets to successful listing is to determine the problem and to convince the owner that you are in a position to solve it by negotiating a satisfactory sale of the property.

Three Ways to Spot Problem-Motivated Sellers

1. Listen to *shop talk.*

    Conversations with brokers, investors, businessmen, bankers, barbers—anyone—can reveal that Mr. Owner is experiencing one or more problems. For example, you meet Fred, the fuel oil salesman, on the street and in conversation he asks, "Hey, what's the matter with John Owner? He hasn't paid his oil bill in several months." Or your local barber says, "You know, I think John Owner and his partner are ready to split up." Flag these conversations and *follow up.*

2. Read your *trade journals* with an eye open for problems.

    By following sales, mortgages, attachments, and liens in your trade journals and financial papers, you can keep on top of problem situations. Records of attachments and liens are particularly significant because someone is unhappy with an owner, and you can be quite sure that Mr. Owner is quite unhappy because his property has been attached. Flag these indicators and *follow up.*

3. Watch for *rental signs* and *rental ads* (as mentioned in Chapter 2).

    Any sign of vacancy or turnover is an indicator of some degree of mental anguish to the owner—it represents loss of income. Flag these signs and ads, and *follow up.*

The Profit-Motivated Seller

Just as ice cream is tempting to most people—so is profit. Many owners are rightfully tempted by the potential profit they will derive from the sale of their income property. Usually the new owner is most susceptible to this motive. The speculative builder falls into this category, or the investor who recently purchased an apartment building or has owned it for less than two or three years.

For example, Lenny Ross, one of my sales managers and one of the finest natural salesmen I have ever known, checks back, as a routine procedure, with all investors who have bought buildings from him. He does this every six months. This usually yields him several fine listings, with which he is already familiar. Once Lenny checked with a doctor who had invested in an eleven-unit brick apartment building in the Back Bay area of Boston and suggested that, having owned the property for almost two years, the doctor might be interested in selling if we could find a buyer who would buy at a reasonable profit. The doctor was agreeable and gave Lenny the listing. Three months later the building was sold to an engineer. The doctor received a significant profit, and Lenny brought another commission check back for his effort.

This is not by any means an unusual example. There's a store block on Commonwealth Avenue in the Brighton section of Boston that we've sold three times in two years. The motive—*profit!*

Let's assume that, using the instructions in Chapter 2, you have spotted several new owners from newspapers, trade journals, and financial papers. Keep in mind that in some cases a new owner has an abiding fear—a nagging anxiety—about the wisdom of this recent purchase (something will go wrong, he thinks). This is a natural fear and because of it, your call to sell his property will often be most welcome, if only because his ego is bolstered by knowing that someone else thinks it desirable.

Expect the owner to say, "But, I just bought it!" Your answer should be right to the point, "Yes, Mr. Owner, and this might be the right time to consider a profit. With the profit you could acquire a larger property that will support a full-time custodian. . . ."

Don't ever be shy about offering an investor a profit. That's what he's after! Make those calls and you will generate many fine listings. Properly handled, ten calls to new owners should produce three or four listings. Fifteen calls will generally yield at least one prime listing. Not a bad day's work, considering the fact that the average commission on each income sale is over $50,000.

Put the builder in the profit-motivated category. After all, he's used to profits—that's why he works twelve hours a day. We saw in Chapter 2 that apartment-for-rent ads in the real estate sections of the local newspapers gave us hundreds of potential sellers. Among these ads, and usually at the top of the page in big display sections, are ads for new complexes under construction or recently completed.

Remember that while these ads are running, the builder is troubled by two big questions: "Will my apartments rent?" and "Should I sell the units as condominiums?" The builder will not express these doubts, but they're there, even with the biggest of them.

How to Speak the Builder's Language. Most builders will discuss a possible sale before or at this stage, and once you have opened the door there is a good chance he will let you sell, after he fills his building—if you show him a p-r-o-f-i-t.

First of all, you have to cut through *his* sales pitch. Remember, that despite his fear of vacancies or other problems, he's had to convince himself of the "great financial possibilities" of his new building. After all, he built it. His spoken attitude will not reveal his unspoken fears.

"Why should I sell or convert? I've got a potential gold mine here in this new building."

Well, I have never met a builder who didn't have dreams of building something bigger and better. You must argue his own dream.

Also, you explain, "Mr. Builder, by selling this building now as a whole or as condos, you can relieve yourself of all management problems. Look, you're in the building business. You certainly can generate a significantly higher return if you sell, and use the equity to build something larger. Take your well earned profits now and reinvest them in your exceptional talent for building profitably."

Don't ever be afraid to approach a builder—large or small. No harm can come from asking, and ten calls to builders currently advertising apartments for rent in new projects will usually yield one or two, of which one will be prime.

The Growth-Motivated Seller

A growth-motivated owner is usually concerned by profit, problems, or maybe both. As pointed out earlier, there is often no clear-cut dividing line between them. Either or both can motivate an owner to sell.

In profiling the growth-oriented seller, you can start from the premise that a current owner of a multi-family house has already been indoctrinated into the why's and how's of property ownership. The owner of an investment property knows what economic growth and amortization of debt, acting together, have done for his personal net worth statement. He knows how much additional income he has derived from his investment, and—if he has lived in one of the apartments—how much less he had to pay for his own shelter.

Most periods over the past few decades have been boom periods for real estate investment. It would be difficult to find any income-producing property, from Maine to California, that didn't significantly appreciate. Many buildings doubled or even tripled in value over those years. The result is that a majority of established owners now have considerable trapped equity in their properties. Why leave this equity dormant? Why not show growth-oriented owners who have already met with success in real estate that it still makes financial sense to sell and reinvest in today's market?

How to Handle the "Yes, But . . ." Owner. Every six to twelve months, the brokers at Peckham Boston will sit down with each client and conduct an Annual Portfolio Review. The purpose of this review is to ascertain whether each individual building in the investor's portfolio is performing to its highest and best use? How can rental income be maximized? How can expenses be reduced? Is this an appropriate time to refinance, convert, or sell and reinvest?

Often you'll hear the growth-oriented investor say, "Yes, I can see that I've accumulated a $500,000 equity base in this building and a $600,000 base in the other building but, under present economic circumstances, it doesn't appear that I have any alternative but to wait for the market to stabilize. But since I've done so well with my last two purchases, I'll consider selling and buying a larger property when things cool down."

I'm sure you've heard this type of reasoning in the past. It's typical of the thousands who have read "Get Rich Quick In Real Estate" books. They're motivated but often indecisive. It's always easier not to make the decision, not to take the risk, to procrastinate and wait for lower prices or lower interest rates. Such investors will always be waiting for a better market.

It is important for you not to allow this kind of reasoning to guide the thinking of your established investors. Remember, every "Yes, but . . ." owner that is persuaded to sell and reinvest means *two* commissions for you! Growth-oriented owners want to be sold. They've made money, and they want to make more money.

Later on you will see how leverage can magnify the benefits of income property ownership. With that information in hand you will also have the tools to demonstrate to the growth-motivated seller that it is often clearly a major advantage to "move on and move up." With your help this type of owner will be able to understand that the disposition of a currently held property replacing it with a larger better leveraged income property is a common and often highly effective strategy for creating wealth.

How to Defer the Capital Gains Tax. As pointed out, in income property there is often a very thin line between buyers and sellers, and in the case of the growth-motivated seller, he is by necessity a prime candidate for the purchase of a larger property.

It may come as a surprise to the residential broker that the seller of income property must pay a capital gains tax even if he reinvests in a larger property. This is one of the marked tax differences between a home sale and the sale of an income property. But there is one way to avoid the immediate payment of a capital gains tax on income property, and that is by negotiating what is commonly referred to as a "tax-free exchange" (made accurately a tax deferred exchange).

The Tax-Deferred Exchange. Exchanging income property is a specialty which has been described fully in many publications. The CCIM Institute, an affiliate of the National Association of Realtors (NAR), conducts various courses and publishes several books on the subject. In addition, Chapter 7 discusses this topic further. The art of exchanging is so broad in scope and so detailed in application that these separate publications are needed to do justice to its unique tax advantages. For now, keep in mind that income property may be exchanged, and under certain circumstances payment of a long-term capital gains tax may be temporarily avoided.

How to Proceed When You Have No Indication the Owner Is in the Market to Sell

Earlier we noted that the best approach to an owner who has decided to sell is to use the direct question, "Have you sold your building yet?" Obviously, this question is inappropriate when you have no indication that the owner has considered selling. Having spotted a situation where the owner may be motivated by problems, profit, or desire for growth or having assembled a list of buildings without any particular knowledge of the owner's motivations, you are ready to contact him regarding a possible sale.

On your first contact with him (usually by telephone), you must impress the fact that you hold the key to:

1. Solving his problems;
2. Realizing him a profit; or
3. Assisting him to create a larger estate.

A cold-turkey call asking to list the property with you will get you a big fat "No," 99 calls out of every 100 you make.

In this situation, it is true that your immediate goal is to get a listing on the property. But, remember, you're talking to a person who, so far as you know, has never seriously considered selling. By all means, avoid using the word *listing!*

To many an owner, the term *listing* is a scary word. It conjures up all kinds of foreboding images. If you use it, he may imagine dire consequences; for him, listing evokes the thought of a big commission to pay or a possible lawsuit to face. (Unhappily, there are a few brokers who seem to make a practice of suing their clients on a very thin pretext. It is, frankly, unfortunate for the whole profession that an owner's fears of listing may sometimes be justified.)

Try to take stock of—and sympathetically appreciate—all the owner's fears and apprehensions about putting his property on the market. Your sympathetic attitude will work to your advantage. Avoid the word *listing* in your initial approach and attempt to appeal to a known owner motivation, to uncover an unknown motivation, or to create the motivation and desire to sell.

A Tactful and Effective Opening

Most brokers who have even a limited clientele of buyers capable of investing in income property will immediately let the owner know of buyer interest in his or her area. By using this approach—"I have a sincere client interested in buying an apartment house (or store block or whatever) in Quincy (or wherever)"—the broker has effectively converted the "cold-turkey" approach into a real, vivid, easily pictured situation where the owner can visualize the broker's client eventually buying his property.

Here is a typical phone conversation—and how you might handle it successfully:

Broker: Hello, Mr. Owner. My name is Bill Broker from the XYZ Realty Company. I'd like to talk with you about your property at 10 Main Street. I have a buyer who is anxious to invest in your area.

Owner: You mean somebody wants to buy my building?

Broker: The person I have in mind might well be interested. The market is good, my buyer is very sincere, and I'd like an opportunity to talk the matter over with you.

Owner: Well, I hadn't even thought of selling.

Broker: Frankly, Mr. Owner, the buyer is quite anxious to put his money into a property investment. I'd consider the matter immediately. Let's get together and talk it over.

Owner: (*The owner may still be hesitant.*) Well, give me a call in a couple of weeks.

Broker: (*as if you hadn't heard him*) Say, I'm going to be in your area tomorrow afternoon. Would that be convenient?

Now, if he replies that he won't be in at that time, you pursue it and pin him down to a definite appointment. Keep your expressed purpose urgent, however.

If the owner will give you all the information you need on the phone, then by all means take it. However, the sooner you get to know the owner personally, the less complicated will be your actual sales negotiations with him.

Step 2: How to Persuade the Owner to Use Your Services

Let us assume that you have approached the owner and, by appealing to the proper motives, convinced him that selling is in his best interest. You must now persuade him to use *your* services.

What do you answer when the owner asks, "Mr. Broker, what can you do for me? If I do decide to sell, why not do it myself?"

Show the owner-seller that you spend 10 hours a day, 6 days a week, 52 weeks per year, dealing with investment buyers. Also, tell him that, because this is your specialty, it is not only worth his while to employ you to sell his property, but that without your assistance, he will be in for weeks, perhaps months, of aggravation. Impress that if and when he sells his property, it is quite possible that he will sell it for a price which is lower than one you can obtain, even after he pays your commission!

The next question that will arise is this: "Why, Mr. Broker, are you able to do this?" Here you must point out that:

- You have hundreds (perhaps thousands) of ready buyers, the names of which you have built up in the course of your business dealings;
- You have qualified these buyers, and you have records of what their requirements are;
- You are equipped to prepare a professional brochure describing the property—you know how to write ads that bring results;
- You are qualified to obtain offers and negotiate terms;
- You are in a position to obtain additional financing for a buyer if he needs it;
- You are acting as a middle man, and a buyer will place much more weight in your analysis of the situation than he will in an owner's statements regarding his own property; and, finally,
- You have sold so many (insert your dollar volume) dollars' worth of the type of property in the area that you must be doing something right.

Use This Clincher: Faced with these truths, it is very difficult for an owner who has finally decided to sell to refuse. As one final, irrefutable argument, if all others fail, say, "Mr. Owner, you are asking $250,000 for your property. If we can get you $250,000, and take all of the burden, bother and aggravation of the selling process off your shoulders by asking $265,000, which includes our commission, certainly it should make sense to you." What owner could refuse such a fair proposal?

Naturally, you must point out that if you are successful in obtaining a price that is acceptable to him, even though it is lower than the "asking" price, he will have to pay your commission from this price; but that, if your price is less, he is the judge as to whether it is acceptable or not.

If these arguments are properly presented, nine out of ten owners will be impressed with your ability, and you will walk away with the listing!

How to Use Visual Aids to Tell Your Story

There are several visual aids which you may use in convincing an owner that you are the man to handle his negotiations. Institutional advertising may be used as a *handout.*

Our office ran a centerspread in our trade paper, the *New England Real Estate Journal.* It showed our office inside and out, and showed a sampling of properties recently sold. The narrative section was our "hard sell" and showed why we felt we were the office to negotiate for an owner. We had several thousand extra copies printed at the time the ad was run, and our brokers have found it to be a very effective sales aid when approaching an owner not familiar with our office.

That ad was recognized by the New England Realtor's Convention as one of the top three ads during that year.

Other convincing sales aids are:

1. Publicity clippings of past sales.
2. Photographs of sold buildings.
3. News articles regarding your office.
4. Mock-ups or displays of your advertising campaigns.
5. Copies of well prepared property brochures and operating statements.

By constantly using any or all of these, you will reassure the owner of his need for your professional services.

Step 3: How to Gather the Necessary Information

Assuming that the owner has decided to sell and has decided that it is to his benefit to use you as his broker, you are ready to take the listing.

There are two ways to gather the information. One is to scratch down a bunch of figures and information on a brown paper bag. The other is to develop and use a step-by-step listing form which makes taking the listing almost automatic.

The Listing Form, and How to Use It

Take a long look at the listing form on pages 56 to 59. This is a specimen listing form, and is typical of those used in the business of income property brokerage.

Now, let me anticipate an obvious question: How does the listing form differ from the operating statement (which we will discuss in Chapter 6)? The difference is really one of *purpose*. Whereas the operating statement is intended for the prospective buyer, the listing form is for the seller and the broker. The information recorded on the listing form is translated into the language of the operating statement. The listing form must contain all the information that is to be included in the operating statement, plus additional administrative items. It may help to think of this form as a *listing information-gathering form*.

Look at the front of the listing form. The name of the brokerage company goes right on top. Then, we have the address of the property, the type of building, the number of stories, number of apartments and/or stores and offices. The next obvious features of interest to both broker and buyer are the tax assessment, the tax rate, and the total annual income. Following those is a section to record the regularly recurring expenses, such as taxes, heat, electricity, insurance, and so forth.

Financing: The Heart of the Form (and the Problem)

You will notice at this point that almost all the rest of the front of the listing form is devoted to financing information. This large portion of the form is, of course, quite consistent with the relative importance of financing to brokerage in general; *financing is 80 percent of the battle.*

Net Income: Now, skip down to Item *E.* Note how the amortized principal is recorded, both by itself (under Item *F*) and as a part of the total yield under *G.*

Next, in order, is the price information; the name and address of the owner; also, the sales picture from the owner's standpoint. The last item on the front of the form (i.e., on the portion shown on page 58) is a code for computing various of the totals called for.

On the back of the form (i.e., on the portion shown on the bottom of page 58) is included specific information about the operation of the building. Remember, the information recorded on the listing form should: (1) be accurate; and (2) include as many strong sales points as possible. The owner should be encouraged to supply many of these sales points; you, the broker, should be able to supply others.

The space under *separate notes* is for confidential information that is of use to the broker. Of course, separate sheets should be used when necessary.

Keep in mind that the form that follows is designed for an apartment building listing. The form can easily be modified or annotated for use with any other form of income property.

The Peckham Boston Company—LISTING FORM

File # _____ Date _____

LOCATION: _____

ADDRESS: _____

DESCRIPTION: _____

TYPE: Brick/Frame Other _____ Number of Stories _____

       Number of Apartments _____ Offices _____

               Stores _____ Other _____

ASSESSMENT—Building _____ Land _____ Total _____

                              Tax Rate _____ 20 _____

(A) Total Annual Income $ _____

EXPENSES:

Taxes _____

Heat _____

Electricity _____

Water (& sewer) _____

Gas _____

Insurance _____

Maintenance _____

_____

_____

(B) Total _____

(C) NET BEFORE FINANCING $_____

FINANCING:

FIRST MORTGAGE: existing/proposed   (circle one)

$ _____ balance   originally $ _____

term balance _____ years   original term _____ years

interest rate _____%

mortgagee:_____

can be prepaid: yes/no   (circle one)   penalty_____

can be assumed: yes/no   (circle one)

_____

SECOND MORTGAGE: existing/proposed   (circle one)

$ _____ balance   originally $ _____

term balance _____ years   original term _____ years

interest rate _____%   principal payments _____

mortgagee:_____

can be prepaid: yes/no   (circle one)   penalty_____

can be assumed: yes/no   (circle one)

_____

THIRD MORTGAGE: existing/proposed   (circle one)

$ _____ balance   originally $ _____

term balance _____ years   original term _____ years

interest rate _____%   principal payments _____

mortgagee:_____

can be prepaid: yes/no   (circle one)   penalty_____

can be assumed: yes/no   (circle one)

_____

FINANCE EXPENSES:

first mortgage interest _____

first mortgage principal _____

second mortgage interest _____

second mortgage principal _____

third mortgage interest _____

third mortgage principal _____

(D) Total _____

(E) NET INCOME $ _____ per year (F) PLUS $ _____ principal

(G) TOTAL YIELD $_____

*Gross price: _____   Net to owner _____
**Gross cash: _____   Net cash to owners _____
Owner _____   Address _____
Home telephone _____   Business telephone _____
Exclusive: _____ Expires _____   Key board # _____
Listed by: _____   Source _____
Owners reason for selling: _____

CODE: A − B = C   C − D = E   E + F = G   F = Total all principal payments
DOUBLE CHECK: 1st mtg. bal. + 2nd mtg. bal. + 3rd mtg. bal. + Gross cash =
             Gross price
DOES THE ABOVE BALANCE?   yes/no
                 (front page of actual form ends here)

                 (back page of actual form begins here)
Rental Information: Rent range _____
                Breakdown of Apts.   ____ studios   ____ 3 bedrooms
                                      ____ one bedroom   ____ other_____
                                      ____ two bedrooms
Rent Roll:

Suite	Apartment Description & tenant (include # of rooms & baths)	Rent per month	Lease and other information
.....	....	....	....
.....	....	....	....
.....	....	....	....
.....	....	....	....
.....	....	....	....

(use additional sheet when needed)

Notes:
kitchens (description) _____
baths (description) _____
heat: type _____ supplied by owner/tenant (circle one)
parking _____
janitor _____ RESIDENT/Non-RESIDENT (circle one)
          If resident, is janitor's apt. income included in Gross?   yes/no
Insurance coverage _____
Furnished apartments (# and type of furniture) _____

Tenants pay own utilities?   yes/no   (circle one)
Elevator?   yes/no   (circle one)
Other sales points: IMPORTANT   (add here any other useful information owner can supply: e.g., new roof, extra land, new wiring, strategic location, etc.). Suggestion—ask owner to list the 10 best selling points.

(use additional sheet when needed)

Separate notes to selling brokers: (e.g.,—contact for key information—flexibility of price, etc.)   * & **
                                       MOST IMPORTANT
                                       Seller understands:

Net cash	yes/no
Net price	yes/no
P.M.M. Amount	yes/no
P.M.M. Interest	yes/no
P.M.M. prin.	yes/no
P.M.M. Term Years	yes/no

(use additional sheet when needed)

How to Obtain and Record the Information

In taking a listing, you have to remember two fundamental facts: (1) The seller, who must supply most of the information, will naturally be prone to painting a completely rosy picture (he wants to sell the building); and (2) All the information recorded must be verifiable—and extensive enough for translation into an operating statement.

Also, you should keep in mind the fact that other brokers may have, or be attempting to obtain, a listing on the same property. Your listing form should be formulated for your use, according to your brokerage capabilities, and according to customary local usage.

The first part of the form offers few problems. Once you have the address, you can go out and actually examine the place in order to complete your description. This shouldn't be necessary from the standpoint of verification; but an on-the-spot examination will actually be of help in your choice of descriptive phraseology.

How Much of the Building Should Be Inspected?

The question often arises, "How much of the building should I inspect in the course of listing it?" There is no clear-cut answer to this; however, see the exterior, public hallways, boiler room—any accessible parts of the building. In addition, try to see a representative sampling of the apartments if it is convenient. Don't hold up the listing procedure if it is impossible to see the property. You can always get back to see it later, and for now the owner will fill you in with an oral description.

Watch Out For Owner's Optimism

When you get to taxes and especially expenses, you must be on guard, for in many questions about income and expense, the owner may be overly optimistic.

Taxes are easily verified; it's a different story, however, in regard to the other operating expenses. The owner's estimate of income will give you not only that information, but also an indication of the reliability of the other information he furnishes.

How to Gather Accurate Financial Statistics (without Offending the Owner)

You should begin your pleasant interrogation of the owner with the question: "What is the income of the building, fully rented?" If he replies, "Oh, the income is *about* $50,000," you must press him for an exact figure; because, remember, all information will ultimately have to stand up to the test of verification.

At this point to assist the owner in his computation estimate, you might say: "Since, of course, we need an *exact* figure, let's break the income down by actual rentals." Now you have a good opening through which you can get to some of the intimate details that only the owner may know.

Here, at this juncture, flip over the listing form and fill in as much information as you can—and have the time to obtain. (If it seems ironic to you that eliciting accurate information from an owner should be difficult, remember that it is human nature to exaggerate when the result is beneficial, and to minimize or conceal when it is not. This is true in all negotiating situations—from marriage to labor-management disputes to real estate brokerage.)

After you obtain all the descriptive information about the rent roll, total up the rents and transfer it to the proper space on the front of the form. (Be careful to multiply the monthly income figure by twelve to arrive at annual income. This sounds elementary, yet I have seen experienced brokers make this simple error, and as a result the final figure just doesn't make sense.)

In the end, you have to take the owner's word as to the accuracy of the information. Nevertheless, you should make all reasonable and tactful efforts to discourage him from giving an unrealistic total picture of his property.

Prevention and cure: There is the safeguard, of course, whereby any deposit we take on a sale will have written into it "subject to verification of expenses and income." However, if you, the broker, try to obtain and record only accurate information on the listing form, you will be, in effect, obviating any problems in verification before they arise.

How Best to Phrase Your Questions

Remember, as you continue with your interrogation, that you must ask each question in a positive manner. I have heard some brokers ask, "You don't know the taxes, do you?" The easiest answer to that question is "No." Some brokers say, "Could you tell me how much your taxes are?" This also is an easy question to answer in the negative.

Always interrogate in a positive, affirmative manner by politely asking a question which requires a specific answer. For example:

"How much were your taxes last year, Mr. Smith?"
"What is the annual cost to heat 100 Main Street?"
"How much does your insurance cost?"

Return now to taxes. As we have noted, usually there are no problems here. Taxes paid on a property are a matter of public record and can easily be verified. Although there is usually no time for the process of verification at this point, to get an accurate tax figure, it is helpful to see either the assessment or the recent tax bill.

How to Do Your Own Rough Verifying On Expenses

On the listing form, under *heat,* the second item of "Expenses," record the total annual expense of heating the building. To tell whether the owner is giving an accurate estimate, simply use your rule of thumb for comparable buildings in your area: multiply the total number of units by the amount that it costs to heat one unit with the type of heating fuel used. Again, in the case of the other utilities, *electric, water,* and *gas,* use your rules of thumb for estimating expenses. If the figures you arrive at disagree considerably with those given by the owner, question him about them.

For the next item, *insurance,* make sure you get complete information as to the coverage. A good practice is to call your own insurance agent and find out what an adequate amount of insurance on this building should cost.

What to Do When You Have to Challenge the Owner's Figures

What do you do when you feel an owner's income or expense estimates are unrealistic? Whatever you do in challenging the figures, it should be done with the utmost tact. After all, you don't want to accuse him of dishonesty.

In general, your challenge should take the form of a "discovery"—a discovery that the owner may have made a natural, innocent mistake in computing his income or expenses. If this doesn't work, try to encourage the owner to look at the matter objectively, to assume the position and attitude of a cautious buyer or a mortgage loan officer: "These figures, of course, will have to stand up under the scrutiny of *all* parties concerned. Could you give me something that will serve to substantiate your estimates?"

Further, you might spell it out to the owner: "When we go to purchase and sale agreements, and the buyer asks for substantiation, will we be able to give it to him? If not, the sale will probably fall through—and all the time we've spent in the negotiations will have been wasted."

The best argument of all to present to the owner about making his expenses and income estimates accurate and realistic is this: "If the buyer challenges these figures and can prove his point—that they are inaccurate—he will have the upper hand, and we'll be on the defensive. Then, we'd never be able to bargain successfully for your price."

When to Put the Buyer On Guard

If you run into a situation where the owner simply insists that he can heat his ten-unit building in Boston for $3,000 per year, ask him why the building is so economical to heat. He may have a very logical reason—perhaps he has a tap on the adjoining owner's fuel tank! Seriously, he may have an extremely efficient system and a well-insulated building. If so, you must include this supporting data on your form. If he can give no logical reason, and if the figure in question is so blatantly out of line with similar existing buildings, then these conditions must be noted and the prospective buyer must be informed until the figures have been verified.

On the other hand, sometimes a broker will be able to point out features of the property, promotional amenities, that the owner himself was not aware of. A long-term owner, especially, may be so close to his building that he loses his sense of objectivity. In this case, the broker should be able to supplement his argument for accuracy with suggestions on how to capitalize on the special features of the building.

Financing: The Critical Part of the Listing Form

It is the financing—the recruitment and involvement of other interested parties and their money—that particularly distinguishes the sale of income property. The possibilities of financing may be the most powerful key you hold to earning your brokerage commission. We will study the power of financing in depth in Chapter 4. For now, let's see how to gather the information in this section of the listing form.

Since financing is the vital force in income property brokerage, it should be given special treatment and attention when the listing is taken. Here again, as with the information on taxes, the financing picture can be readily verified. An owner will rarely hedge on this information. As a matter of fact, it is often the case that he will be surprisingly unaware of just where he does stand, how much interest and principal he's been paying on the property, for example, and even the extent to which his mortgage has been amortized during his period of ownership. Even after referring to the figures, he may reveal a shocking lack of knowledge about the simplest aspects of financing. This is where you, the knowledgeable broker, must step in and utilize your professional skill.

Remember: Your competence—your ability to analyze the financing structure of the property—will enable you to ask the appropriate questions. Your operating statement depends on this.

Keep in mind that your all-important operating statement will be compiled from data supplied on the listing form. The information must be accurate. It must also be extensive enough to enable you to determine how the financing might be made more effective from a new owner's standpoint—and particularly, how much the available financing will cost the new owner.

But, we're talking to the seller now. Let's proceed with filling out the listing form.

Filling Out the Financing Section of the Form

Let us assume that the building in question has a first mortgage and that it's fairly new. Fill in the *balance* and, under *originally,* the original amount; then the *original term* and the *interest rate.* The next two items—*mortgagee* (who holds the mortgage), and whether it can be prepaid with or without penalty—are not absolutely essential at this juncture; this information could, if necessary, be omitted for the time being—but will become essential later, so do your best to obtain it now. Be sure to determine whether the loan can be assumed. This information can help to pave the way for a creative transaction.

> *A sample case:* Let's say the first mortgage was for $700,000, and it was placed five years prior to this date. Under *originally,* you write $700,000.
> "Now, what is the balance, Mr. Owner?"
> "Well, it's about $670,000."

You record this (to be confirmed by computation later). Then you continue, and find out that the *original term* was a 25-year D.R. The *term balance* thus comes out to be 20 years. And the interest rate is 8 percent. This information can then be summarized in the appropriate section of the form.

How Financing Can Be Rearranged For the New Owner

Notice that the listing form provides room for recording information on secondary financing. The data called for here are much the same as those necessary to compute the financing expenses of a first mortgage.

All the secondary mortgages—no matter how many there may be—must be described. It is quite important, however, that you record every detail of each mortgage carefully. You will discover that, in some cases, the existing financing can be assumed—leaving the door open to providing a below-market rate to a new owner.

Caution: You will observe that all the financing expenses will later be computed on an annual basis. Whenever it may be necessary to break the figures down to monthly costs, simply divide the annual costs by twelve. Remember that all income, as well as costs, should be on the same basis for the sake of comparison.

Eliminating Costly Mistakes

At the bottom of the listing form you will see that there is a *code* and a *double check.* Let's look at these more closely. They are your important guides to computing the "bottom-line figure"—your net return.

All the computations on the listing form are quite simple and require only basic arithmetic. However, an arithmetical error can prove costly. Therefore, a code to double-check the arithmetical steps can be very important.

CODE: On our form, you'll note that A is *Total Annual Income;* B is *Total Expenses;* and C is *Net Before Financing*

At the bottom of the form there is the formula: $A - B = C$ (Expenses subtracted from income equals the net before financing).

D is *Total Finance Expenses;* and E is *Net Income.*

Then, $C - D = E$ (Financing expenses subtracted from net before financing equals net income).

F is *Principal Payments;* and G is *Total Yield.*

Then, $E + F = G$ (Net income plus principal payments equals the total yield).

Double Check. Under *Double Check* you now have all the information needed—except *Gross Cash* and *Gross Price.*

Getting the Owner's Price

You say to the owner at this point, "What is the *minimum* price that you'll sell this building for?"

Let's assume his answer is "$900,000."

There are two very important considerations here—and you overlook either at your peril! First of all, you must determine whether the difference between the total mortgage notes and the gross price is required *all in cash*.

Secondly, you must come to a crystal-clear understanding with the owner in regard to your commission.

> I assume, then, Mr. Seller, that the $900,000 includes the commission, so that you will net $850,000 (or whatever your commission rate produces).

If he replies that he wants the $900,000 for himself, what then?

You explain to him that the commission for this sale will be $50,000—and that, therefore, the gross asking price must be $950,000.

If this asking price, in your opinion, is too high for the current market, then you must begin the task of counseling him about a realistic price. Make sure, however, that he understands how your commission is to be paid!

A point of ethics—and practicality: Unfortunately, there are a few brokers who will add the amount of their commission on to the gross asking price without the concurrence of the owner. This practice is not only very foolish (the price being quoted is then higher than competitive brokers' prices, if it is an open listing), but generally considered unethical, as well.

How to Arrange Owner Financing, but Safeguard Your Commission

Once the gross price is established, your next step is to determine the minimum amount of cash an owner will take. (Of course, most owners would like all cash above existing financing, but it is a financial fact of life that a large percentage of income property sales involve a purchase-money mortgage that is taken back by the seller.)

Let's assume that the first mortgage balance is $670,000, and that there is no other financing. It is important to negotiate your commission on the basis that it *must* come from the gross cash realized from the sale.

If the owner in our example wants $100,000 cash for himself, obviously, he will require $100,000 plus $50,000, or $150,000 cash, to cover the commission. Again— make sure that he understands how the commission will be paid.

A false assumption: Occasionally, a broker will assume when a seller says, "I want $100,000 in cash," that this is gross, and that the seller will pay the commission from it. By falsely assuming this, the broker has, at the outset, given away his cash commission. Even if he finds a buyer on the terms set forth on his offering sheet, he has not obtained a cash commission—he has worked for paper! This is so important that there is a line in the operating statement under *Financing Expenses* (see page 57) in which *net cash to owners* must be clearly filled in; thus, the seller understands exactly what he or she will net from the price in cash and in purchase-money mortgage terms.

When there is a differential between the amount of cash the seller wants to receive (*plus* the commission) and the owner's equity, you must then negotiate the terms of the purchase-money mortgage (PMM)—the mortgage that the seller will take back.

In the case we are considering, your purchase price of $950,000 so far is made up as follows:

$ 670,000   First Mortgage Balance
+150,000   In Cash
_____
$ 820,000

The balance then ($950,000 less $820,000) of $130,000 will be the amount of the purchase-money mortgage. The price then breaks down as follows:

$670,000   First Mortgage
+130,000   PMM (to be taken back by seller)
+150,000   In Cash (includes $50,000 commission)
_____
$950,000   Price (includes $50,000 commission)

Thus, the seller will receive $100,000 in cash plus a $130,000 mortgage after paying the $50,000 commission in cash.

How to Handle the Seller's Most Common Objection: Terms

In this case, it is necessary for the seller to take back a purchase-money mortgage in order to realize the price he wants. His major objection to this financing arrangement will probably be the terms. He will sometimes have the idea that he can get a comparatively high interest rate, something comparable to the rate for commercial second mortgage loans.

Here, again, you must counsel him in the financial facts of life. Usually, he'll be able to see the wisdom in his taking back a purchase-money mortgage on bank terms for a reasonable length of time. The argument that must be used to convince a seller to take back a PMM is this:

> There are many more buyers who have a small amount of cash to invest than there are those with large amounts. To eliminate 90 percent of the buying market by asking for a high down payment will tend to depress the eventual sales price. In addition, by taking back a purchase-money mortgage at a "bank" rate, you can maximize your capital gain (taxed to low rates) while minimizing your interest, which is ordinary income (taxed at high rates).

How to Win an Owner's Respect

Remember that there is nothing wrong in negotiating with a seller when you are taking a listing. If he asks a price that is way out of line and you don't question him or indicate that you feel that this price is way out of line, or if he suggests outlandish terms and you don't react by pointing out how unrealistic they are, he is going to think very little of your knowledge of real estate. He will also think very little of your capability of selling the property.

You must list at a realistic price and on practical terms or you are wasting your time. We will spend considerable time discussing financing in Chapter 4, and pricing to sell in Chapter 5. By combining the information in those chapters with your understanding of the listing techniques in this chapter, you should have no trouble in obtaining and negotiating the proper price and terms from any realistic owner.

Gathering the Significant Details

Now, finally, to return to the listing form, look at the items included under *Notes*.

If you examine these items, you'll see that they comprise the basic information required by a buyer who is concerned with the obvious needs of his prospective tenants. These are the things a tenant will look for (such as type of kitchen and bath, air-conditioning, parking, etc.).

Wherever possible, list the utilities and conveniences as *luxuries*. Use the respective manufacturers' trade names and descriptions. And be sure to include every item that might serve to make the building more salable. Spell out in detail the unique features of the building.

Of course, even though your listing of the amenities will be designed to make the property attractive as an income property investment, you should include any deficiencies and faults that may exist. This kind of honest presentation is actually more convincing to a buyer than one that is couched in superlatives. The owner, furthermore, when pressed to reveal the detrimental aspects of the building, will be less likely to persist in an unrealistic appraisal of the building's virtues.

Cyber Assists for the Listing Process

There are innumerable resources on the Internet that can help when you need more than your personal experience to guide you through the process of evaluating the reliability of information taken in the process of listing an income property.

For example a single search on the term "apartment statistics" at this writing yields 694 resources. You will find that many of the *big boys* will do a lot of your statistical work for you. Simply go to the web sites for any of the major commercial brokerage firms (i.e., CB Richard Ellis, Grubb and Ellis Colliers International). Look for their local market reports—and shazam, you have your own research and statistics department!

In addition you can often obtain any information you may need from the various listservs that bring together real estate professionals of common interest. Some of the more popular ones at this writing include many investment categories and several apartment investment groups.

You can also access information on other similar properties for sale at the major commercial property sales portals. At this writing two of the more popular are www.Loopnet.com and www.ccimnet.com. These resources are open to all and contain a wealth of information so you can acquaint your self with the nuances of the local market in question.

CHAPTER 4

How to Use Today's New and Ingenious Ways to Finance Income Property

Many comparative newcomers to the income property brokerage field shudder when the word *financing* is mentioned. For some reason, the word implies complicated computations and sophisticated theoretical concepts—both designed, it seems, to create terror and confusion in the mind of the sales-oriented broker.

Set your fears aside! There are no complicated formulas involved. And there are no theoretical concepts. *Mathematical computations* is just a fancy-sounding phrase that, in income property financing, means nothing more than adding, subtracting, and multiplying. Only on very rare occasions you may have to divide, but tables have been prepared for these times, which can save you that bother. The calculations required usually don't go past sixth-grade math. And to make it even easier, today's calculators remove all of the remaining vestiges of drudgery!

The more you learn about financing, the more effective you will be in negotiating income property sales. As you will see in Chapter 6 on operating statements, many brokers present income and expense figures, but say nothing about financing methods or costs. They leave it to the buyer's imagination to figure out how the property will be financed.

This chapter will help you fill that gap. It will show you how to project the maximum amount of available financing, and will assist you in showing how much it will cost the buyer. It will also show you the minimum down payment the buyer will need, and will give various financing options for different investment objectives.

The Importance of Strategic Thinking

You may ask, "Why should I learn to do these calculations or use tables when I can turn on my computer, use a mortgage calculator, or run all sorts of programs that will do all of these calculations for me?" The answer is both easy and logical.

You can use these programs to do all of your calculations—and you will. For now, however, by working through the calculations and strategic logic presented in this chapter you will not only learn the reasoning behind the math, but you will train yourself to think through financial strategies to keep you way ahead of the competition by providing exceptional service to the buyers and sellers you represent. In short you will be able to recognize opportunities that others overlook.

A Note about Financing Rates and Terms

Over the years in earlier editions (this being the fourth) I have tired of changing interest rates and terms every time the winds of the mortgage market shift. (For example, in previous editions examples have raged from 5% to 18%.) For this reason I will use a variety of rates and terms in the examples in this edition, being pretty confident that over a period of time you will see them all. Please know that the basic principals we share here should pass the test of time no matter where rates go!

Other People's Money: A Primary Source of Financing

The potential in financing income property lies in the fact that it can be purchased by borrowing a high percentage of the purchase price with Other People's Money (O.P.M.). O.P.M. for the purchase price comes in many forms, but the highest percentage usually comes in the form of a bank first mortgage (or first trust deed). For simplicity, in this chapter and throughout the Guide, we will use the term *mortgage* to refer to both mortgages and trust deeds.

First mortgages are generally referred to as primary financing. Second, third, fourth, and so on, mortgages are referred to as secondary financing. Primary financing is usually obtained from savings banks, federal savings and loan associations, insurance companies, and pension funds.

In Chapter 3 on listing, you learned how to assemble the information on existing financing—the amount and the terms. In many cases, if the existing financing can or must be paid off, it is wise to project new financing.

Keep in mind that many income property sales are made by conveying the property to a new buyer who either assumes a mortgage, or takes title subject to the existing financing. In periods when interest rates are considerably higher than the rate on an existing loan, a lender holding a "callable" (alienable) loan will often renegotiate the interest rate to a point midway between the existing loan and prevailing rates.

Even when there is an alienation clause, the bank will usually assent to the sale if it obtains the signature of the buyer on the note, or if there is an adjustment in the interest rate (in a time of increasing rates). The following sections will focus on sales in which new financing is required or desirable.

How Financing Ingenuity Can Make You a Winner

In the example, beginning on page 63, Chapter 3, we discussed a situation where an income property was listed as follows:

$ 670,000	existing first mortgage
+130,000	purchase money mortgage (to be taken back by seller)
+150,000	cash (includes $50,000 commission)
$ 950,000	price (includes $50,000 commission)

Thus, the seller was to receive $100,000 in cash, plus a $130,000 purchase-money mortgage after paying the $50,000 commission. In order to accomplish such a sale, you as a broker must find a buyer with $150,000 in cash to invest as the down payment.

Assume now that, after reviewing the income and expenses, you estimate that you can obtain a new first mortgage of $765,000, and that the seller will still take back a $130,000 second mortgage. In effect, he just wants $100,000 net in cash, plus the $130,000 mortgage. By projecting a $765,000 first mortgage, you can work up the price as follows:

$765,000	first mortgage ($105,000 more than existing mtg.)
+130,000	purchase-money mortgage
+ 55,000	cash
$950,000	price

By analyzing the listed property with a keen eye to possible new primary financing, you have reduced the cash required significantly. Now the listed property can be offered to any one of the many buyers in the market who can invest $55,000, but who do not have the $150,000 previously needed for a down payment.

How to Multiply Your Selling Chances

Carefully analyzing the listing can enable you to come up with ten times as many potential buyers as the competitor who just takes the figures as presented. As a result, the odds are ten to one that the selling broker will be *you* and not your competitor. Carry this one step further, and compare your position with the broker who didn't negotiate the purchase-money mortgage with the seller. That broker is scurrying around looking for buyers with $280,000 in cash to invest!

Keep in mind, however, that if the amount and terms of the existing financing are favorable, it is usually wise to leave it as is. Even if you project new financing and reach an agreement between your buyer and seller, you still have the job of obtaining the projected financing.

Here's what can happen as a consequence of projecting financing that is unrealistic under current market conditions:

Say you have listed a property and projected a $700,000 first mortgage at 6.75 percent interest on a 20-year direct reduction basis. Your parties agree to the sale, contingent upon the buyer obtaining the mortgage projected. Once the property is under agreement, you roll up your sleeves and try to obtain the projected financing, but can obtain only $650,000 at 6.75 percent interest on a 15-year direct reduction basis. Your sale has about a 30 percent chance of going through. Under the foregoing circumstances with all other things being equal, if the sale goes through, the parties are affected as follows:

1. The seller will have to take $50,000 less in cash if the buyer won't pay $50,000 more down;

or

2. The buyer must put up $50,000 more in cash if the seller won't pick up the difference on his purchase-money mortgage;

73

or

3. The broker may have to take most of his commission as a mortgage if neither the buyer nor seller will budge on his cash-down requirements;

and

4. The buyer will receive less cash flow because of the increased interest and principal costs to carry the mortgage.

Six Rules to Help Project Potential Financing

Your job as broker is to project financing that makes the property as salable as possible, but to be conservative enough so that when the time comes you can reasonably expect to obtain that financing. The following rules should be helpful:

Rule 1. When to Project New Financing

Generally, new financing should be projected when:

A. There is an adequate supply of mortgage money at competitive rates through conventional lending sources.

B. The existing first mortgage is paid down well below its original level, or well below the level at which the property can now be financed. (Usually the spread must be at least 10 percent, i.e., you would not generally refinance a mortgage from a balance of $300,000 to a new first mortgage of $325,000, but you would consider refinancing a $250,000 balance to $350,000.)

C. The end result of your refinancing either improves the percentage return on equity or reduces the cash down required to purchase the property.

Rule 2. When to Use the Existing Financing

Most of the time, you should not project new financing, but should set up your offering using the existing financing when:

A. You are in a period of "tight money" with very little money available for mortgage loans.

B. There is a relatively new assumable first mortgage on the property at a competitive rate.

C. The end result of possible refinancing would not improve the cash flow picture, or reduce the cash down requirement.

D. The existing financing is "locked in" and cannot be prepaid.

Rule 3. How to Determine the Amount of Money You Can Borrow

The amount of money you will be able to borrow depends on several variables:

A. The type of property.

B. The location of the property.

C. The credit and net worth of the borrower.

D. The selling price of the property.

E. The lender's appraised value of the property.

F. The lending practices of your mortgage source.

G. The lender's money supply.

A good rule of thumb to start with is that you should generally not project a new first mortgage of over 80 percent of the fair market value of the property. Be careful to base this "80 percent rule" on a reasonable estimate of fair market value, and not on an optimistic owner's inflated asking price. Also keep in mind that this "80 percent rule" can quickly become the "70 percent rule" depending on changes in the mortgage market.

The "80 percent" rule should be applied only to well-located, well-constructed, well-managed properties. There are many exceptions to this rule. Let's examine the variables:

■ Variable A: The Type of Property.

Following are listed the percentage ranges you might expect for first mortgages on various types of well-located income properties:

Apartment houses	70 to 85%
Store blocks	60 to 70%
Office buildings	70 to 85%
Shopping centers	70 to 85%
AAA1 net-net leased buildings	80 to 90%

■ Variable B: Location of the Property.

Depending on location, you should adjust your expected loan as follows:

excellent location—as projected previously
average location—deduct 5 to 10%
poor location—deduct 10 to 20% (if you can get a loan!)

■ Variable C: The Credit and Net Worth of the Borrower.

The lender will normally look primarily to the property in evaluating the amount he will lend. However, he will "bend" somewhat depending on the credit and net worth of the individual borrower or borrowers in a partnership or joint venture transaction. If your borrower qualifies as an excellent credit risk and will "guarantee" the loan, then use the upper figures from the basic projections in Variable A. If he is an average borrower, use the lower limits. If he has a poor credit history, you'd better not project financing for him, because the odds are you won't get it!

■ Variable D: The Selling Price.

Usually the lender will look primarily to its own appraisal of the fair market value of the property. Keep in mind, however, that the lender will need some convincing to peg the fair market value at a level above selling price. You might convince the lender to "hang his hat" on the selling price if it is above his estimate of fair market value. However, if your selling price is below the lender's estimate, be prepared with facts and figures to show him why he should base his loan ratio on fair market value and not on selling price.

To achieve the best possible loan it may be wise to have the seller make application for the loan prior to offering it for sale. By doing this, the seller—who still owns the property—can maximize his financing without being tied to a stated contract price. He should make sure, of course, that the lender's standard loan agreement does not include an alienation clause, which would prevent a sale of the property to your buyer without the bank's approval.

Earlier it was mentioned that many income properties are transferred to buyers who either assume an existing mortgage or take title subject to an existing mortgage. In the absence of an alienation clause, this is of course possible. The seller's risk in transferring title in this manner is far less in income property sales than in single-family sales. This is true for two reasons.

1. First mortgages rarely exceed 80 percent of the value of income property, while single-family loans often exceed 90 percent.
2. In the event an income property loan is foreclosed, there is generally rental income present to support the existing first mortgage. In homes, when a foreclosure occurs, there is no income present to support the mortgage debt service.

If a property warrants a loan in excess of the rules of thumb outlined above, and you can document the reasons why, by all means do so. It is often necessary for you and your buyer to look at a property imaginatively, and to ask: How can the profit potential of this building be maximized? What is the highest and best use? Will retrofitting reduce energy and other expenses? What cost effective improvements could increase its income? Is a condo option viable? Are investment tax or historical tax credits available?

Generally, your buyers will have solid reasons for purchasing investment properties even in an era of higher interest rates. They may believe that a 5 million dollar apartment building will be worth 10 million dollars after conversion to condominiums. Or, they may think that a continuing housing shortage, the rush toward conversion by other investors, or a sensible improvement program will enable them to upgrade rents and make the $300,000 property they're buying today worth $500,000 in a reasonable period of time. And if they believe this, it's because you've sold them.

You can use these same persuasive arguments to convince the bankers. Support your logic in writing with demographic data, contractors' estimates, and projected income and expense figures. For example, you can say, "Yes, Mr. Loan Officer, we are looking for a $900,000 mortgage on this $1 million purchase. As you can see, we reasonably expect this property to be worth $1.2 million in three years, and $1.5 million in five years."

Don't be shy in preparing and defending your case this way to lenders. Ask for the financing you need. If you believe in the profit potential for a property, you can *sell* it to the lender as well as the buyer.

■ Variable E: The Lender's Appraisal of the Property.

Get to know the appraisal practices of the lenders in your area. Some lenders are more liberal than others in arriving at their estimate of fair market value. Often their final figure depends a great deal on your presentation of the property. Certainly a few figures scratched on the back of an envelope aren't going to make much of an impression on the loan officer.

Remember that you may have as big a selling job to do with the lender as you had with your buyer. Therefore, you should give the loan officer a well-prepared brochure containing the following:

1. An accurate operating statement on the property, including a complete rent roll (see Chapter 6);
2. A good photograph of the property;
3. A signed net worth statement of your borrower;
4. A completed loan application on the bank's form; and
5. A covering letter in which you explain why you feel the requested loan will be a good investment for the lender. A well-prepared application will greatly enhance your chances of obtaining the requested loan.

■ Variable F: The Lending Practices of the Lender.

Get to know the lenders in your area. The amount they will lend and the types of property they will lend on or favor vary from lender to lender. Some lenders prefer lending only on single-family dwellings. Some stick to apartment houses. Some like shopping centers. Some only like the core city, while others will prefer lending only in the suburbs.

Follow your local reporting journal, such as the *Banker and Tradesman* in our area, which reports all mortgages given each week. This will give you a good indication of which lenders prefer which areas and what types of properties they will lend on. Also keep in mind that most lenders go through a period where they are temporarily "loaned out." When you run into this situation, try to determine when they will be back in the lending business.

■ Variable G: The Lender's Money Supply.

How do you find out this information? Ask the lender. If a mortgage application that you assist your buyer in placing is rejected—and this happens to everyone from time to time in the normal course of business—there is very little extra effort involved in asking the loan officer for an explanation. Perhaps the bank is presently "loaned out," but would be willing to re-evaluate the loan proposal at a later date. Perhaps the amount requested or interest rate desired is unacceptable, but the lender would be willing to negotiate on different terms. Find out. At the very least, a rejecting lender can provide input that may be helpful to you in writing a new application to a different lender.

Also, don't be shy about asking the rejecting lender if he can give you a lead as to what other lenders in the area might be attracted by your offering. This is simply another application of the networking principle!

By acquiring knowledge of all the local factors included in Variables A to G, you should be able to estimate quickly the amount of money you will be able to borrow, and safely project new financing for any listing that calls for it. *Remember to keep your projections realistic.*

Rule 4. How to Determine the Interest Rate You Will Pay

Generally, interest rates on prime income property loans will range from 1 to 2 percent higher than the rate for residential loans. For example, if in your area a conservative home loan currently costs 5 percent, then a conservative income property loan will cost 6 to 7 percent. Assuming the prime residential rate to be 5 percent, the following interest rates would be indicated on income property:

Apartment houses (depending on quality)	6 to 7%
Store blocks (depending on quality)	7 to 8%
Office buildings (depending on quality)	6 to 8%

In certain periods interest rates can fluctuate significantly and, occasionally, a well-secured income property loan has actually been placed at a rate below the prevailing single-family home rate.

Marginal properties would command even higher interest rates if any loan could be obtained. The six variables mentioned in Rule 2, which control the amount of loan, will also have a bearing on the interest rate.

Rule 5. How to Determine the Length of a Conventional Loan

Conventional mortgage loans have historically been written on a *direct reduction* basis. That is, they are written for a certain period of years, and by paying constant amounts (usually monthly), the loan is completely paid off at the end of the direct reduction term. Currently, however, a great number of loans are written with due dates that are much shorter than the direct reduction term.

The term of the loan is critical to your brokerage job. Obviously, the longer the term, the lower the annual payments. Some of your investors will be looking primarily for *cash flow* (how much cash the investment puts in their pockets at the end of the year). They may also expect to pay off the mortgage or mortgages, but this goal is usually secondary to their desire for cash flow. Your job is usually to project the potential mortgage for the longest possible term without giving yourself an impossible job when it comes time to place the loan.

How Longer-Term Financing Can Increase Cash Flow. The following comparison will make the importance of the direct reduction term clear:

New $1,000,000 loan @ 6% interest	New $1,000,000 loan @ 6% interest
20-year D.R. Carrying costs: Interest $60,000 Principal 26,000 Total $86,000	15-year D.R. Carrying costs: Interest $60,000 Principal 43,000 Total $103,000

Thus, if you as broker can provide 20-year direct reduction financing rather than 15-year, you have added $17,000 to your cash flow.

In the next section you will learn how to arrange the most favorable financing terms that will add many dollars to the potential selling price of the property, and how this will also put many thousands of dollars in extra commissions in your pocket!

The following is a current guideline of what to expect on well-located prime income properties:

Apartment houses	20 to 30 year D.R.
Office buildings	20 to 30 year D.R.
Store blocks	15 to 18 year D.R.

Loans on marginal properties will generally demand a 12-to-15-year direct reduction, if you can obtain a loan!

Important: Find out which lenders in your area will write a loan on a long-term pay-back basis *with a short-term note.* Some lending institutions will, for example, write a loan on a property that might normally command a 15-year direct reduction, on a 20-year direct reduction basis, but with a 5- or 10-year note. In effect, the bank is saying, "We will compute your payments as though this were a 20-year direct reduction, but the note will be due in five years."

This is a sound financing technique for the bank, because if interest rates rise, or the area declines, the bank can either adjust the rate or call the loan in five years (or ten or whatever). The borrower then must refinance the property either with that bank or with another lender.

This is but another method of increasing your cash flow and making a sale that otherwise might not have been made.

Rule 6. How and When to Explain Your Projections to the Owner

Understanding how much new financing you can obtain, at what rate, and for what pay-off period is necessary, but all of this is useless if you cannot negotiate the use of your new financing with the seller. I have seen some of the best natural sales-people fall down miserably when the time came to explain the use of new financing to an owner. It's a real shame to see an otherwise competent salesperson miss a large commission because he didn't take a half hour to sit down and work out a financing presentation before approaching the owner.

Look again at the example on page 63. Mr. Owner has listed his property as follows:

$ 670,000	first mortgage
+130,000	purchase-money mortgage
+150,000	cash (including $50,000 commission)
$ 950,000	(including $50,000 commission)

Assume that you have analyzed the financing make-up and have determined that you can obtain a $765,000 first mortgage on the owner's property.

You hope to effect a sale on the following basis:

$765,000   first mortgage
+130,000   purchase-money mortgage
+ 55,000   cash
$950,000   price

Setting aside, for now, any consideration of interest rate or direct reduction term, let's see how an astute broker might approach the owner to convince him to sell on the basis of obtaining the new first mortgage.

How to Persuade a Seller to Lower the Cash-Down Requirement

"Mr. Owner, I have analyzed the figures you gave me yesterday, and have some concrete suggestions on how we can effectively merchandise your property so that you can obtain the best possible price.

"By using your existing $670,000 first mortgage, even with your taking back a $130,000 purchase-money mortgage, we must find a buyer with $150,000 in cash to invest. There are ten times as many potential buyers for this property with $55,000 to invest as with $150,000—and most of the investors with $150,000 want a much larger property. So our chances of obtaining the highest price are improved about 20 times if we can sell this property with $55,000 down."

Mr. Owner interrupts, "Look, I said I need $110,000 net to myself. I have certain obligations to pay out of that $110,000, and I won't drop it a nickel."

The astute broker continues, "Mr. Owner, let me show you how we can get you the highest price and still find a buyer with lower cash down. My office maintains excellent relations with several lenders, and I am quite confident that we can obtain a $765,000 first mortgage. If we can do this and find the right buyer at your price with $55,000 down, then you will have $105,000 net from the new first mortgage, plus the buyer's $55,000. After our commission you will have $110,000 net to yourself, plus the $130,000 purchase-money mortgage. I would like to suggest that we write it up that way."

Keep This Rule In Mind for Timing Your Proposal

Brokers frequently ask me, "When do you approach the seller with your proposal?" Hopefully, you will be able to spot a situation where new financing will be desirable early in the listing procedure. The earlier you analyze the situation and convince your seller that this is the most effective way to sell the property, the greater your competitive advantage will be, and you will sell the property quicker.

Once you have the owner's agreement to present the property with your projected financing, rework your listing sheet, and retype your operating statement. (In Chapter 6 you will see how to incorporate projected financing into the operating statement.) Keep in mind that you will use the same procedure to convince the owner to sell with a new larger first mortgage when a buyer proposes new higher financing in conjunction with an offer. It's always better, however, for you to propose the financing first, because if a buyer spots the potential of more favorable financing, he's doing your job!

When to Place a New First Mortgage

We've already discussed where to obtain new first mortgage financing and what items you must provide the lender to help make his decision. The next step is to make an application for the loan—and it's important to know *when* to do this. If you have estimated the needed financing properly, you can be reasonably confident that—once you find a buyer for the property—you can negotiate on the terms you have projected.

Some inexperienced brokers will rush out and *shop* for new mortgage financing the day they obtain a listing. This is a particularly dangerous step to take on an open listing. It's much better to get your parties to agree on a sale first. If you go shopping for your financing before your buyer and seller have agreed on terms, you may have wasted valuable selling time. You may also run the risk of arranging financing, only to see a competitor (or the owner himself) sell the property, and take advantage of the loan you have arranged.

Another danger of shopping for a loan before your parties have reached an agreement is that—sooner or later—the lenders in your area will become wary of your running them ragged on sales that never happen. Once your parties have executed a proper purchase and sales agreement—including discussing, negotiating, and agreeing upon the best mortgaging options—then you can swing into action and arrange the financing. If you have done a realistic job of projecting financing options and alternatives, that task should be easy.

The Importance of Breaking Down Financing Costs

Throughout this Guide I will compare what the *average broker* does with what *you* must do to get a competitive edge. Among the most important jobs you must be able to accomplish is that of breaking down financing costs. It's important for your investor to see just how beneficial your proposed acquisition will be after figuring all financing costs. In the residential field, all brokers are capable of computing monthly carrying costs on first mortgage loans—with a handy pocket calculator or online program. But it's a different story with investment properties.

There are two critical differences between financing for the home buyer and financing for the investor:

1. The home buyer thinks and talks in terms of *monthly* carrying costs, while the experienced investor thinks *annually.*
2. The home buyer, although concerned with his equity buildup through amortization of his mortgage, does not actually show the high degree of interest evidenced by the investor. The home buyer knows that at the end of 20, 25, or 30 years he will own his house free and clear. The investor, however, is vitally interested in the amount of principal savings he is building up year by year—and one of your jobs is to show him this by separating the interest from the principal payments.

How to Compute Financing Costs Fast
Using the "Peckham Translator"

Income brokers speak in terms of "annual constants." You might overhear a sophisticated investor say to his broker, "If we can get 6 percent financing, what's the constant for a 20-year direct reduction?" What he is asking is, "At 6 percent interest, what percentage of the borrowed amount will I have to pay each year to liquidate the loan in 20 years?"

If the residential broker were to calculate monthly payments, he would find that a 6 percent 20-year loan would require $7.1643 per $1,000 loaned, or .71643 percent each month for 20 years. An annual constant merely expresses this percentage on an annual basis, that is, .71643% times 12, or

.0071643
×   12
.0859716 or 8.60%

We will talk in terms of annual constants for loans requiring monthly payments. The constants used would be different if the payments were required on a quarterly or annual basis. Generally, however, income property loans are paid monthly; and for simplicity's sake, we will run all of our computations on the assumption that payments are made that way.

Look now to *The Original Peckham Annual Constant Payment and Mortgage Principal Payment Translator* in the illustration on page 89. Don't let the long, tongue-in-cheek title in this chart obscure its simplicity. The Translator is designed to meet the needs of the income property broker who is interested in thinking strategically about *annual* financing costs. The use of an annual constant percent eliminates one step in computing financing costs. By using the Translator, it will not be necessary to multiply a monthly payment by twelve.

Experienced brokers usually commit a few common constants to memory so they don't even have to pull the Translator out. For example: assuming that the most common direct reduction loan available on well-located apartment houses in your area is currently a 6 percent, 20-year direct reduction, you would commit the constant 8.6 percent to memory.

Now I can see a number of you wondering why you should bother with the Peckham Translator after you've just spent a hundred dollars on a pocket calculator or a thousand dollars on a computer. Both get you to the same place, right? Right.

The reason is that, as an investment broker, you are often placed into the role of educator. You are expected to be capable of taking and explaining alternate routes and approaches to the same destination—the completion of a successful transaction. During the various phases culminating in such a transaction, you will deal with many figures. At some point, a client, buyer or seller, with a blank expression may ask, "Excuse me, but where did you get that number?" You could hesitate, stammer, and cover up with, "Well, I pushed this button. See, I'll push the button again and the same number will come up again." This is the answer of a robot broker who only knows what the machine tells him. This is certainly not the best approach.

The right approach is to explain patiently *how* the calculator arrived at a particular answer—and, if necessary, to take out the Translator and explain the calculation. While you won't often be asked for such explanations, you should be ready to give them.

You should be familiar, of course, with computer calculation programs, calculators, and the Translator. They can all serve a useful purpose. Over time, everyone develops preferences for solving different types of calculations. You pick your favorite tool, and have the use of all the others as a back up.

How the Translator Works

It's easy to use the Translator (or, for that matter, any Constant Table). Look for a minute at its construction. The vertical column farthest to the left is a series of yearly lengths for some of the most commonly written direct reduction terms. They run from ten to thirty years, skipping some of the uncommon lengths.

The topmost horizontal column is an ascending arrangement of interest rates. Beneath each listed interest rate are two vertical columns; the one labeled *P & I* contains a percentage figure required to service both *principal and interest* on the loan. This is the *constant* percentage we have been discussing.

The column to the right of the P & I column is marked *P*, and contains a percentage figure that represents an approximation of the amount of *principal reduction* that will occur in the *first* year. This is a convenience column, but is only for use on a new or projected loan. The reason this gives an approximation and not an exact figure is that each month on a direct reduction loan the interest declines and the principal savings increase by a small amount. The importance of this approximation is primarily to enhance strategic financial thinking.

The *P* column is computed as though the first year's principal savings were equal to 12 times the first month's principal savings. This is a technical point, but it should be noted because all of the principal payment figures you will compute for final use on your operating statement will be slightly less than the actual amounts amortized on the loan. The Peckham Translator can also be used to:

- Compute total debt service for any loan.
- Compute the breakdown between interest and principal on a new loan.
- Compute the breakdown between interest and principal on an old existing loan.

Using the Translator For a New Loan

You can compute annual interest and principal payments in two easy steps:

Step 1. To Find the Approximate Annual Interest

You really don't need the Translator for this one. Simply multiply the loan amount by the annual interest.

Example: $100,000 loan @ 6% interest (.06)

$$
\begin{array}{r}
\$100{,}000 \\
\times \quad .06 \\
\hline
\$ \quad 6{,}000
\end{array}
$$

Step 2. To Find the Approximate Annual Principal Reduction (Amortization)

Refer to the Translator in the *D.R. Term* column for the loan term. Move across to the right until you reach the correct interest rate column. The percentage under *P* applied to the loan amount will give you the approximate principal reduction.

Example: $100,000 loan @ 6% interest, 20-year direct reduction. Go to 20-year D.R., and read across to the left until you are under 6% interest. The percentage under the *P* column is 2.60. This = .0106

$$
\begin{array}{r}
\$100{,}000 \\
\times \quad .0260 \\
\hline
\$ \quad 2{,}600
\end{array}
$$

Using these two steps, you now have the annual payments for principal and interest.

Interest	$ 6,000
Principal	+2,600
Total	$ 8,600

As a double check on a new loan you can take the percentage figure in the P & I column under 6 percent interest, 20-year direct reduction term (8.6 = .086) and multiply it by the loan amount:

$$\begin{array}{r} \$100,000 \\ \times \quad .086 \\ \hline \$ \quad 8,600 \end{array}$$

Your answer, then, is correct, as these two figures are equal.

Remember that the total P & I amount will remain *constant* throughout the life of the loan. However, the amount of this $8,600 annual payment that must be used for interest will *decrease* with each payment; and, because the total payment remains the same, the amount that will be used to reduce the principal amount will *increase* with each payment.

How to Compute Principal and Interest Payments On an Existing Loan

Unlike residential transactions, income property sales are sometimes consummated with the buyer taking the property subject to existing financing or by assuming the existing financing. The legal mechanics are well known to any licensed broker. If any of the existing lower rate primary or secondary mortgages can be utilized by a new buyer, it will be advantageous to build your financing package from this base.

When computing the breakdown between interest and principal payments on an existing loan, do not use the *P* column; it is designed only for new mortgages.

There are four steps required to compute interest and principal on an existing loan:

THE ORIGINAL PECKHAM ANNUAL CONSTANT PAYMENT AND MORTGAGE PRINCIPAL PAYMENT TRANSLATOR

	INTEREST RATE																									
	5%		5¼%		5½%		5¾%		6%		6¼%		6½%		6¾%		7%		7¼%		7½%		7¾%		8%	
D.R. TERM	P & I	P	P & I	P	P & I	P	P & I	P	P & I	P	P & I	P	P & I	P	P & I	P	P & I	P	P & I	P	P & I	P	P & I	P	P & I	P
30 yr.	6.45	1.45	6.63	1.38	6.82	1.32	7.01	1.26	7.20	1.20	7.39	1.14	7.59	1.09	7.79	1.04	7.99	.99	8.19	.94	8.40	.90	8.60	.85	8.81	.81
25 yr.	7.02	2.02	7.20	1.95	7.37	1.87	7.55	1.80	7.74	1.74	7.92	1.67	8.11	1.61	8.30	1.55	8.49	1.49	8.68	1.43	8.87	1.37	9.07	1.32	9.27	1.27
20 yr.	7.92	2.92	8.09	2.84	8.26	2.76	8.43	2.68	8.60	2.60	8,78	2.53	8.95	2.45	9.13	2.38	9.31	2.31	9.49	2.24	9.67	2.17	9.86	2.11	10.04	2.04
18 yr.	8.44	3.44	8.60	3.35	8.77	3.27	8.94	3.19	9.10	3.10	9.27	3.02	9.44	2.94	9.62	2.87	9.79	2.79	9.97	2.72	10.14	2.64	10.32	2.57	10.50	2.50
17 yr.	8.75	3.75	8.91	3.66	9.07	3.57	9.24	3.49	9.40	3.40	9.57	3.32	9.74	3.24	9.91	3.16	10.08	3.08	10.25	3.00	10.43	2.93	10.61	2.86	10.78	2.78
16 yr.	9.10	4.10	9.26	4.01	9.42	3.92	9.58	3.83	9.74	3.74	9.91	3.66	10.07	3.57	10.24	3.49	10.41	3.41	10.58	3.33	10.75	3.25	10.93	3.18	11.10	3.10
15 yr.	9.49	4.49	9.65	4.40	9.81	4.31	9.97	4.22	10.13	4.13	10.29	4.04	10.46	3.96	10.62	3.87	10.79	3.79	10.96	3.71	11.13	3.63	11.30	3.55	11.47	3.47
14 yr.	9.95	4.95	10.11	4.86	10.26	4.71	10.42	4.67	10.58	4.58	10.74	4.49	10.90	4.40	11.07	4.32	11.23	4.23	11.40	4.15	11.56	4.06	11.73	3.98	11.90	3.90
12 yr.	11.10	6.10	11.25	6.00	11.41	5.91	11.56	5.81	11.72	5.72	11.87	5.62	12.03	5.53	12.19	5.44	12.35	5.35	12.51	5.26	12.67	5.17	12.83	5.08	12.99	4.99
10 yr.	12.73	7.73	12.88	7.63	13.03	7.53	13.18	7.43	13.33	7.33	13.48	7.23	13.63	7.13	13.78	7.03	13.94	6.94	14.09	6.84	14.25	6.75	14.41	6.66	14.56	6.56

Notes: 1. P & I (Principal and Interest) column represents constant annual percent needed to amortize a principal amount that requires monthly payments.
2. P column approximates first years amortization on a new loan. (Use only for new loans or projected financing.)

Step 1: Ascertain the constant percent (P & I) required from the Translator.

Step 2: Multiply this constant by the *original* loan amount.

Step 3: Multiply the interest rate by the *balance* of the loan.

Step 4: Subtract the interest payment (result of Step 3) from the total constant payment (Step 2). This equals the current annual principal reduction.

Example:

Original mortgage amount	$1,000,000
Mortgage balance	$800,000
Interest rate	6¾%
Term	20-year direct reduction

This existing $800,000 loan had an original amount of $1,000,000. The owner is still making the same constant payments; however, more of the payment is going to principal and less to interest. Here's the solution step by step:

Step 1: From the Translator, we find that the constant percent required is 9.13 (down the *D.R.* column to 20 years, then across to the 6¾ percent *P & I* column = 9.13).

Step 2: $1,000,000 (the original loan)
  ×   .0913 the annual constant (from Step 1)
  $ 91,300 (the annual dollar payment to service the loan)

Step 3: $ 800,000 (loan balance)
  ×   .0675 (interest rate)
  $ 54,000 This is the annual amount now being paid for interest on the loan.

Step 4: $ 91,300 (P & I from Step 2)
  –   54,000 (interest from Step 3)
  $ 37,300 This equals the annual principal reduction at this stage of the loan.

The final result of your calculations for either a new (proposed) loan or an old (existing) loan will then be entered on your listing sheet, and will appear on your operating statement.

How to Figure Mortgage Balances

As you can see from your computations, the portion of each payment going toward debt reduction (i.e., the principal savings or amortization), is steadily increasing. Taking an example of a *new* $1,000,000 loan at 6½ percent interest, 20-year direct reduction, we figured the first year's principal would be approximately $24,500 (2.45 percent from the Peckham Translator × $1,000,000).

The uninitiated investor might assume that in ten years, his total amortization would amount to $245,000, and that his mortgage balance would be $755,000. Many times an investor will ask, "Mr. Broker, what will the mortgage balance be in ten years?" You must be prepared to give him an accurate answer.

To figure the balance simply go to any online mortgage reduction program or mortgage calculator and you will find that the balance will be $655,589.

This is a far cry from the $755,000 balance we would have obtained by simply multiplying ten times our first year's amortization, and deducting it from the original loan.

The well-known fact that the amortization increases with each payment is obvious to most brokers and to experienced investors, but must be made vividly clear to the new investor. If you fail to make this clear to the novice, he will have missed $100,000 in equity built up over a ten-year holding period! You will see why the ability to compute mortgage balances becomes critical when we finish the next section on secondary financing.

Creating Maximum Leverage with Secondary Financing

Primary financing usually makes up 60 to 80 percent of the purchase price. A proper understanding of the use of primary financing in income brokerage puts you in the position to make the sale ten times quicker and ten times more effectively than the broker untrained in the intricacies of primary financing.

In Chapter 7, you will learn more about the magic of leverage. For now, keep in mind that leverage in the investment field refers to the extra investing power one gets through the use of other people's money. For example, if an investor had to make a 50 percent cash down payment for a certain building and could obtain only 50 percent financing, that would be comparatively poor leverage. On the other hand, if he could buy the same property with a 15 percent down payment and 85 percent financing, that purchase would be considered highly leveraged.

Secondary financing picks up from the primary financing level and often, combined with primary financing, can make up 80 to 100 percent of the purchase price! A proper understanding of the use of secondary financing can put you in the position to make the sale 100 times quicker and 100 times more effectively than the broker untrained in its use.

How a Purchase-Money Mortgage Helps Both Buyer and Seller

Secondary financing can help both the buyer and seller—and you! An investor once told me a story that vividly points out how an understanding of the proper use of a purchase-money mortgage is essential to the income broker. Fred (investor) related how he had just acquired a $2,500,000 apartment building which he had bought through Broker A. He had obtained a $2,000,000 first mortgage, and the seller took back a $500,000 second mortgage that was personally endorsed by Fred, who has substantial assets and an impeccable credit rating. This story in itself is not too startling, because income property is often purchased with little or no cash down.

Fred continued by telling me that a few days after he had signed a purchase and sales agreement with the seller, another broker, whom I'll call Broker B, brought him a "statement" on the same property. Broker B's statement set forth minimal details of the offering, including the price. At the bottom of the statement in big bold print was the warning: "Owner not interested in taking back any paper."

Probably the owner had told the broker that he wanted all cash. The broker then, without pursuing the matter with Mr. Owner, translated this desire to his statement. Broker A, who made the sale, had explored the question further: "Of course, Mr. Owner, most sellers *want* all cash; however, it may be possible to find a buyer who will pay a higher price—with you taking back a mortgage—than he would be willing to pay on an all-cash basis. If we can obtain your price and find a buyer who will sign the note personally, and whose credit rating and financial stability you approve, would you take back a reasonable purchase-money mortgage?"

Broker B didn't pursue this line of questioning. While he was wasting his time looking for an investor with $500,000 in cash, or for an investor smart enough to figure out just how he could buy and finance the building (and figure out how much he would have left over after paying for his financing), Fred was sharpening his pencil and negotiating with Broker A. After negotiations were completed, Fred had purchased the property with no cash down, and Broker B was still looking for a buyer who would figure out how to buy the property and finance it. Broker A, in the meantime, was counting his commission!

If Broker B had been lucky enough to find a buyer who was able to shape up an acceptable sale due to his (the buyer's) superior knowledge of financing, the broker would have been paid his commission—but he wouldn't have *earned* it.

The Benefits of Taking Back a Purchase-Money Mortgage

Many times it is to the *seller's* advantage to take back a purchase-money mortgage because:

1. He can usually obtain a higher price for his property.
2. He can sometimes defer paying part of his capital gains tax until he actually receives his cash.
3. He can usually sell his property in a shorter time, because more potential buyers are available with the lower cash down payment required.
4. He may receive a higher rate of interest than he would if he deposited the funds in a money market account.

The purchase-money mortgage almost always works to the *buyer's* advantage because:

1. He can acquire more property.
2. He can experience economic growth on a larger parcel.
3. He can conserve his cash for physical improvements to the property.

Naturally, the ability to negotiate the purchase-money mortgage on realistic terms is to the broker's advantage, because by doing so, he automatically increases the number of potential investors for his offering tenfold!

How the Purchase-Money Mortgage Is Written

We already know what a direct reduction payment is, and what a constant payment is, but the term *balloon mortgage* may be a bit foreign. The *balloon* is the balance of the loan remaining unpaid when the loan must be paid off. Usually the purchase-money mortgage is taken back for a relatively short term, running anywhere from one to ten years (occasionally less, occasionally more). The average purchase-money mortgage runs about five years. If these short-term mortgages were written on a direct reduction, or self-liquidating basis, the drain on cash flow would be too great because of the heavy amortization required.

Earlier in this chapter we mentioned that some lending institutions will lend on a 20-year direct reduction basis, but with a five-year note. This is nothing more than a balloon mortgage. There will be a substantial balance due at the expiration of the note. Back in the 1920s, lending institutions wrote *standing mortgages.* These were loans secured by real estate on which only interest payments were required. There was no requirement to make regular payments to reduce the principal amount of the loan. Many purchase-money mortgages are now written on this same basis—for example, a $100,000 loan at 6 percent interest—only, for a term of five years. At the due date the loan balance is still $100,000. In addition to the interest-only form, there are many other ways the purchase-money mortgage can be written, with principal payments being made in various ways.

Five Basic Types of Purchase-Money Mortgages

The purchase-money mortgage can be written on any terms agreed upon by the buyer and seller, but generally it is written in one of five basic ways:

1. Interest only—with a *balloon.*
2. Interest on the declining balance, *principal constant,* with a balloon.
3. Interest and principal on the declining balance.
4. Interest and principal on a *constant direct reduction* basis.
5. Interest on a *constant payment* basis with a balloon.

Look at the following illustration. This summary of types 1 to 5 gives you a handy reference, for comparison, of some of the characteristics of the five basic methods of writing a purchase-money mortgage.

Type	Description	Example	Balloon?	Principal Payments Constant?	Total Payments Constant?
1	Interest only with a balloon	$10,000, 6% interest, no principal, term 10 years.	Yes	None	Yes
2	Interest on the declining balance, principal constant, balloon	$10,000, 6% interest, plus $25 per month principal, term 10 years.	Yes	Yes	No (decrease)
3	Interest and prin-cipal on the declin-ing balance with a balloon	$10,000, 6% interest, plus 2% principal. Both on the declining balance, term 10 years.	Yes	No (decrease)	No (decrease)
4	Interest and principal on a constant direct reduction basis	$10,000, 6% interest, 20-year D.R. $111.11 per month includes interest and principal payments.	No (unless note term is shorter than D.R. term)	No (increase)	Yes
5	Interest and prin-cipal on a constant payment basis with a balloon	$10,000, 6% interest, 2% principal, term 10 years. Constant payments of $75 per month include interest and principal.	Yes	No (increase)	Yes

How to Compute Purchase-Money Mortgage Debt Service

The most common type of purchase-money mortgage is type 5, where interest and principal are paid on a constant basis, but with a balloon payment required. Types 1 to 4 are very easy to compute. So, let's tackle them first:

Type 1. This is the easiest of all because only interest payments are required.

> *Example:* $10,000 loan amount
> × .06 interest rate
> $ 600 annual interest (no principal payments are required)

Type 2. This one is easy, too. Simply multiply the interest rate times the loan balance. This gives you the annual interest. Then multiply the constant monthly principal payments by twelve, to give you the annual amortization.

Example: (for a new loan)

	$10,000	loan
×	.06	rate
$	600	annual interest
$	25.00	
×	12	
$	300.00	annual amortization

Example: (for an old loan)

	$ 8,400.00	loan balance
×	.06	interest rate
$	504.00	annual interest
$	25.00	per month—principal
×	12	months
$	300.00	annual amortization

Type 3. Another easy one! Simply multiply the interest rate by the loan balance for annual interest. Then multiply the principal rate by the loan balance for annual principal.

Example: (new loan)

	$10,000.00	loan
×	.06	interest rate
$	600.00	annual interest
	$10,000.00	loan
×	.02	principal rate
$	200.00	annual amortization

Example: (old loan)

	$ 9,800.00	loan balance
×	.06	interest rate
$	588.00	annual interest

$ 9,800.00 loan balance
×   .02 principal rate
$ 196.00 annual amortization

Type 4. This type of purchase-money mortgage is written exactly the same as a direct-reduction first mortgage loan. Use the same steps as outlined earlier in this chapter for computing debt service on both new and old loans. Keep in mind that if a Type 4 purchase-money mortgage is written—where the length of the loan is not sufficient to amortize the loan fully during the term—there will be a balloon. Such a loan would be called, for example, a $10,000 second mortgage at 6 percent interest on a ten-year direct reduction basis, but with a five-year due date.

Type 5. This type of purchase-money mortgage is very similar to the direct-reduction loan in that the total payments remain constant; the interest (as in all types except Type 1) decreases with the loan balance; and the principal payments increase with each payment. It differs from the standard direct-reduction loan in two respects:

1. It has a balloon (it is not self-liquidating).
2. It is not expressed as a direct reduction loan. Usually it is expressed, for example, as "a $10,000 purchase-money mortgage at '6 + 3' for five years." This means that the original loan is $10,000, that the interest rate is 6 percent per annum, and the constant payment is 9 percent (6 + 3). The term of the loan (five years) does not enter into your calculation of interest and principal payments at all. In this case, it only tells you when the loan must be paid off; and as you will see later in this chapter, it will be used in calculating the balloon payment due at that time.

A Type 5 purchase-money mortgage can also be expressed as "a five-year $10,000 purchase-money mortgage at 6 percent interest, requiring total monthly payments of $75, which includes both interest and principal." This is just another way of expressing the method by which the loan will be paid during its term. $75 per month equals $900 per annum which, based on the original loan amount, is 9 percent *constant.*

How to Compute Type 5: You can easily compute the annual interest and principal payments on this type of purchase-money mortgage, by using the same steps as used on a direct-reduction first mortgage.

For a new loan you merely multiply the interest rate by the loan amount, and the principal rate by the original loan amount.

Example: A $10,000, 6% interest, 3% principal constant payment P.M.M.

Interest $10,000.00   loan amount
$$\times \quad\quad .06 \quad \text{interest rate}$$
$ 600.00   annual interest

Principal $10,000.00   loan amount
$$\times \quad\quad .03 \quad \text{principal rate}$$
$ 300.00   annual principal

(Remember that here, as in a direct-reduction first mortgage, when payments are made monthly, the total annual interest payments will actually be a bit lower and the principal payments correspondingly higher. But for the sake of projecting our financing costs, the results obtained are sufficiently accurate.)

For an old loan, you learned the four steps (see page 90) to computing the breakdown between interest and principal. Steps 2, 3, and 4 are exactly the same for a Type 5 purchase-money mortgage. The only difference is in Step 1. In a direct-reduction first mortgage, you went to the Peckham Translator to find the constant percent required. In a Type 5 purchase-money mortgage this step is unnecessary, because you already have the constant percent. If the loan is a "6 + 3" constant, then your constant annual payment is 9 percent, or 6 plus 3. If it were a "7 + 3" loan, for example, your constant would be 10 percent.

Example: An $8,000 loan *balance* at 7% interest and 2% principal for ten years. The *original* loan amount was $10,000.

Step 1: The constant is 9% (7 + 2)

Step 2: $10,000.00   original loan
$$\times \quad\quad .09 \quad \text{constant annual payment rate}$$
$ 900.00   constant annual payment (P & I)

Step 3: $ 8,000.00 loan balance

         ×   .07 interest rate

         $ 560.00 present annual interest payment

Step 4: $ 900.00 annual P & I payment

        −   560 annual interest payment

        $ 340.00 annual principal payment

Computations Can Mean Commissions!

When you gather information on an existing second (or third, etc.) mortgage, it may well have been a purchase-money mortgage connected with a previous sale. Make sure that you find out enough information to determine which category the loan belongs in. After obtaining the information, if you combine the foregoing guidelines with basic common sense, you should have no difficulty in projecting your prospect's carrying costs for any mortgage. You will see how your ability to make these computations paves the way to a successful sale in Chapter 15.

Work with various practical problems, and you will find that, after a while, computing debt service will become second nature. You will use this ability daily in taking a listing, preparing an operating statement, and in closing a sale. By working with these day-to-day problems, you will develop an ability to compute mortgage costs quickly. Without this practice, you will revert to presenting properties to a prospect without enough information for him to see exactly what the property will do for him. If you can't show him this, he won't buy!

How to Make a Balloon Mortgage Palatable to Your Buyer

As you can see from the discussion of secondary financing, there is often a *balloon* left when the note comes due. This is because there has been insufficient amortization to reduce the debt to zero (as opposed to a direct-reduction mortgage).

The unsophisticated investor sometimes thinks that when this balance comes due, he will have to reach in his pocket to pay it off. Unless the secondary financing is written for too short a term, this should not be necessary.

The ideal solution to this problem is to write the second mortgage for a long enough term, so that the buyer can then consolidate his financing by refinancing his first mortgage with the present lender or with a new lender. This, of course, assumes that the mortgagee (the holder of the note) is not interested in renegotiating the existing loan.

How to Figure the Balance on Various Kinds of Second Mortgages

Earlier in this chapter, you learned how to calculate the balance left on a first mortgage loan at any given time in the future. Before you can project your client's position to a future date when the *balloon* in the secondary financing will be due, you must compute the remaining balance on the secondary financing. Here's how to do it:

1. *To find the balance for a Type 1 secondary loan:* This presents no problem at all! There are no principal payments required—so the balance on the due date will be the same as today.
2. *To find the balance for a Type 2 secondary loan:* Again no problem! The principal payments are constant. You simply multiply the monthly payment by the number of months remaining before the note falls due, and deduct that amount from the current balance.
3. *To find the balance for a Type 3 secondary loan:* This one is not so easy. But it is also a very uncommon type of loan. Because the calculations are complex, I would suggest you "rev up" your computer and print out a month-by-month progress chart for any specific loan.
4. *To find the balance for a Type 4 secondary loan:* Because this is a direct-reduction type loan, you figure the remaining balance just as though it were a first mortgage and you follow the same procedure as outlined on page 97 of this chapter.
5. *To find the balance for a Type 5 secondary loan:* The illustration on page 98 will assist you in handling a Type 5 loan. By referring to this chart, you can quickly compute the balance remaining when the *balloon* comes due.

The left-hand vertical column gives you the total constant annual rate. The next column in to the right shows various interest rates. The next set of columns show you the percentage of the loan which is paid off at five, ten, fifteen, and twenty-year intervals. The last vertical column gives you the length in time that the loan would have to be written to completely amortize itself. Obviously, for any term shorter than that given in this column there will be a *balloon*.

Here's a problem and its solution from the chart: Your seller will give a $20,000 "6 + 2" second mortgage for ten years. Your buyer wants to know how much will remain unpaid at the end of ten years.

Step 1. Enter the chart with the annual constant rate—8% (6 + 2).

Step 2. In the next column, pick out the interest rate—in this case 6%.

Step 3. Move across to the ten-year column—you find that 27.3% will be paid off.

Step 4. Multiply the percentage paid off by the original loan amount:

$20,000.00 original loan
×   .273 % paid off
$ 5,460.00 amount paid off

Step 5. Deduct the amount paid off from the original balance:

$20,000.00 original loan
− 5,460.00 amount paid off
$14,540.00 balance

Thus, the loan balance will be $14,540 in ten years.

How to Figure the Balance On Odd-Year Terms. If the term of the loan is somewhere in between the given five-year intervals, you must interpolate. A scary word, maybe, but not difficult at all.

CONSTANT PAYMENT PROGRESS CHART (Monthly Payments)

Total Constant Rate	Interest Rate	Percent Paid Off In:				
		5 Yrs	10 Yrs	15 Yrs	20 Yrs	Full Term
5%	3½%	8.2%	17.9%	29.5%	43.4%	34 Yrs.-6 Mos.
	3¾%	6.9%	15.1%	25.1%	37.2%	37 Yrs.-1 Mos.
	4%	5.5%	12.3%	20.5%	30.6%	40 Yrs.-4 Mos.
5½%	3½%	10.9%	23.9%	39.4%	57.8%	29 Yrs.-0 Mos.
	3¾%	9.6%	21.2%	35.2%	52.0%	30 Yrs.-8 Mos.
	4%	8.3%	18.4%	30.8%	45.8%	32 Yrs.-7 Mos.
	4¼%	7.0%	15.5%	26.2%	39.3%	35 Yrs.-0 Mos.
	4½%	5.6%	12.6%	21.4%	32.3%	38 Yrs.-0 Mos.
6%	3½%	13.6%	29.9%	49.2%	72.3%	25 Yrs.-1 Mos.
	3¾%	12.4%	27.2%	45.2%	66.9%	26 Yrs.-3 Mos.
	4%	11.0%	24.5%	41.0%	61.1%	27 Yrs.-7 Mos.
	4¼%	9.7%	21.8%	36.6%	55.0%	29 Yrs.-1 Mos.
	4½%	8.4%	18.9%	32.1%	48.5%	30 Yrs.-11 Mos.
	4¾%	7.0%	16.0%	27.3%	41.6%	33 Yrs.-2 Mos.
	5%	5.7%	12.9%	22.3%	34.9%	35 Yrs.-11 Mos.
6½%	3½%	16.4%	35.9%	59.1%	86.1%	22 Yrs.-2 Mos.
	3¾%	15.1%	33.3%	55.3%	81.7%	23 Yrs.-0 Mos.
	4%	13.8%	30.7%	51.9%	76.4%	24 Yrs.-0 Mos.
	4¼%	12.5%	28.0%	47.1%	70.7%	25 Yrs.-1 Mos.
	4½%	11.2%	25.2%	42.7%	64.7%	26 Yrs.-3 Mos.
	4¾%	9.9%	22.7%	38.2%	58.2%	27 Yrs.-9 Mos.
	5%	8.5%	19.4%	13.4%	51.4%	29 Yrs.-5 Mos.
	5¼%	7.1%	16.4%	28.4%	44.1%	31 Yrs.-6 Mos.
	5½%	5.7%	15.3%	23.2%	36.3%	34 Yrs.-2 Mos.
7%	3½%	19.1%	41.8%	68.9%		19 Yrs.-10 Mos.
	3¾%	17.8%	39.4%	65.3%	96.6%	20 Yrs.-6 Mos.
	4%	16.6%	36.8%	61.5%	91.7%	21 Yrs.-9 Mos.
	4¼%	15.3%	34.2%	57.6%	86.5%	22 Yrs.-0 Mos.
	4½%	14.0%	31.5%	53.4%	80.9%	23 Yrs.-0 Mos.
	4¾%	12.7%	28.7%	49.1%	74.9%	24 Yrs-0 Mos.
	5%	11.3%	25.9%	44.5%	68.5%	25 Yrs.-2 Mos.
	5¼%	10.0%	23.0%	39.8%	61.7%	26 Yrs.-6 Mos.
	5½%	8.6%	19.9%	34.8%	54.5%	28 Yrs.-1 Mos.
	5¾%	7.2%	16.8%	29.7%	46.7%	30 Yrs.-1 Mos.
	6%	5.8%	13.7%	24.2%	38.5%	32 Yrs.-7 Mos.

CONSTANT PAYMENT PROGRESS CHART (Monthly Payments) (*continued*)

Total Constant Rate	Interest Rate	Percent Paid Off In:				
		5 Yrs	10 Yrs	15 Yrs	20 Yrs	Full Term
7½%	3½%	21.8%	47.8%	78.8%		18 Yrs.-0 Mos.
	3¾%	20.6%	45.4%	75.4%		18 Yrs.-7 Mos.
	4%	19.3%	42.9%	71.8%		19 Yrs.-2 Mos.
	4¼%	18.1%	40.4%	68.0%		19 Yrs.-9 Mos.
	4½%	16.8%	37.8%	64.1%	97.0%	20 Yrs.-5 Mos.
	4¾%	15.0%	35.1%	60.0%	91.5%	21 Yrs.-2 Mos.
	5%	14.2%	32.4%	55.7%	85.6%	22 Yrs.-1 Mos.
	5¼%	12.8%	29.5%	51.2%	79.3%	23 Yrs.-0 Mos.
	5½%	11.5%	26.6%	46.5%	72.6%	24 Yrs.-2 Mos.
	5¾%	10.1%	23.6%	41.5%	65.4%	25 Yrs.-5 Mos.
	6%	8.7%	20.5%	36.4%	57.9%	26 Yrs.-11 Mos.
	6½%	5.9%	14.0%	25.3%	40.9%	31 Yrs.-1 Mos.
8%	3½%	24.5%	53.8%	88.6%		16 Yrs.-6 Mos.
	3¾%	23.3%	51.5%	85.4%		16 Yrs.-11 Mos.
	4%	22.1%	49.1%	82.0		17 Yrs.-5 Mos.
	4¼%	20.9%	46.6%	78.5%		17 Yrs.-11 Mos.
	4½%	19.6%	44.1%	74.8%		16 Yrs.-5 Mos.
	4¾%	18.3%	41.5%	70.9%		19 Yrs.-1 Mos.
	5%	17.0%	38.8%	66.8%		19 Yrs.-8 Mos.
	5¼%	15.7%	36.1%	62.5%	97.0%	20 Yrs.-5 Mos.
	5½%	14.4%	33.2%	58.1%	90.8%	21 Yrs.-3 Mos.
	5¾%	13.0%	30.3%	53.4%	84.1%	22 Yrs.-2 Mos.
	6%	11.6%	27.3%	48.5%	77.0%	23 Yrs.-2 Mos.
	6½%	8.8%	21.1%	37.9%	61.3%	25 Yrs.-10 Mos.
	7%	6.0%	14.4%	26.4%	43.4%	29 Yrs.-10 Mos.
8½%	3½%	27.3%	59.8%	98.5%		15 Yrs.-3 Mos.
	3¾%	26.1%	57.5%	95.4%		15 Yrs.-7 Mos.
	4%	24.9%	55.2%	92.3%		16 Yrs.-0 Mos.
	4¼%	23.6%	52.8%	89.0%		16 Yrs.-5 Mos.
	4½%	22.4%	5.0%	85.5%		16 Yrs.-10 Mos.
	4¾%	21.1%	47.9%	81.8%		17 Yrs.-4 Mos.
	5%	19.8%	45.3%	78.0%		17 Yrs.-10 Mos.
	5¼%	16.5%	42.6%	73.5%		18 Yrs.-5 Mos.
	5½%	17.2%	39.9%	69.7%		19 Yrs.-0 Mos.

CONSTANT PAYMENT PROGRESS CHART (Monthly Payments) (*continued*)

Total Constant Rate	Interest Rate	Percent Paid Off In:				
		5 Yrs	10 Yrs	15 Yrs	20 Yrs	Full Term
8½%	5¾%	15.9%	37.1%	65.2%		19 Yrs.-9 Mos.
	6%	14.5%	34.1%	60.6%	96.3%	20 Yrs.-6 Mos.
	6½%	11.8%	28.1%	50.6%	81.7%	22 Ys.-4 Mos.
	7%	8.9%	21.6%	39.6%	65.1%	24 Yrs.-11 Mos.
	7½%	6.0%	14.8%	27.6%	46.1%	28 Yrs.-8 Mos.
9%	3½%	30.0%	65.7%			14 Yrs.-2 Mos.
	3¾%	28.8%	63.6%			14 Yrs.-5 Mos.
	4%	27.6%	61.4%			14 Yrs.-9 Mos.
	4¼%	26.4%	59.1%	99.4%		15 Yrs.-1 Mos.
	4½%	25.2%	56.7%	96.2%		15 Yrs.-6 Mos.
	4¾%	23.9%	54.3%	92.7%		15 Yrs.-10 Mos.
	5%	22.7%	51.8%	89.1%		16 Yrs.-4 Mos.
	5¼%	21.4%	49.2%	85.3%		16 Yrs.-9 Mos.
	5½%	20.1%	46.5%	81.3%		17 Yrs.-3 Mos.
	5¾%	18.8%	43.8%	77.1%		17 Yrs.-10 Mos.
	6%	17.4%	41.0%	72.7%		18 Yrs.-5 Mos.
	6½%	14.7%	35.1%	63.2%		19 Yrs.-10 Mos.
	7%	11.9%	28.8%	52.8%	86.8%	21 Yrs.-7 Mos.
	7½%	9.1%	22.2%	41.4%	69.2%	24 Yrs.-0 Mos.
	8%	6.1%	15.2%	28.8%	49.1%	27 Yrs.-7 Mos.
9½%	3½%	32.7%	71.7%			13 Yrs.-2 Mos.
	3¾%	31.5%	69.6%			13 Yrs.-5 Mos.
	4%	30.4%	67.5%			13 Yrs.-9 Mos.
	4¼%	29.2%	65.3%			14 Yrs.-0 Mos.
	4½%	28.0%	63.0%			14 Yrs.-4 Mos.
	4¾%	26.7%	60.7%			14 Yrs.-8 Mos.
	5%	25.5%	58.2%			15 Yrs.-0 Mos.
	5¼%	24.2%	55.7%	96.7%		15 Yrs.-5 Mos.
	5½%	23.0%	53.2%	92.9%		15 Yrs.-10 Mos.
	5¾%	21.7%	50.5%	89.0%		16 Yrs.-3 Mos.
	6%	20.3%	47.8%	84.8%		16 Yrs.-9 Mos.
	6½%	17.7%	42.1%	75.9%		17 Yrs.-10 Mos.
	7%	14.9%	36.1%	66.0%		19 Yrs.-2 Mos.
	7½%	12.1%	29.7%	55.2%	92.9%	20 Yrs.-11 Mos.
	8%	9.2%	22.9%	43.3%	73.6%	23 Yrs.-2 Mos.

CONSTANT PAYMENT PROGRESS CHART (Monthly Payments) (*continued*)

Total Constant Rate	Interest Rate	Percent Paid Off In:				
		5 Yrs	10 Yrs	15 Yrs	20 Yrs	Full Term
10%	3½%	35.5%	77.7%			12 Yrs.-4 Mos.
	3¾%	34.3%	75.7%			12 Yrs.-7 Mos.
	4%	33.1%	73.6%			12 Yrs.-10 Mos.
	4¼%	32.0%	71.5%			13 Yrs.-1 Mos.
	4½%	30.8%	69.3%			13 Yrs.-4 Mos.
	4¾%	27.6%	67.0%			13 Yrs.-8 Mos.
	5%	28.3%	64.7%			13 Yrs.-11 Mos.
	5¼%	27.1%	62.3%			14 Yrs.-3 Mos.
	5½%	25.8%	59.8%			14 Yrs.-7 Mos.
	5¾%	24.6%	57.3%			14 Yrs.-0 Mos.
	6%	23.3%	54.6%	96.9%		15 Yrs.-4 Mos.
	6½%	20.6%	49.1%	88.8%		16 Yrs.-3 Mos.
	7%	17.9%	43.3%	79.2%		17 Yrs.-3 Mos.
	7½%	15.1%	37.1%	69.0%		18 Yrs.-7 Mos.
	8%	12.2%	30.5%	57.7%	98.2%	20 Yrs.-3 Mos.
10½%	3½%	38.2%	83.7%			11 Yrs.-8 Mos.
	3¾%	37.1%	81.7%			11 Yrs.-10 Mos.
	4%	35.9%	79.8%			12 Yrs.-1 Mos.
	4¼%	34.8%	77.7%			12 Yrs.-3 Mos.
	4½%	33.6%	75.6%			12 Yrs.-6 Mos.
	4¾%	32.4%	73.4%			12 Yrs.-9 Mos.
	5%	31.2%	71.2%			13 Yrs.-0 Mos.
	5¼%	29.9%	68.9%			13 Yrs.-3 Mos.
	5½%	28.7%	66.5%			13 Yrs.-7 Mos.
	5¾%	27.4%	64.0%			13 Yrs.-10 Mos.
	6%	26.2%	61.5%			14 Yrs.-12 Mos.
	6½%	23.6%	56.1%			14 Yrs.-11 Mos.
	7%	20.9%	50.5%	92.4%		15 Yrs.-9 Mos.
	7½%	10.1%	44.5%	82.8%		16 Yrs.-11 Mos.
	8%	15.3%	38.1%	72.1%		18 Yrs.-0 Mos.
11%	3½%	40.9%	89.6%			11 Yrs.-0 Mos.
	3¾%	39.8%	87.8%			11 Yrs.-2 Mos.
	4%	38.7%	85.9%			11 Yrs.-4 Mos.
	4¼%	37.5%	83.9%			11 Yrs.-7 Mos.

CONSTANT PAYMENT PROGRESS CHART (Monthly Payments) (*continued*)

Total Constant Rate	Interest Rate	Percent Paid Off In:				
		5 Yrs	10 Yrs	15 Yrs	20 Yrs	Full Term
11%	4½%	36.4%	81.9%			11 Yrs.-9 Mos.
	4¾%	35.2%	79.8%			12 Yrs.-0 Mos.
	5%	34.0%	77.6%			12 Yrs.-2 Mos.
	5¼%	32.8%	75.4%			12 Yrs.-5 Mos.
	5½%	31.6%	73.1%			12 Yrs.-8 Mos.
	5¾%	30.3%	70.7%			12 Yrs.-11 Mos.
	6%	29.1%	68.3%			13 Yrs.-3 Mos.
	6½%	26.5%	63.2%			13 Yrs.-10 Mos.
	7%	23.9%	57.7%			14 Yrs.-6 Mos.
	7½%	21.2%	51.9%	96.6%		15 Yrs.-4 Mos.
	8%	18.4%	45.7%	86.5%		16 Yrs.-4 Mos.
11½%	3½%	45.6%	95.6%			10 Yrs.-5 Mos.
	3¾%	42.5%	93.9%			10 Yrs.-7 Mos.
	4%	41.4%	92.0%			10 Yrs.-9 Mos.
	4¼%	40.5%	90.1%			10 Yrs.-11 Mos.
	4½%	39.2%	88.2%			11 Yrs.-1 Mos.
	4¾%	38.0%	86.2%			11 Yrs.-3 Mos.
	5%	36.8%	84.1%			11 Yrs.-6 Mos.
	5¼%	35.6%	82.0%			11 Yrs.-8 Mos.
	5½%	34.4%	79.8%			11 Yrs.-11 Mos.
	5¾%	33.2%	77.5%			12 Yrs.-2 Mos.
	6%	32.0%	75.1%			12 Yrs.-4 Mos.
	6½%	29.4%	70.2%			12 Yrs.-11 Mos.
	7%	26.8%	64.9%			13 Yrs.-6 Mos.
	7½%	24.2%	59.3%			14 Yrs.-2 Mos.
	8%	21.4%	53.4%			15 Yrs.-0 Mos.
12%	3½%	46.4%				9 Yrs.-11 Mos.
	3¾%	45.3%	99.9%			10 Yrs.-1 Mos.
	4%	44.2%	98.2%			10 Yrs.-2 Mos.
	4¼%	43.1%	96.4%			10 Yrs.-4 Mos.
	4½%	42.0%	94.5%			10 Yrs.-6 Mos.
	4¾%	40.8%	92.6%			10 Yrs.-8 Mos.
	5%	39.7%	90.6%			10 Yrs.-10 Mos.
	5¼%	38.5%	88.5%			11 Yrs.-0 Mos.

CONSTANT PAYMENT PROGRESS CHART (Monthly Payments) (*continued*)

Total Constant Rate	Interest Rate	Percent Paid Off In:				
		5 Yrs	10 Yrs	15 Yrs	20 Yrs	Full Term
12%	5½%	37.3%	86.4%			11 Yrs.-3 Mos.
	5¾%	36.1%	84.2%			11 Yrs.-5 Mos.
	6%	34.9%	81.9%			11 Yrs.-7 Mos.
	6½%	32.4%	77.2%			12 Yrs.-1 Mos.
	7%	29.8%	72.1%			12 Yrs.-7 Mos.
	7½%	27.2%	66.7%			13 Yrs.-2 Mos.
	8%	24.5%	61.0%			13 Yrs.-10 Mos.

Suppose, in the example cited, the loan is to be written for seven years rather than ten years. When you reach step 3, simply take the following sub-steps:

Step 3A. Enter the chart for the next *longest* term—in this case ten years. You find 27.3%.

Step 3B. Enter the chart for the next shortest term—in this case five years. You find 11.6%.

Step 3C. Subtract the smaller percentage from the larger:

$$\begin{array}{r} .273 \\ -.116 \\ \hline .157 \end{array}$$

Step 3D. Because seven years is two-fifths of the way from five years to ten years, multiply the difference 2/5 times .157:

$$\begin{array}{r} .157 \\ \times\ 2/5 \\ \hline .0628 \end{array}$$

Step 3E. Add the result obtained in Step 3D to the percentage paid off in five years; your result is the percentage paid off in seven years:

$$\begin{array}{r} .116 \\ +\ .0628 \\ \hline .1788\ \text{or}\ .179 \end{array}$$

Paying Off a Second Mortgage

You are now equipped to compute mortgage balances for both primary and secondary financing. Use it. You didn't go to the trouble of learning how to do this just for mental gymnastics—it's vital to your job as an income broker. (Of course you will use your handy calculator or investment analysis programs on the computer or online from here on out!)

You have been preparing for the day a prospect looks you in the eye and says, "O.K., Mr. Broker, this deal looks pretty good to me, but what happens when this second mortgage comes due?" You had better have the answer for him—or forget the whole thing! With a good set of financing tables, a good financial calculator, or an online program you should be ready.

(You may wonder why we have gone through the pain of doing these calculations when most of today's hand-held financial calculators or online investment analysis programs can do them directly. We did this because it is absolutely necessary that you have a *feel* for the numbers. Once you have acquired this natural flair, a calculator will speed the process immeasurably.)

How to Overcome a Buyer's Fears

What follows is a simple form to show a prospect where he should stand when his second mortgage comes due. My brokers have saved many a sale by using this projection to overcome a buyer's fears. This is a section of an overall investment analysis form that will be discussed further in Chapter 6 on Operating Statements, in Chapter 7 on Taxes, and in Chapter 15 on Closing the Sale.

With this easy-to-use form, you can quickly let your prospect know if, when the secondary financing comes due, he can obtain a new first mortgage that will be sufficient in dollar amount to pay off the remaining balances on his existing financing. If the buyer cannot obtain a large enough loan, the form allows you to project his income picture after utilizing secondary financing.

How to Use "Economic Growth Rate" to Make the Sale

Before using the form, you must be familiar with the growth pattern in your area. In Chapter 7, you will learn how general economic growth affects real estate values.

For now, it is sufficient to realize that inflation in the United States has run at an increasing rate almost unabated for decades. Real estate values in most areas generally increase at an even greater rate. You should determine what a conservative economic growth rate for your area is for property that is maintained in its present condition—for example, in the Greater Boston area, a 6 percent rate is generally considered a conservative estimate. This rate will vary from city to city, neighborhood to neighborhood, and certainly year to year.

PRINCIPAL SAVINGS ANALYSIS

Secondary due date _____ (SDD)

23. Fair market value now   _____

24. Annual growth % × years   × _____

25. FMV at SDD   = _____

26. Estimated loan/FMV %   × _____

27. Estimated new first mtg. @ SDD   = _____

28. Total existing mtg. bal. @ SDD   − _____

29. Surplus/or Bal. required   = _____

New first mortage (line 28)

30. Amount _____ Debt. serv.   _____

31. Secondary amount _____ Debt. serv. + _____

32. Total debt service   = _____

33. Debt service now (line 8)   _____

34. Debt service after SDD (line 31)   _____

35. Cash flow before taxes (Increase/Decrease)   _____

A case in point, using the analysis form: With this as background, let's assume that your prospect is about to make an offer to purchase 100 Main Street, which is a 20-unit brick apartment building worth $1,000,000. He has only $100,000 in cash. He will offer $1,000,000 with financing as follows:

$700,000 first mortgage @ 6½% interest, 20-year, direct reduction,
$200,000 purchase-money mortgage @ 7-2% principal (9% constant) 5-year term.

Then he turns to you and says, "Mr. Broker, what will happen in five years when I have to pay off that $200,000 second mortgage?"

Follow the solution through using the analysis form:

Line 23: "Mr. Buyer, the fair market value of this property is $1,000,000 now." (You enter $1,000,000.)

Line 24: (You have already explained economic growth to him.) "Mr. Buyer, 3 percent is considered a conservative growth rate in this area. Your purchase-money mortgage will run for five years. In five years if you maintain the property in its current condition, it should be worth 1.15 × its current value. (.03 × five years = .15 without compounding.)

Of course, if you let the property deteriorate, this will not hold true, but if you improve the property the figure should be higher." (You enter 1.15.)

Line 25: Multiply 1.15 times $1,000,000, and your result indicates a probable fair market value of $1,150,000 in five years (without compounding).

Line 26: "Mr. Buyer, today we can obtain a 70 percent first mortgage at 6½ percent interest on a 20-year direct reduction basis. No one can project mortgage terms five years ahead, so we must go on the assumption that similar rates and terms will be available. They may be less favorable, but on the other hand, they may be more favorable. (You enter 70 percent.) However, we should be able to arrange a new first mortgage in five years, at 70 percent of the appreciated value."

Line 27: You multiply 70 percent times $1,150,000, and enter your estimated new first mortgage loan at the secondary due date . . . $805,000.

Line 28: You calculate that the first mortgage balance will be $599,200. You also know that the second mortgage balance will be $176,200. Your total mortgage balance then will be $775,400. You enter it and explain, "Mr. Buyer, the total balance due in five years on both of your present mortgages will be $775,400."

Line 29: You subtract the remaining balance on the mortgages (line 28) from the new first mortgage obtainable (line 27), and enter $29,600 on line 29. "Mr. Buyer, based on these projections you will only have to refinance to $775,400 to eliminate your present mortgages. You should be able to refinance to $805,000, which means that if you refinance to this higher amount, you would put the $29,600 surplus in your pocket at that time—and this $29,600 would be tax-free!"

The illustration below shows the completed form for the preceding presentation:

PRINCIPAL SAVINGS ANALYSIS

Secondary due date __5 years__ (SDD)

23. FMV Now		$1,000,000
24. Annual growth 6% × years	×	1.15
25. FMV at SDD	=	1,150,000
26. Estimated loan/FMV %	×	.70
27. Estimated new first mtg. @ SDD	=	805,000
28. Total existing mtg. bal. @ SDD	–	775,400
29. Surplus/or Bal. required	=	29,600

Using lines 30 to 35, you can carry your analysis a step further and show Mr. Buyer how his spendable income will be affected when he refinances.

New first mortgage

30. Amount __$775,400 (6½% 20 yr.)__ Debt. serv.		$69,400
31. Secondary amount _____ Debt. serv. +		None required
(If necessary) (line 28)		
32. Total debt service	=	69,400
33. Debt service now (line 8)		80,650
34. Debt service after SDD (line 31)		69,400
35. Cash flow before taxes (Increase/Decrease)		11,250

Assume that Mr. Buyer refinances to $775,400, which is the total amount he needs to liquidate his existing mortgage balances as shown on line 28.

You calculate that $775,400 at 6½ percent interest, on a 20-year direct-reduction basis, will cost $69,400 per year for principal and interest, and you explain, "Mr. Buyer, when you refinance in five years you will need $775,400. Notice that your total debt service will be $11,250 less than your current costs. This, of course, will be a very small amount when rent increases over the five-year term are considered."

What to Do If the Purchase-Money Mortgage Term Is Too Short

If your calculations show that the purchase-money mortgage term is too short, so that a new first mortgage could not be obtained to cover the existing balances, there are still several alternatives. Here are a few:

1. The prospect can try to negotiate the term of the purchase-money mortgage for a sufficient period to accomplish proper refinancing.
2. If this is not possible, your prospect can still acquire the property and when the secondary financing comes due, he can either make up the required amount from other funds; or
3. He can renegotiate the purchase-money mortgage with the holder; or
4. He can obtain the excess required by borrowing that amount from a commercial lender. (The cost of this borrowing can be calculated on line 31 of the Analysis Worksheet.)

Of course, if your prospect follows the fourth alternative, he will have to pay commercial money interest rates, which generally run at a higher rate than charged by regular lending institutions. In most cases, however, your prospect's gross spendable income should not be adversely affected, even with the higher interest rates. This is possible because of the lower total mortgage balance combined with anticipated increased rental income.

How, Why, and When, to Use Commercial Secondary Financing

Primary financing, as we have seen, usually is provided by traditional lending institutions. Secondary financing, many times, can be arranged with the seller in the form of a purchase-money mortgage at interest rates close to prevailing bank rates—and quite frequently less.

If secondary financing is needed and cannot be arranged with the seller, then you as the broker must often be prepared to arrange a second mortgage loan with a commercial second-mortgage lender.

The commercial second mortgage lender is a firm or individual who will provide money to the buyer that he can add to his equity-capital and use as a down payment. The loan is secured by a second mortgage on the property. The interest rates, as you will see, are greater than those you would pay to a first mortgage lender.

Don't let the fact that we call this mortgage lender a commercial lender confuse you. He can advance funds for the acquisition of an apartment house, a shopping center, land—in fact, he may lend on any type of real property, including homes. The market rates charged by the commercial lender will be governed by the supply and demand for money in his area, and also by local usury laws.

Some Common Uses of Commercial Secondary Financing

Commercial lenders serve a very useful purpose in the income property field. They are able to provide funds in excess of normal first mortgage lending limits—and because the risk is greater, the interest rates they command are greater.

Builders and converters many times will use commercial money to complete a project when their construction financing and equity money run short. In the same way, professional investors will utilize commercial money if they need additional equity capital to acquire a property when the seller will not take back an adequate purchase-money mortgage. They also, as we noted earlier, will use commercial money when a short-term purchase-money mortgage comes due and the refinancing proceeds are not adequate to pay off the existing financing.

What Rates to Expect For Commercial Loans

Commercial loans are often written at interest rates that are approximately 2 to 4 points higher than those of primary mortgage loans. For example: if the current first mortgage rate is 7 percent interest, you would expect to pay 9 to 11 percent for a commercial second mortgage, if allowed by local usury laws. Repayment of principal is usually negotiable on commercial loans, and can range from straight interest type loans requiring no principal payments, right up to direct-reduction type loans. For ease of illustration, in the next few pages we will assume that all the commercial second mortgages in our examples require no principal payments during their term.

How to Cope with the Buyer's Fear of High Interest Rates

Many investors are frightened by 9 to 10 to 11 percent interest rates, believing that this type of loan is overly dangerous, or that there is something wrong with the property if such high interest rates must be paid for a second mortgage. Because of this fear, many lenders will arrange an *add-on* second mortgage. This type of loan is very similar to an automobile loan you obtain from a bank—in that the true interest rate is higher than the stated rate. The add-on second mortgage, however, can be very useful to the buyer and to the broker, and an understanding of this type of loan will help you make many sales that otherwise might have been lost.

If the current bank rate for first mortgages is 7 percent, for example, a commercial lender might refer to his "add-on" loan as a "7 and 4 add on." This means that the lender will compute the add on or bonus at 4 percent per year, each year, for the length of the loan. Then the total bonus will be added to the actual amount loaned, and the promissory note will be written at that figure, with 7 percent interest to be paid on the higher amount, which must be paid off at the due date. Financial Disclosure Regulations require that the rate of interest on these types of loans be divulged. However, we shall see how they can be helpful in structuring a transaction.

How to Show a Buyer the Cost of an Add-On Mortgage

Suppose you are sitting with a client and he says, "Can you get me a $20,000, 7 and 5 add-on loan for five years? And if so, how much will my current carrying cost be?"

Use these four steps, and you can figure the cost of an add-on mortgage:

Step 1. Multiply the actual amount loaned by the annual add-on rate = annual bonus. $5\% \times \$20,000 = \$1,000$

Step 2. Multiply the annual bonus by the term of the loans = $\$1,000 \times 5$ (years) = $\$5,000$

Step 3. Add the total bonus to the actual cash loaned = the face amount of loan to be repaid at the due date. $20,000 + $5,000 = $25,000

Step 4. Multiply the face amount of the note by the basic interest rate = the annual carrying cost. $25,000 × .07 = $1,750

Why the Add-On Mortgage Is an Effective Brokerage Tool

The true interest rate of this loan is in excess of 12 percent, because the borrower is in effect paying interest on the amount borrowed plus interest on the bonus—and when he repays the loan, he is paying the bonus. The "7 + add-on" mortgage, despite its higher interest rate, is a very effective brokerage tool for two reasons.

1. The note is not written at 12 to 14 percent interest, which in itself tends to provide a psychological block to the average investor.

2. The carrying costs of the loan, during its term, are actually lower than the straight interest type loan.

   For example: A $20,000 loan at 12 percent interest only will cost $2,400 in annual carrying costs. However, a $20,000 loan written on a "7 + 5" add-on basis for five years will cost only $1,750 annually to carry during its term.

   Hence, the borrower who borrows on a "7 + 5" basis will have $650 more in annual cash flow during the term of the loan.

Most buyers would rather have that extra cash flow for the first few years of ownership, while they are developing the potential of their investment—and, in return, are willing to pay the slightly higher actual interest rate, and contend with the bonus when the loan comes due.

You must, of course, point out to your client exactly how the loan is obtained and computed, and show him that his true interest rate is actually higher by using an add-on type loan.

How to Solve a Knotty Brokerage Problem

Here is a typical situation you may find in the course of your brokerage business: As a broker you have a buyer who will actually pay a higher price than the seller wants, and is willing to do this if he can purchase the property with a limited cash down payment. After much negotiation, you find that the seller will not take back a purchase-money mortgage; the untrained broker might throw his hands up and lose the sale.

Here's a summary of your problem, followed by the solution:

The problem: A suburban office building has a $700,000 first mortgage @ 6 percent interest, 20-year direct reduction, and the property can be sold subject to this mortgage. (Assume that all figures are gross and include commission.)

Buyer will pay	Seller will sell for
$100,000 Cash	$220,000 Cash
+700,000 1st mortgage	+700,000 1st mortgage
+156,000 2nd mortgage (13 + 0, 7 years)	
$950,600 Price	$920,000 Price

The solution: It appears that, although the buyer will pay a higher price than the seller wants, you have a stalemate! The seller will not take less than $220,000 in cash, and the buyer has only $100,000. You arrange a commercial add-on mortgage as follows:

Lender gives buyer $120,000 in cash, and in return receives a $156,000 second mortgage at 6 percent interest, no principal (6 + 0) for five years. You have arranged a "6 + 6" add on.

Referring to our four steps, here's the math:

Step 1: $120,000 \times .06 = $7,200
Step 2: $7,200 \times 5$ (years) $= $36,000
Step 3: $120,000 + $36,000 = $156,000
Step 4: $156,000 \times .06 = $9,360

Everyone is happy. The seller gets his $100,000 in cash. The buyer gets the property with $100,000 down, and the terms he wanted. The broker gets his commission (and he deserves it!).

The Profit-Moral of the Story. Whenever you run into a brokerage situation where the buyer's cash down is limited, but who is willing to pay a higher price than the seller is asking, pull out your pencil and paper and make the sale with an add-on mortgage from a commercial lender!

You, as the income property broker, must explain financing to your clients within the context of the specific transaction. In the section in Chapter 15, making a presentation using the income analysis worksheet, you will see how to tailor an entire package—including financing—to the particular investment objectives of your buyer. One buyer may be primarily interested in appreciation, another in cash flow, and a third in tax sheltering. Different financing options will be available to accommodate different buyer's and seller's requirements; and you will want to be able to explain them all.

A Proven Method for Obtaining Low-Rate or No-Rate Mortgages

If you were lending money yourself, would you charge a low interest rate? Of course not. This is the simple rationale behind the growing trend toward including lenders as equity partners. Many new large-scale (million plus) developments are financed in this manner. Certainly, investors and developers used to the whole ownership pie don't necessarily like the idea of sharing their profits; but if equity partnerships are to be a part of this business in the future, realistic buyers will agree to listen.

As a broker, your theme will of course be that a good deal—however it's put together—is a good deal. A 50 percent or 40 percent equity interest in something is better than a 100 percent interest in nothing! Many lenders therefore are taking advantage of the ownership benefits of investment property, and will be willing to discuss the exchange of low-interest mortgages, all-cash transactions, and even no-money-down opportunities for buyers with development and/or property management experience.

Opportunities for Today's Brokers

Many engineers over age 35 are presented with a career dilemma. The engineering science curriculum has been almost completely revamped in the ten to fifteen years since they left college. So they have a choice: they can study and relearn, or they can step aside for the young rising students of the new technology.

Investment brokers must face the same challenge. In this chapter, we've outlined the essentials of financing. You now have a solid foundation on which to build your understanding of the intricacies involved in custom designing financing for specific buyer, seller, and property objectives.

You are not alone. The principals involved in investment transactions are rarely naive "babes in the woods." Buyers and sellers of income properties who may be investing hundreds of thousands or millions of dollars are, in fact, apt to be quite sophisticated in the realm of finance. And they will bring plenty of ideas and suggestions to the bargaining table. Your job as broker is to listen to these ideas, analyze them, transmit them in a clear manner to the other party and then, finally, use one of them to negotiate a successful transaction.

To become a successful negotiator/broker, you must be prepared to study the literature. You must be prepared to brainstorm with your staff. You must be prepared to exchange information with other professionals in real estate, banking, law, and accounting. You must be prepared to accept the fact that investment property financing has changed and will continue to evolve in the future. Understanding financing, then, is an ongoing process.

Finding Income Property Financing in Cyberspace

The Internet has opened the door to matching investors needs to the offerings of lenders. The mortgage business has become much more global and the time to process loans from start to finish is decreasing because of the interconnectedness the Internet brings to this specialty.

As of this writing there are a myriad of ways to hook up with a lender for your deal. The problem is often sorting through the huge volume of sources. For example a quick search on Google (the search engine of choice today) for "income property financing" brings 4,420 results in .21 seconds. Similarly a search on "apartment financing" brings 13,000 results. "shopping center financing" brings 1,400.

So where do you turn? We looked and the current online favorites at the Real Estate CyberSpace Society are C-Loan and LoopNet. Both can be accessed at www .REcyber.com in "25 Top E-Tools" and "Find a Lender For Your Deal." Because

Internet sources change so often through sale, merger, and even more earthshaking events you may find other sources there if you are using this Guide well after its release date. The beauty of the Internet is that the Society updates its sources regularly so you can stay ahead of these changes at that one location.

It is also sound advice to develop a personal relationship with a human being in the lending business—especially someone connected to a firm that maintains a web site with a depth of information on income property financing. A good example of this is the firm I often turn to, Fantini and Gorga at www.fantinigorga.com.

Analyzing Financing with Today's Tools

Throughout this chapter I have alluded to the fact that once you learn to think strategically, you can use the "high tech" tools to analyze financing and real estate investment performance much more effectively.

There are a plethora of mortgage calculators available on the Internet. A quick search using: "mortgage calculator" + "income property" yields 46,800 results at this writing. You can always find an up-to-date calculator for just about any need at www.REcyber.com in the "25 Top E-Tools" section.

You may benefit from a program I currently use (and have for over 20 years) called PlanEase www.planease.com. This and programs like it take all of the drudgery of "doing the math" (I can hear you now—"Now he tells us!"). Remember though that you now understand the basis for these calculations and are miles ahead of the competition. These programs just make it sweeter!

A Final Word on Financing

All of the problems and calculations you have encountered in this financing chapter apply equally to apartment buildings, office buildings, shopping centers—in fact, any type of income producing property. The bricks and mortar are different, but the method of handling the calculations is the same.

Master the principles in this financing chapter and you will have a ten-to-one advantage over the average broker. You will be able to put more sales together with less effort, make sales that would otherwise be lost—and you will be able to put the miracle of leverage to work for your clients.

The judicious use of the purchase-money mortgage, to the advantage of your buyers and sellers, is one of the things that makes your services so valuable in the sale of real estate.

It is to financing with other people's money that we can attribute the magnificent, unparalleled development of our American economy. The same principle, wisely applied, will make you and your clients prosper.

CHAPTER 5

How to Price Income Property to Sell Quickly

Without proper counseling, almost every seller of income property will list his offering at a price that he would like to obtain. Similarly, almost every buyer of income property will submit his initial offer to buy at a price he would like to acquire the property for. Using a simplification, you can equate this procedure with what happens in the over-the-counter stock market. The owner's price is asked. The buyer's price is bid. As a rule, the eventual selling price lies somewhere in between.

Based on a study of over a billion dollars of income property sales at Peckham Boston, we have determined that the eventual selling price averaged 92.5 percent of asking price. Of course, in our area during this period, there were hundreds of other offerings that did not sell; and if they had sold, the spread between the asking price and eventual selling price would have been greater. The main reason that they did not sell was because the asking price was so far out of line with reality that very few buyers considered them serious offerings.

In the stock market, if the spread between *bid* and *asked* is too great, sales volume drops off due to the inability of the broker to bring the two parties together on agreeable terms. In the real estate market, if this spread becomes great, sales volume also drops off; and if the spread becomes too great, sales practically stop.

This background is necessary to understand why you must arm yourself with the tools to evaluate quickly and effectively if a listed property is priced realistically.

Estimating Value

The project of formally estimating value belongs to the qualified appraiser. The appraiser is a specialist who has spent years preparing himself through formal training and in-the-field experience to qualify for professional designation and recognition. Certainly if you have not already achieved the background to qualify as a recognized appraiser, you don't want to wait for years to enter the income brokerage field—and you don't have to. There are dozens of excellent books that will teach you the formal approach to appraising income property. If your leanings are toward acquiring a background in this specialty, then by all means study these books and take special courses in appraising. However, the purpose of this Guide is much simpler.

When I started in the income brokerage business, I cornered everyone who would talk to me, looking for some guidelines—some rules of thumb to help determine if a listing was priced within reason, and to determine if other brokers' listings were worth expending my effort to sell.

Working Guidelines—Imperfect, but Useful

As you start out in this exciting field, you will need some guidelines. This chapter is dedicated to giving you a basic understanding of what price, for any particular listing, is within reason.

Before you study these proven and practical guidelines you must understand that rules of thumb, although easy and convenient to use, have serious limitations. I have received angry protests from a few appraisers who have talked to some of my former students. The gist of their complaints goes like this, "What in blazes do you mean by telling a bunch of novices that they can do an appraisal with your half-baked rules of thumb!"

Caution: Any of the rules of thumb that you learn here are not for purposes of arriving at a professional estimate of fair market value. That is the appraiser's province. Our working guidelines are only to help you quickly estimate whether the seller's asking price is "in the ball park."

Without belaboring this point, I can almost guarantee you that over the years whenever an appraiser in a crusading mood reads sections of this chapter out of context, he will angrily call me and repeat the "What in blazes . . ." question. If he reads your copy of this Guide and calls you instead, give him my answer . . . "Mr. Angry Appraiser, please read the caution on page 122 of Chapter 5."

The guidelines we will study are aimed at giving you an indication of the price level at which a property should be listed to bring the owner action and result in the best sale possible. I refer to this as the *Action Price Level* or APL.

What Is the Action Price Level?

The Action Price Level of any property should be close enough to the eventual selling price to interest you, your associate brokers, and prospective buyers. By listing an income property at an unrealistically high price, the seller hurts only himself, because the broker receiving an operating statement on the property will quickly file the sheet in his incidental information file. He only has time to sell, and he is going to spend it on those listings that are offered at the action price level. Even if, by chance, the broker finds time to offer the overpriced property to a prospect, the prospect will set the offering aside because of its unrealistic price. The end result is that the owner who grossly overprices eventually suffers, by accepting a lower price than he could have obtained by pricing the property fairly, and developing wholehearted effort from the broker and sincere negotiations from the buyer.

How to Estimate Action Price Level

Upon receiving an operating statement on any property, there are four things a broker or prospect looks at immediately to determine if an offering warrants further investigation. The four guides for establishing the APL are:

APL Guide 1. The gross income/price ratio.
APL Guide 2. The net income before financing/price ratio.
APL Guide 3. The per-unit cost.
APL Guide 4. The net return on equity.

APL Guide 1: "The Gross Multiplier" (And How to Use It)

The most commonly used rule of thumb among investors is the Gross Multiplier. It works like this: An investor arrives at a "magic" figure for his area, which he multiplies by the total annual income (gross income) of the property under consideration. The total annual income represents all of the income the property would bring in if it were fully occupied throughout the year. No expenses have been deducted from this figure, which is also referred to as the *scheduled gross income.*

You will often hear an investor say, "I wouldn't pay a nickel over 7 times the gross for any building in Littletown." He is saying in effect that if the gross income of the property is $100,000, he thinks the maximum value of the property to him is $700,000 (seven times $100,000). In another area, the Gross Multiplier might be six or eight. In the case of six, the investor would peg the value of the property with the $100,000 gross income at $600,000. In the case of eight, at $800,000.

As an income broker, you must understand the use and limitations of the Gross Multiplier for several reasons. Many prospects' understanding of the value of an income property rarely goes past the use of the Gross Multiplier. And because it is so easy to use, many prospects have heard of it, and many apply it dangerously either to the point of overpaying for a property, or to the other extreme of overlooking an exceptional buy because of their misunderstanding of its use.

The sophisticated investor and broker use the Gross Multiplier, but only as a quick check to determine whether to spend additional time investigating an offering. Convenient as it is, the Gross Multiplier has numerous inadequacies, and these limitations are obvious when you think how many important factors are necessarily ignored, because the result is arrived at without considering such essentials as operating expenses and financing. Still the Gross Multiplier, when used with discretion, can be most helpful for a quick on-the-spot estimate of APL. You can determine Gross Multiplier bases for your area by using the following guidelines.

How to Determine the Gross Multiplier for Your Area.
   Step 1. Start by selecting the most common type of income property sold in
           your area. Make this selection based on:
           A. The type of construction.
           B. A specific neighborhood.
           C. The type of rental arrangements:
               1. furnished/unfurnished;
               2. owner heated/tenant heated;

3. weekly rents/monthly rents;
4. leased/month-to-month tenancy.

Step 2. Then select ten typical recent sales of this common type of income property.

Step 3. Divide the sales price in each case by the total annual income.

Step 4. The average result of the computations is your *Base Gross Multiplier.*

Remember that the properties selected for your analysis must be as similar as possible. If there are two or more distinct types of property, either group them separately and work out separate multiples for them, or apply the variations given later in this section to your Base Gross Multiplier.

A Case in Point: To give you an idea of how the Base Gross Multiplier is derived, consider this example of a suburban garden apartment building:

Let's assume that most representative sales of these residential income properties are in good shape and the vast majority of these properties range from ten to thirty years old and are of brick veneer construction. A typical property is a two-and-one-half story garden-type apartment building. It is heated by the owner and consists of unfurnished one- and two-bedroom apartments of moderate size. The number of rental units per complex ranges from twelve to several hundred. Let's say for demonstration's sake that a typical 24-unit building generates a gross income of approximately $300,000 and would sell for around $2,100,000.

By taking this as a typical sale, we divide $2,100,000 by $300,000, and our resulting Base Gross Multiplier is seven. Our typical building, then, sells for "seven times the gross." This is our *suburban base.*

If your typical area is Georgetown, in Washington, D.C., you will calculate your Georgetown base; if it is Bal Harbor, in Miami, it will be your Bal Harbor base. These calculations will be based on the current sales and circumstances in your area.

Let's look at how variations from our typical sales affect variations in our Base Multiplier.

If the apartments in the building under consideration are furnished, take ½ to 1 point *off* this Gross Multiplier. If your base is 7 times, this building should sell for somewhere in the vicinity of 6 to 6½ times the gross. The reasoning behind this is as follows: The furnishings are generating income in excess of what this building would normally rent for, if it were not furnished. These furnishings have to be replaced, and it costs money to replace them. Their useful life might be about three to four years. The building, therefore, is not worth as much, on a Gross Multiplier basis, as it would be unfurnished. You are multiplying an income that is ballooned from furnishings.

On the other hand, if the property is *tenant heated,* that is, if the tenant pays for the heat, depending on your area, it may be marketable at as much as one point higher than the base. The reason for this *addition* is that you're multiplying an income from which you don't have to deduct fuel costs to heat the building. So, taking our "Base," of seven times the gross, if all else is equal, the market value of this building would become eight times the gross. Also, a building with separate utilities for each unit may have greater condominium conversion potential. Conversion potential is a feature many investors look for in today's market.

If your base is a 30-year-old building, and the property under consideration is relatively new, generally you may add ½ to 1 point to your Gross Multiplier. This is because you will suffer less loss of income for repairs and maintenance.

How to Adjust for Buildings of Inferior (or Superior) Construction. Along the same line, if your base is a brick building (as it is in our demonstration "Base") and the property in question is of frame construction, take one point off. Frame buildings require more maintenance, and they have to be painted from time to time. On the other hand, if the property is of superior construction to your base, you will add ½ to 1 point.

Observe these guidelines: If you are operating in several areas, then you must get a sense of your base for each particular community. The factors affecting the base are:

1. Tax climate;
2. Desirability of the neighborhood; and
3. General condition of the property in the area under consideration.

The same Gross Multiplier can be derived for non-apartment-type properties such as office buildings, store blocks, and shopping centers. Simply select a typical kind of sale, and average out the price/gross income ratio for a series of recent sales. The principle is the same.

Important: You must understand that the broker does not establish the base—the market does. And factors not generally under the control of the broker, the buyer, and the seller determine the market. You must also recognize that the base can change.

An unusual example of a base that changed dramatically was seen in a town north of Boston. Up until a few years ago, this town was taxing apartment owners at the rate of 12 to 13 percent of the gross income. Buildings were selling at 7 to 7½ times the gross. A few years ago, the town changed the tax structure, so that about 20 to 22 percent of the total income from an average property was going to taxes. The people who had paid 7 or 7½ times the gross were frantic. Many buyers who had a fine net return before this move ended up with much less cash flow, just because of this change in tax climate. The Gross Multiplier in that town immediately tumbled to 6½ to 7 times the gross.

Examples of Dramatic Variation within One City. The Base Gross Multiplier will sometimes vary dramatically within the same city. This is due to neighborhood desirability and the general condition of the property in the neighborhood. Nearly any city in the country could illustrate this point.

In the cities and towns directly adjacent to a core city, we sometimes see the market establish multipliers that run higher than the core city base. For example, a well-run town with a solid tax base and a healthy tax climate will often contain buildings that will sell at a base multiplier in excess of the multiplier experienced in the core city.

The important point to remember here is that the Gross Multiplier is, at best, an inadequate system of estimating value. Novice investors, many times, will use it as a sole guide to value and will: (1) disregard an offering because the asking price exceeds their rule of thumb; or will (2) unfortunately, purchase a property only because the price falls below their beloved "7 times the gross." As an agent or broker you need to be familiar with this rule of thumb to help you read your client's mind.

A Checklist for Varying the Base. As an income property broker, you must understand the use of the multiplier. And, in order to interpret it competently to the layman, you must understand that it will vary from area to area, and that there are variations from the basic Gross Multiplier within a neighborhood. Again, the variations, which you, as broker, must be able to recognize and interpret are:

1. Construction   Brick   (+1)
                         Frame   (−1)
2. Heat   Owner-heated   (−1)
                         Tenant-heated   (+1)
3. Furnishings   Owner-provided   (−1/2 to 1)
                         Tenant-provided   (+1/2 to 1)
4. Age   Older, requiring maintenance   (−1/2 to 1)
                         Newer, requiring less maintenance   (+1/2 to 1)

The most important point to remember from this discussion of Gross Multipliers is the weakness of the system. It should not be developed as a guide to value. It is merely a quick means to let you judge if a listed property is priced at the APL. Remember: An income property offered at 2 times the gross may be greatly overpriced, while another income property offered at 10 times the gross, may be the steal of the century!

APL Guide 2: "The Net Multiplier" (And How to Use It)

A more accurate method of determining the APL is by applying a net multiplier. In Chapter 3 we studied the format of the income property listing form. Item *C*, net (income) before financing, represents how much income is left over after paying the building's operating expenses, but before accounting for financing costs and other items such as vacancy and repair allowances, management fees, and the investor's return on his equity investment.

In Chapter 6 on operating statements you will see how we will adjust this figure, which is commonly called *seller's net before financing,* to reflect the true operating income derived from the property. Until you have an opportunity to analyze this seller's net before financing figure, however, you need a quick check to see if the owner is listing his property at the APL.

The net multiplier as used here will fluctuate in proportion to ratios between a property's ability to produce income and the demand for that income at any particular point in time. A good starting point for well-maintained, well-located income property might be ten to twelve times the seller's net before financing. This will give you a quick estimate of whether the property is listed at the APL.

Consider this example: You have listed a building with $500,000 gross scheduled income, fully rented. You have deducted from this figure taxes, heat, electricity, water, sewer tax, insurance, superintendent—the works! However, you don't have enough information yet to deduct for vacancies, repairs, or management. You arrive at a seller's net before financing of $350,000. Take this net and multiply it by 10. You think to yourself, "This building should be listed, and it should be salable somewhere in the $3,500,000 range." If the owner's asking price is near this figure, my listing is at the APL and I can give the owner action.

Suppose your owner is asking $5,000,000 for this building; no one in his right mind is going to buy it as an *income* property. If the owner is looking for $4,000,000, you are going to have a tough time interesting a serious buyer. Your job, as broker, is to convince Mr. Seller to price his property at a level that will be reasonably attractive to potential buyers.

How the Net Multiplier Eliminates Variables

Now, you must realize that this example of "10 times the net" will vary from location to location. However, we have eliminated some of the major variables from the Gross Multiplier:

1. Tax climate (we have deducted the taxes to arrive at our net).
2. Heat (we have deducted our fuel costs, if any, before arriving at our net).
3. Other extraordinary expense items (for example, the owner pays all utilities, including electricity and cooking gas).

Even though you have eliminated these variables, by using the Net Multiplier, you are *not* considering building construction, age, neighborhood desirability, or the effect of financing on value. However, you *are* using a more reliable guideline. You are getting away from the haphazard "7 times the gross." But don't make the error of forgetting that the Gross Multiplier exists. It does exist, and it affects the market because so many potential buyers are arbitrarily applying it when they attempt to analyze a prospective purchase.

In the Net Multiplier you have a quick guide to the APL. It can vary from 5 times the net to 13 times the net, depending upon the location and growth potential of the property in question. Ten times the net is a quick and easy guide to apply, but you must determine the variations for your own area. Once you have, you will find it a most useful tool.

As mentioned earlier, what is commonly called the *seller's net before financing* has not accounted for several items, such as an allowance for vacancies and repairs and a fee for management. You will see in Chapter 6 that we will account for these expenses after we have had the opportunity to study the property in depth. Until then, our net multiplier has given us another quick tool to use to determine whether the owner has priced his property at the APL.

APL Guide 3: "Per Unit Cost" (And What It Tells You)

A useful rule of thumb to assist in determining if an owner has listed at the APL is the per unit cost guide. Many sophisticated investors look first to how much per unit they are being asked to pay for a proposed investment. To determine your guidelines, simply divide the selling price by the number of rental units. If 100 Main Street sold for $700,000 and the building contains ten apartments, then the cost per unit was $70,000.

You can quickly determine the average per unit selling price for various types of properties in your area. Once you have assembled this information, apply it as a quick check to be sure that your owner has listed his property at the APL.

APL Guide 4: "Equity Return" (How to Figure It and How to Use It)

Another way to estimate whether your listing is priced at the APL is to look to the percentage return on equity (down payment). This boils down to the most important question your investor will ask: "How much return am I going to get on the cash that I put down?"

In order to determine this, we must apply an allowance for vacancies and repairs to our seller's net. For example, in looking at a listing that requires $500,000 down, a buyer might say to himself, "I would like to see this property show me a 6 percent cash return, after I allow 10 percent for vacancies and repairs (V&R). If the gross income is $500,000, and the cash required is $500,000, I would like this property to have a minimum seller's net (before V&R allowance) of $80,000. Then I can apply a 10 percent for V & R, take the $50,000 off that seller's net, and see a net of 6 percent of my cash in. With a down payment of $500,000, a cash flow of $30,000 would give me a 6 percent cash return on equity."

This approach comes down to the fact that our buyer, when he decides to buy, is asking himself: "How much cash do I put into the building, and how much cash does the building, in return, put into my pocket on an annual basis?"

How to Put the APL Guides Into Action

For a moment, imagine yourself at an owner's office taking a listing on a 50-unit apartment building. You know, for example, that comparable buildings are selling at six times the gross (APL Guide 1); that they are selling at about ten times the seller's net (APL Guide 2); that they are selling for about $50,000 per unit (APL Guide 3); and that investors expect a 6 percent return on their equity (APL Guide 4).

After you assemble the information on Mr. Owner's building, you have the following basic facts:

Gross income, $400,000
Seller's net before financing, $50,000
Seller's net after financing (before V & R) $60,000
Total existing financing $2,000,000

The owner tells you he wants $1,000,000 in cash above the existing first and second mortgages, which total $2,000,000, for a total price of $3,000,000, and looks to you for an opinion of his pricing. Now you have an opportunity to put your APL guides into action. Let's see how this offering shapes up.

Use these simple computations:

APL Guide 1. (Gross Multiplier)

$\quad$ \$ 400,000 Gross Income

$\quad \times \underline{\qquad 6}$ Gross Multiplier

$\quad$ \$2,400,000 APL

APL Guide 2. (Net Multiplier)

$\quad$ \$ 250,000 Seller's Net before Financing

$\quad \times \underline{\qquad 10}$ Net Multiplier

$\quad$ \$2,500,000 APL

APL Guide 3. (Per-Unit Cost)

$\quad$ \$ 50,000 Per Unit

$\quad \times \underline{\qquad 50}$ Units

$\quad$ \$2,500,000 APL

APL Guide 4. (Equity Return)

$\quad$ \$ 60,000 Seller's Net before V & R

$\quad - \underline{\quad 40,000}$ V & R Allowance at 10%

$\quad$ \$ 20,000

$\quad \div \underline{\qquad .06}$ To yield 6% on equity

$\quad$ \$ 333,333 Justifiable cash investment

$\quad$ \$2,000,000 Existing Financing

$\quad + \underline{\ 333,000}$ Equity

$\quad$ \$2,333,000 APL

You now have four action price levels . . . .

$\quad$ \$2,400,000 APL1

$\quad$ \$2,500,000 APL2

$\quad$ \$2,500,000 APL3

$\quad \underline{\$2,333,000}$ APL4

$\quad$ \$9,733,000 ÷ 4 = \$2,433,250

What to conclude: You know from experience that if he insists on his price of $3,000,000 ($1,000,000 above the existing financing) that (1) prospective investors will not take his offering seriously, and (2) associate brokers will expend their efforts on more salable properties to the exclusion of his offering.

Stating Your Conclusion to the Owner

You ask Mr. Owner if there is anything about the property that would warrant an extraordinarily high selling price. If there is no special reason for his asking price other than personal whims (such as greed), you continue by explaining, "Mr. Owner, I have analyzed your property using four approaches in order to arrive at a price level which I feel would interest prospective investors. The four approaches yield four price levels ranging from $2,333,000 to $2,500,000. If this property is offered at a level much over $2,500,000, you are hurting yourself because investors will not take your offering seriously. I would suggest that we offer this property at a price not too far from the upper level indicated."

If Mr. Owner is serious about selling, he will alter his sights to a more realistic level and you will have an investment priced at the APL.

How Location Can Push the APL Above the Norm

Certain unique properties will sell at prices that exceed normal estimates of the APL. The APL for a "one of a kind" property, or a property in a location that is in great demand, will often exceed the usual averages for the area.

An example of this in the Boston area is property located on the waterside of Beacon Street. One side of this fashionable Back Bay Street looks out over the Charles River. The view from most of these buildings is spectacular. While buildings on the side of Beacon Street that does not overlook the water may sell at relatively ordinary multipliers. Buyers will often pay a significantly higher multiplier to own the desirable waterside buildings.

The same holds true in fashionable sections of Chicago, along the lake, in New York, along the river, or in San Francisco, high on the hills. I'm sure that there are similar exceptions in your area.

Exceptional Financing Can Change the APL

Financing plays a very important role in establishing the APL. Your APL guides will be based on the usual financing available and employed in your area. Any deviation from this will affect the price a prospect will pay. If the existing financing is undesirable and cannot be rearranged—if it bears a high interest rate or requires extraordinarily heavy amortization, then a seller will find that he must adjust his price downward from the norm in order to list at an APL.

On the other hand, if exceptional financing is available with a low interest rate or a low rate of principal reduction, or if a property can be purchased with a very low down payment, then the property can be priced at a higher level and still sell.

As a general rule of thumb, if the cash down payment required is high in relation to the price (40 to 50 percent, for example), then the property must be priced below the average APL. If, on the other hand, the required cash down is low in relation to the price (10 to 15 percent) and favorable financing is available, then the property can be sold above the average APL.

A Final Word

You now have the tools to evaluate quickly whether an owner has priced his property at the APL. Always be alert to the fact that the market establishes price—not the broker. Remember, too, that these rules of thumb must be flexible and are only rough guidelines to assist you while you accumulate the most reliable knowledge available—that gained from experience.

For now, you are equipped to avoid the humiliation of accepting a grossly overpriced listing without letting the optimistic owner know that you recognize his price level as sheer fantasy.

These guides will not make you an appraiser, but they will put you several giant steps along the road to effective and realistic pricing—Action Pricing!

Cyber Assists for the Pricing Process

Surprisingly, many of the pricing guides used in a particular geographic area are often learned by a new agent when he leans out the window and yells to an associate "What's a good gross multiplier for Plainville today?" The associate yells back "Try

8 times the gross!" This is the easy way, but a good understanding of the process as outlined in this chapter will put you miles ahead of the competition. It will put you inside the investor's head and give you a fast start if you are new to this field.

In addition there are many resources on the Internet that can help when you need more substantive information to guide you through the process of justifying your APL estimates, or in getting a better handle on what rules of thumb are applicable in your area.

The cyber comparable to "yelling out the window" is a quick visit to the web sites for any of the major commercial brokerage firms. There you can check local sales statistics in their local market reports and also access information on comparable properties they have for sale.

In addition you can often obtain pricing information from the various listservs (mentioned earlier in Chapter 4) that bring together real estate professionals of common interest. A quick "yell out the window" here will get you almost instant input—and often for multiple participants.

You can also access information on other similar properties for sale at the major commercial property sales portals. At this writing two of the more popular are www.Loopnet.com and www.ccimnet.com. These resources are open to all and contain a wealth of information so that you can acquaint yourself with the nuances of pricing in your local market. As URLs change often and mergers raise havoc with cited URLs you may have to do a search for the most recent favorite sales portal. On Google try "apartments for sale" + "Albany" (or wherever).

In addition, some of the sites that report recent single family sales prices often include income property sales in their areas.

CHAPTER 6

Setting Up Operating Statements That Promote Sales

There are giants specializing in income property brokerage! But more income property sales are made by the smaller companies and residential brokers who sell an occasional income parcel. This chapter will provide you with a guide to help you adjust your merchandising techniques to the demands of the income market—no matter what market niche describes your activities.

In residential sales, the major emphasis is on the physical features of a property and its value compared to similar properties. Income brokers, on the other hand, rightfully rely upon a merchandising tool that is unique to their specialty—the operating statement. The most important single sales aid the income broker can use is a well-prepared presentation of the facts and figures in a compact easy to comprehend operating statement.

How many automobiles would the dealer on "Auto Row" sell if he didn't: (1) show his wares in their best light; and (2) arrange for the low down payment—the financed deal? Not many. Then, why do so many brokers shove a hastily typed statement at an investor and say in effect, "Here it is, buddy. Now you've got the income, the expenses, and the price. You figure out how to finance it, and come back to me and we'll phone in your offer."

Let me admit that I'm painting the worst possible picture. But believe me, even though you don't operate this way, look around; many of your competitors do! (You may be sure, however, that they are not your strongest competitors.)

Setting Up an Operating Statement

Following are *before and after* versions of an operating statement. Let's compare them. The *before* statement is as poorly prepared as possible; this was done intentionally to give you a striking comparison.

Before Statement—The Wrong Way!

JOHN DOE, Licensed Broker
1 MAIN STREET, LITTLETOWN

"Specializing in all types of real estate—
Sales, Rentals, Financing, Leasing, Exchanging, etc."

Free Counseling Services

8 units at 200 Main Street
Littletown, Massachusetts

Income: About $90,000
Expenses: About $30,000
Nets: About $60,000

Price: Make Offer

This is a red-hot listing and must be seen to be appreciated! Better make a quick offer, or it'll be gone!

Remember that an investor can't take the building home to study, but he can and will spend time with your statement in the privacy of his den or office.

The *before* statement shown here is a waste of effort, paper, and ink. It doesn't give the prospect the slightest idea of how much cash he needs, or what type of financing is available. He has no indication of what the financing would cost or how much would be left over for him after paying the debt service. Many operating statements end with *net before financing* and give no consideration to financing. This, as we saw in Chapter 4, is the phase of this specialty that separates the pros from the amateurs.

Now let's look at the *after* version of the statement. Keep in mind that although our operating statement example is an apartment building, you can effectively use the same general format for office buildings, store blocks, and shopping centers.

THE PECKHAM BOSTON COMPANY

Four Longfellow Place
Boston, Massachusetts 02114
617-555-1212

LOCATION: Well-located one block from the ocean in Littletown, Massachusetts

TYPE: Solid brick building containing 8 two-bedroom apartments
ASSESSMENT: $322,000 (land $60,000), improvement $262,000
TOTAL ANNUAL INCOME: $87,000   TAX RATE: $46.85   2006

RENTALS: Each apartment contains: living room, 2 bedrms, kit., and bath

Apt. #1	$870 TAW (14 yrs.)	Apt. #5	$935 Leased to 6/30/07
Apt. #2	$910 Leased to 6/30/07	Apt. #6	$925 Leased to 6/30/07
Apt. #3	$920 Leased to 6/30/07	Apt. #7	$910 TAW (3 yrs.)
Apt. #4	$900 Leased to 6/30/07	Apt. #8	$870 TAW (5 yrs.)

ESTIMATED EXPENSES:

Taxes	$15,086
Heat	$ 9,600
Electric	$ 3,225
Water	$ 1,195
Insurance	$ 3,200
Janitor	$ 6,000
	$38,306

NET BEFORE FINANCING: $48,694

First Mortgage (assumable) $280,000   8% interest. 20 years D.R.
Second Mortgage (proposed) $40,000   8% interest. No principal
    Term 5 yrs.

FINANCE EXPENSES:

First Mortgage interest	$ 22,400
First Mortgage principal	$ 5,704
Second Mortgage interest	$ 3,200
Total	$ 31,304
NET INCOME:	$ 17,390
PRINCIPAL SAVINGS:	$ 3,200
TOTAL YIELD:	$ 20,590
PRICE:	$410,000 CASH REQUIRED: $90,000

Additional Notes: Please see Page 2.
Exterior photograph: Please see Page 3.

THE ABOVE NET RETURNS, UNLESS OTHERWISE NOTED, ARE COMPUTED AFTER FIXED EXPENSES BUT BEFORE ALLOWANCE FOR VACANCY AND REPAIRS. THE ABOVE INFORMATION WAS RECEIVED FROM SOURCES DEEMED RELIABLE AND IS OFFERED SUBJECT TO ERRORS AND OMISSIONS. CHANGES IN PRICE AND PRIOR SALE OR WITHDRAWAL WITHOUT NOTICE.

Notes:

1. All kitchens are completely equipped with stoves and refrigerators and have built-in dining nooks.
2. Heat: #2 oil-steam. Four automatic zones. Rebuilt burner and boiler.
3. Janitor: Resident janitor receives $500 per month applied against rent.
4. Located near stores and schools. Transportation at the front door. One block from a sandy beach.
5. Financing: The new first mortgage may be assumed by new owner. Second mortgage: Seller will take back second mortgage at 8% interest. No principal payments required, term 5 years.
6. Well-proportioned apartments recently renovated.
7. Exterior painted last year.
8. Public halls recently paneled and redecorated. New lighting fixtures.
9. Insurance coverage: $350,000 fire and E.C. plus $500,000 liability plus $70,000 rent loss.
10. Rent level appears lower than rentals currently being obtained for comparable units in the area.

A glance shows that you have taken the trouble to arrange a purchase-money mortgage with the seller and prenegotiate its terms. You have computed debt-service costs, making it obvious that $90,000 down will buy the property. You have further pointed out what the return before vacancies and repairs will be.

One additional step will be taken. Later in this chapter, you will learn how to establish a reasonable figure for V & R, and convert all operating figures to reflect a net operating income rather than a *seller's net*. However, this should be done after thorough research, since without this preparation any "guesstimate" would be inaccurate. The essential point to grasp is that we have given the investor, in capsule form, the data he needs to make the decision to further explore the offering.

Now let's examine page 1, step by step, analyzing the arrangement and content of this presentation. It is simplest to think of it in terms of a beginning, a middle, and an end; and to discuss it in these three phases.

How to Prepare the Beginning of an Operating Statement

Location

The prospective investor wants to know where the property is located. There are two ways of doing this on your operating statement: by a simple statement of the address, or by a statement conveying the property's general whereabouts without giving a specific address. At Peckham Boston, we use the latter method because we find it easier to discuss several properties with an investor without exposing him to a volume of addresses. Notice how location is stated in the *after* example: "Well located one block from the ocean in Littletown, Massachusetts." Both the area and some of its amenities are communicated in these ten words. (You can almost smell the salt air!) Another example might be "Well located on the waterside of Beacon Street (Back Bay), Boston, Massachusetts."

Type

"What kind of property is it?" This question is not less important to an investor than location. But keep the description brief. Tell in a very few words the type of structure, what it is made of, its use, its approximate size, and perhaps something of its special character. From the sample form: "Solid brick building containing eight two-bedroom apartments." Here we have supplied the basic information in eight words. Another example of a succinct description would be "Handsome yellow-brick six-story building containing 56 apartments," or "Modern two-story brick office building."

You can include more than this. Some brokers do, and it is really a matter of judgment where to draw the line between brevity and incompleteness. Is it a brand-new structure, or is it 30 years old? Does it have an elevator? Is it air-conditioned? These are facts of description that may be added to the more fundamental data. However, I personally favor being as brief as possible; otherwise the investor's mind might be cluttered right from the beginning. The place for much of this additional information is under *notes*.

Assessment

This figure has special significance to the income property buyer, since it has a direct bearing on the before- and after-tax profit picture. Hence, you should include it with the foregoing items at the beginning of the operating statement.

Tax Rate

Besides the assessment, you should state the amount of tax that is levied per thousand dollars of assessment, and the tax year. Naturally, every broker knows the RAT formula (rate × assessment = tax) for determining the tax bill.

Total Annual Income

Many investors use this figure in their rule-of-thumb formulas for estimating market value; the Gross Multiplier is the most common of these. Hence, it is a good idea to give this statistic in the beginning of the operating statement, so prospective buyers will not have to plow through a long list of rentals to find it.

Remember the fringe revenues, too. To arrive at total annual income (also called the *gross* income), you add up all the actual rentals, the market value of the janitor's apartment, and the market value of the vacant apartments. The total will also include income from laundry machines and parking. In commercial properties, you will also include additional income generated from tax and sales volume averages contained in the tenants' leases. That concludes the beginning, or phase one of the operating statement.

How to Construct the Middle Portion of an Operating Statement

This section is principally reserved for breaking down and presenting expenses and financing details. It contains the statistical background for the conclusions (or totals) given at the beginning and end of the presentation.

Rentals

These are the chief components of total annual income. Actual dollar amounts of monthly rent should be given for each income unit. They are usually itemized by apartment number and show the size of the apartment. You should state whether there is a written lease in effect, or whether it is occupied by a *tenant at will* (TAW). In the latter case, the term of residency of the tenant may be a pertinent fact—even a selling point.

Estimated Expenses

Here list the cost of taxes, heating, electricity, water, insurance, janitorial service, and so on; also, any expenses that may be peculiar to the particular building and not covered by the preceding categories. Make sure you label them as *estimates!* Remember that this information has been provided to you by the owner and is still subject to verification. This fact is further emphasized at the bottom of your operating statement, where the prospect is warned that "the above information was received from sources deemed reliable and is offered subject to errors and omissions, changes in price and prior sale or withdrawal without notice."

The expenses itemized in this section will be the same as those obtained from the owner during the listing process (Chapter 3). You will note that a figure for repairs is not contained in the sample *after* statement. The reasoning behind not including this is much the same as that for not including a vacancy allowance at this stage—you must research the building and the area to arrive at an accurate estimate. The present owner might have spent $300 on repairs—the buyer might have to spend $1,000. You will see later in this chapter how to adjust a *seller's net* to reflect the cost of repairs after sufficient research.

Net before Financing. Subtract the total estimated expenses from the total annual income to arrive at this figure. This figure comes directly from your listing form, as we discussed in Chapter 3, and is particularly significant to you and the investor in applying your Action Price Level Guide #2, the "Net Multiplier" (Chapter 5). Remember that on the preliminary operating statement, this figure represents what income the property generates before (1) financing costs; (2) return on equity; and (3) vacancy, repair, and other allowances.

Financing

How to Use Financing as a Sales Clincher

This is where the pros in our business really distinguish themselves. Their operating statements, unlike the more common ones, will indicate the most effective means by which the property can be financed. The professional broker will package the financing costs in a way that shows the investor how much return he will receive on his equity or down payment.

Under *Financing,* your operating statement should list all the existing and proposed mortgages; but this only if the building is to be conveyed with an existing mortgage. In this situation, you should list the following: (1) the original balance; (2) the present balance; (3) the interest rate; (4) the original term and present-term balances; and (5) the principal payment.

In our example, the building is to be conveyed with a new existing and assumable mortgage.

To illustrate, we list:

FINANCING: First mortgage (existing) $280,000, 8 percent interest, 20-year D.R.: second mortgage (proposed) $40,000, 8 percent interest, term five years.

In the note section of our operating statement, we spell out the complete terms of all financing. For the sake of brevity and clarity it is best to provide the detailed information under the note section. By doing this, you can provide your prospect with a summary on the first page without overwhelming him or confusing him with too much detail.

Finance Expenses

In this section of your operating statement, you demonstrate exactly how much the buyer will pay for debt service on all financing. The costs are broken down as applied to interest and principal. In Chapter 3 you learned how to assemble this data, and in Chapter 4 you learned how to compute the financing costs. Be sure that you break down the costs as illustrated in the *after* statement.

How to Complete the Final Segment of the Operating Statement

After reviewing the income, expenses, and financing data, the investor will silently ask, "What does this all mean to me?" You have, in a mathematical sense, stated your premises. Now it is time to draw your preliminary conclusions.

Net Income

To arrive at the net, you must total the annual financing expenses (or debt service, as it is often called); then you must subtract the total from the net before financing. You have already completed these calculations on your listing form (Chapter 3). In typing your operating statement, you can merely transfer that figure.

Remember that this net income is still a *seller's net* and must be adjusted for vacancy, repair, and other allowances. We will cover this conversion later in this chapter. For now, however, you have summarized all of the preceding information and calculations so that you can show your investor what he will net before the vacancy and repair allowance.

Principal Savings

How to allow for the growth of equity: Take this figure from *first mortgage principal,* as listed under finance expenses. If there is an amortizing (reducing balance) second mortgage, there will also be an amount listed as *second mortgage principal.* Keep in mind that if any of the mortgage payments are made on a constant payment plan, that this principal savings figure will increase with each succeeding year. Make sure your investor also understands this.

Total Yield

How much does the building earn? Add the principal savings to the net income and you have the total yield. That is often a sophisticated investor's major concern. He can use it (after making proper adjustments for vacancies and repairs) to establish an actual percentage return on cash invested. But do keep in mind that at this point it is the yield after fixed expenses and financing costs, but *before* allowances for vacancies and repairs.

Price and Cash Required

In the lower left-hand section of page 1 of the sample operating statement appears "Price: $410,000." To the right appears "Cash Required: $90,000." To repeat a caution contained in Chapter 3: Be sure that your mortgage balances and cash required, when all added together, equal the price.

In our sample:

First mortgage balance	$280,000
Second mortgage	+ 40,000
Cash	+ 90,000
Price	$410,000

Notes

What to include, and what to avoid. This is the last item in the sample operating statement, and appears on page 2. In this section you should include any amenities, anything that might make your property both attractive and salable. Remember the obvious! You have to do the job of selling. If your description of the property you're trying to sell doesn't make the building sound desirable, then you are actually doing something in conflict with your purpose.

Now, of course, there may be facts about the property that should be made known to the buyer but do not belong in the operating statement. Put this information on your listing sheet. If the ceilings are cracked or the bathtubs are on legs, for two examples, put these facts on your listing sheet, so that your brokers and your salespeople will be aware of them.

These facts can and should be pointed out when you show the property, but they do not belong on the operating statement. However, an important exception to this rule should be noted: If you have a building that is a renovator's delight—one that could produce more income after some renovation—then you have an important selling point. Here is an example of what I mean: "The building is in poor repair; however, with a minimal amount of cash outlay and a large amount of imagination, its income could be improved substantially."

Be Sure to Include Photographs with the Operating Statement

Always include an exterior photograph of the property. Remember that the investor will take your operating statement home and will spend considerable time analyzing it. If you are handy with a digital camera, simply take a good clear exterior shot of the property and reproduce it with your statement—a picture is and always has been more effective than a thousand words!

To this point in the chapter, I'm sure that one question has been running through your mind: "All this is fine, but I'm still left with an equity return that really isn't a return at all—even Peckham refers to the net income as *seller's net* and admits that this is not the return an investor will see. He admits that further adjustments must be made to this figure in order to show the investor what true return he will see on his investment."

Why It Is Often Necessary to Use *Seller's Net*

If you are operating in an area where income property is listed on an exclusive basis, you can afford to take the time initially to research each offering and arrive at accurate estimates for vacancy and repair allowances. With this information, you can construct an operating statement that includes these allowances. However, if you operate in an open listing market, you must prepare your operating statement as quickly and as accurately as possible, with the notation that the figures projected are "owner's estimates" and that, at the time the operating statement was prepared, no allowance for vacancies and repairs was included.

The only other alternate method in an open listing market is to apply haphazardly a standard allowance without proper research for each individual offering. This is not only dangerous, but unfair to both the seller and buyer.

How to Convert *Seller's Net* Into *Net Operating Income*

To cope with this chore, we use the Income Analysis Worksheet, which is shown in the following illustration. You saw a section of this worksheet in Chapter 4, where we demonstrated the use of lines 23 to 35, which deal with Principal Savings Analysis. You will learn how to use another section of the worksheet, which deals with tax analysis, in Chapter 7 (special benefits). You will see how to combine all the elements of the sales aid into a comprehensive sales clincher in Chapter 15 (How to Make a Final Presentation That Clinches the Sale).

For now, concentrate on lines 1 to 11 which give you the format for converting *seller's net* to true net.

INCOME ANALYSIS

1. Seller's net before financing   _____

2. Rent stabilization   _____

3. V & R allowance   _____

4. Expense adjustment   _____

5. Net operating income   _____   _____

FINANCING

6. Interest (total)   _____

7. Principal (total)   _____

8. Total   _____   _____

9. Before tax cash flow   =   _____

10. Cash down payment   _____

11. % return on equity   _____

How to Use the Income Analysis Section

Line 1. (Seller's net before financing)

On this line, simply enter the figure arrived at on your operating statement—the figure we have called *seller's net before financing.* In our example, this figure is $48,694.

Line 2. (Rent stabilization)

This figure represents any amount that the present rentals vary from the fair market value of the rental units. To arrive at this figure, you must study comparable rental units in the area.

In our example, surrounding rentals for comparable apartments were five percent higher. By stabilizing the rents on the property under consideration, the investor would add $4,350 per annum to his gross income. We enter + $4,350 on Line 2.

Line 3. (V & R allowance)

How to figure the "V" or Vacancy portion: From our study of surrounding properties rented at fair market value, we find that vacancies and credit losses use up about 5 percent of the gross or scheduled income, which in our property now amounts to $91,350. (This is the sum of $87,000, gross income, and $4,350, the amount by which present rentals could be adjusted upward to fair market value.) The vacancy allowance computation now looks like this:

$ 91,350 scheduled gross income
×   .05 vacancy percentage
$4,567.50 vacancy allowance (say $4,568)

How to figure the "R" or repair portion: By keeping accurate records of what other owners in the area are paying for repairs, including redecorating vacated apartments, as needed, and by combining this with our knowledge of the construction and condition of the property under consideration, we arrive at an estimate of $8,000 for our repair allowance.

Then by combining the two figures

$ 4,568 vacancy allowance
+ 8,000 repair allowance
$12,568 V & R allowance

Enter—$12,568 on line 3.

Line 4. (Expense adjustment)

Remember that usually the figures on the operating statement are owner's estimates. Quite often his estimates must be adjusted to reflect a new owner's expected expenses. Many times, as you saw in Chapter 3, an owner is optimistic in his estimate of how reasonable his expenses will be, and they must be adjusted accordingly. In our example, we examine the owner's estimated expenses, and determine that between an expected increase in the taxes, an expected increase in fuel costs, and the cost of increased insurance coverage, the new owner can expect an increase in expenses amounting to $3,879.

In addition to vacancy and repair allowances, we must deduct an allowance to pay for professional management. This is true even if the buyer intends to manage the property himself. If he in fact does eventually manage the property himself, with the manual assistance of the janitor, which has been allowed for, then the amount we have allowed for management will be reimbursement for his efforts.

Your allowance for management will vary, depending on the type of property, the time required, and local custom. It can vary from 3 percent to 10 percent. The fee for management in our sample is 5 percent. This fee is based on actual collected rents (gross operating income) as follows:

$ 91,350 scheduled gross income
− 4,568 vacancy allowance
$ 86,782 gross operating income
× .05 management allowance
$4,339.10 management fee (say $4,339)

Combining the $4,339 allowed for management with the $3,879 in other expense adjustments, we arrive at a total expense adjustment of $8,218. We enter that figure on line 4.

Line 5. (Net operating income)

By making these adjustments to the seller's net before financing from the operating statement, we have arrived at a net operating income of $40,776.

Lines 6 to 9. (Financing)

The financing costs need no adjustment unless your buyer insists on an analysis based on different terms from those offered. In Chapter 15 you will see what is required to readjust this section if it becomes necessary. Take the total interest costs (first and second mortgages) directly from the operating statement, and enter $25,600 on line 6.

Line 7. (Principal)

As with interest, take the total principal savings from your operating statement, and enter $5,704 on line 7.

Line 8. (Total)

Add line 6 (interest) and line 7 (principal):

$25,600 interest
+ 5,704 principal
$31,304 total debt service

This figure should agree with your total financing costs on the operating statement.

Line 9. (Before tax cash flow)

By deducting your total financing costs (line 8) from your net operating income, you can now show your buyer what return he can reasonably expect from the property. If he manages it himself (as most small investors do), this return will increase as allowed for management, and this will represent just compensation over and above his return on equity.

Line 10. (Cash down payment)

Enter $90,000 from the operating statement.

Line 11. (Percent return on equity)

Simply divide the cash down payment into the before tax cash flow:

$$\frac{\$\ 9{,}472}{\$90{,}000} = 10.5\ \text{percent}$$

This shows your prospect that besides the usual tax benefits, and equity growth, all explained in detail in the next chapter, he should realize a before tax cash flow of 10.5 percent on his investment. Not too bad and even better when we demonstrate the all-important *after* tax cash flow (Chapter 7).

The final computations entered on lines 1 to 11 of the Analysis Worksheet look like this:

INCOME ANALYSIS			
1. Seller's net before financing		$48,694	
2. Rent stabilization	+	4,350	
3. V & R allowance	–	12,560	
4. Expense adjustment	–	8,218	
5. Net operating income		$32,266	$32,266

FINANCING

6. Interest (total)		$25,600	
7. Principal (total)	+	5,704	
8. Total		$31,304	$\quad$ − $\quad$ $31,304
9. Before tax cash flow			= $\quad$ 9,472
10. Cash down payment		90,000	
11. % return on equity		10.5%	

When and How to Use the Operating Statement and Analysis Worksheet

The operating statement can be used before, during, or after showing the property in question. It can be mailed to trusted prospects to interest them in viewing a property. It can be reviewed in the quiet of your office prior to showing an investment. You can use it while showing the property to point out the rentals on the apartment, and to highlight various amenities the building has to offer. Most important, it is handed to the prospect after his inspection of the property and used as a closing tool, as you will see in detail in Chapter 15.

Unless you have researched the property and the area prior to your meeting with the prospect, point out that you must make certain adjustments to the operating statement to show him just what the property will do for him. If he shows a genuine interest in the property, then roll up your sleeves and prepare the Analysis Worksheet.

Once your prospect has shown a genuine interest in the property, complete your research and fill in lines 1 to 11 of the worksheet to show him just what before tax cash flow he should expect.

In Chapter 15, you will see how this *Income Analysis* section (lines 1 to 11) ties in with the *Tax Analysis* section and the *Ten-Year Result* section to provide you with a closing tool the prospect can hand to his lawyer or accountant (or both). If you have properly prepared your figures, your prospect's advisers will say, "This guy is the smartest broker I've ever seen—we'd better sit down with him!" And it isn't difficult to present this information to your prospect. It's just a matter of common sense, accuracy, and a bit of effort to ensure that the result is legible and easily understood. The rewards of these efforts are more sales, more commissions, and the healthy respect of your investors.

Cyber Assists for the Operating Statement Process

These rewards are easily magnified with the powerful tools provided on the Internet. Obviously the online calculators and mortgage calculators mentioned earlier will provide a big time savings (and may be used as a double check against any work you do by hand).

As you will see later, your proficiency in gathering and presenting information in a straightforward operating statement will serve you well when you begin to magnify these skills by bringing in the power of the Internet and e-mail to your marketing process.

You will find that when you apply the networking and information sharing capabilities of the Internet, the basics you learn here will stand you in good stead! You will learn a system for applying these capabilities in Chapter 14.

CHAPTER 7

How to Present the Unique Benefits of Investing in Income Property

More wealth has been created and more rags-to-riches stories have been written about real estate investments than any other field! Small wonder—the advantages of investing in real estate are so great that almost anyone with cash to invest or the courage to speculate can look seriously to real estate to create personal wealth and comfort!

Anyone, man or woman, can invest in income property. Carpenters, plumbers, oil men, insurance agents, stockbrokers, bankers, doctors, airline pilots, teachers, retired people, salespersons, engineers, deep sea divers, vegetarians, video game players—the list is endless—invest in income property. The type of buyer differs, but the motivation remains the same: *To make money!* Your market is limitless!

Showing the Benefits of Owning Income Property to Your Prospect

The problem with selling income property lies not in improving the advantages offered, but in explaining them to your prospect. You must be able to show your prospect just what it is about income property that makes it imperative for him to balance his investment portfolio with real estate. You must also show why income property will put more spendable (after tax) cash in his pocket than assets tied up in savings accounts, stocks, bonds, and insurance (the primary competing outlets for your investor's dollar).

Before bankers, insurance agents, and stockbrokers beat a path to my door and conduct a protest, let me explain that we don't intend to invest our prospect's last dollar in real estate. We always recommend that an investor carefully analyze his position before making any move, and plan his portfolio to include adequate balance in these areas. He should be sure that he has established a comfortable savings account as a ready source of liquid cash, so that he has emergency funds available.

Your investor should often also own adequate *term* life insurance, not as an investment, but to provide for financial protection in the event of the breadwinner's death. Term insurance is the only *pure* form of insurance without investment overtones. Insurance for insurance's sake is a wonderful buy. As so-called investment vehicles, however, insurance policies generally provide an extremely low return on the capital tied up; this additional capital can be used to greater advantage in a true investment situation—such as real estate!

Once your prospect has adequately provided for emergency funds through savings, and for death with a term insurance program, he should weigh the advantages of investing in real estate or the stock market—or a healthy combination of the two. The advantages of a real estate portfolio, as you will see, can be spectacular. The information contained in this chapter will give you a powerful selling and closing tool to prove this point to your prospects.

The Six Big Selling Points of Income Property

Stated briefly, the six main advantages of income property are:

1. Leverage
2. High return on cash invested
3. Tax benefits
4. Stability
5. Control
6. High growth (appreciation) of invested capital

Selling Point 1—Leverage: Using Other People's Money

The number one advantage of investing in income property lies in the type of financing that can assist in acquiring it. I'm referring to the most fascinating phase of the broker's job, namely, arranging *leverage*.

Leverage can be used to the investor's advantage to accomplish two major results: (1) it enables the buyer to acquire more property and pyramid the effect of the economy's growth on his holdings; and (2) it boosts the percentage return on equity. In Chapter 4 we discovered that leverage is created by using "O.P.M."—other people's money (borrowed money), to purchase real estate. The following pages will tell you how to explain the "magic" of leverage to your prospect.

How Leverage Can Multiply Growth to Create Wealth. Real estate has historically outpaced the economy in terms of growth in value, and this trend is expected to continue. However, there may be two exceptions:

Exception 1: If the population were diminished considerably by an immense disaster.

In this case, the ratio of people to land would decrease, and the economic law of supply and demand would take hold. Values of land and improvements would also decrease.

Conversely, if the population is constantly on the increase and there is a limited supply of land, values must increase. The old adage that "God stopped making land long, long ago" still applies.

Exception 2: If a property lies in the path of deteriorating influences.

Certain sections of any area are, from time to time, hit by creeping blight. This fact alone vividly explains the importance of *location* in selecting an investment.

With these two exceptions, well-located real estate can be expected to increase in value at a rate of at least equal to the area's economic growth rate, and generally at a much higher rate. Using, for example, 6 percent per annum as a conservative growth rate for well-selected income property, let's see how leverage, combined with this growth, can create spectacular wealth for your investors.

Assume that an investor buys a small rental property for $300,000 and puts $30,000 down. The economy is pushing the value of his investment up by 6 percent per year, or $18,000 per annum (.06 × $300,000). Because this growth affects the market value of his investment and not just the down payment, his equity return from growth is not 6 percent, but 60 percent per year!

The following illustration shows you how a 6 percent economic growth acts at various levels of financing.

Down Payment	Equity Growth
100%	6.0%
90%	6.6%
80%	7.4%
70%	8.6%
60%	10.0%
50%	12.0%
40%	15.0%
30%	20.0%
20%	30.0%
10%	60.0%

The fact that financing of 80 to 90 percent can be negotiated for the income property buyer provides an enormous advantage, and, if carefully exploited by the investor, with the guidance of an experienced broker, he can amass a huge estate with relatively low cash invested.

Comparing this with margin requirements in the stock market will readily show why so many huge fortunes have been made in real estate. Granted, stock purchases can also be leveraged to some extent, but income property has one big advantage: the fact that the rent-paying tenants are providing the income to pay the regularly recurring expenses (taxes, heat, insurance, etc.) *plus* the financing costs, both interest and principal. And even when the financing costs create a negative cash flow, the tax advantages of investing can turn this situation into a positive cash flow after taxes—as we shall see later in this chapter. The tenants are, in effect, repaying the borrowed money for the investor, while he experiences the economic growth of the total investment! Little wonder that fortunes have been made, and will continue to be made in real estate. You are on the threshold of a rewarding career where you can guide your investors and assist them in creating an estate for their future and for their children's futures.

A Word of Caution: The magic of leverage can also become the nightmare of leverage if the property is not well selected. Obviously, if a property is acquired in an area of declining values, the growth percentages will work in reverse and in equally dramatic proportions. That is all the more reason for the investor to obtain the services of a well-trained and highly reputable investment property specialist. This is why your services will be so valuable.

How Leverage Can Affect a Property's Return. How does leverage affect your buyer's return? Let's take a look at an illustration that shows leverage in action. Note that, as discussed in the financing chapter, you will have used a range of interest rates here anticipating that over the span of your long income property career the chances are good that you will experience a wide range of rates in the real world. In this one also note that often as the investor's leverage increases, his relative cash flow decreases. However, we shall see how our tax advantages will offset this decrease—and then some!

Situation I (without financing)		*Situation II* (with first mortgage)		*Situation III* (with first and second mortgages)	
Price	$300,000	Price	$300,000	Price	$300,000
Scheduled Gross Income	$60,000	Scheduled Gross Income	$60,000	Scheduled Gross Income	$60,000
Net Operating Income	$37,000	Net Operating Income	$37,000	Net Operating Income	$37,000
Debt Service	None	Debt Service	$31,633	Debt Service	$35,968
Cash Flow before Taxes	$37,000	Cash Flow before Taxes	$5,367	Cash Flow before Taxes	$1,032
% Return on Equity	12.3%	% Return on Equity	7.2%	% Return on Equity	2.6%

I. Property is purchased for $300,000, all cash.
II. A) Property is purchased with $225,000 first mortgage at 13% for 20 years.
  B) Debt service: Interest $29,250
        Principal   2,383
        TOTAL $31,633
  C) Cash invested—$75,000.

III. A) Property is purchased with same first mortgage as example II, plus a $35,000 second mortgage at 11% interest for 20 years.

   B) Second mortgage debt service: Interest $3,850

                               Principal   485

                               TOTAL $4,335

   C) Cash invested—$40,000.

Here you see three alternatives to the financing structure of the building. But the financing is the only thing that changes. In each case, the building is the same, the tenants are the same, and the income is the same. Only the financing differs in each example.

Example I. The property is bought for $300,000, all cash. There is no mortgage. The scheduled gross income is $60,000. The net operating income and, because there is no financing, the cash flow before taxes is $37,000; thus, the cash flow before taxes on the investment of $300,000 is 12.3 percent.

In the second alternative, let's put leverage to work.

Example II. The price of the property is still $300,000. It is acquired, however, with the help of a $225,000, 20-year, 13 percent direct-reduction first mortgage. The debt service (annual amount for interest and principal) on the mortgage loan is $29,250 for interest, and $2,383 for principal. The annual debt service is $31,633. The cash flow before taxes, after paying for financing, is $5,367. This seems small in comparison with the $37,000 in the first example. But remember, the buyer hasn't invested $300,000—only $75,000, the balance over the $225,000 mortgage. The cash flow before taxes on the equity is now 7.2 percent.

The buyer in this example now has an interest deduction of almost $30,000, and $225,000 to invest in other properties. However, the buyer in Example I has neither of these advantages. This is what *leverage* is all about, but it still isn't the end of the story.

Example III. Here the property is purchased with the same first mortgage as in Example II, the $225,000, 20-year, 13 percent interest direct-reduction mortgage; however, the seller has taken back a $35,000 second mortgage at 11 percent for 20 years.

The interest on this second mortgage is $3,850; the principal is $485. The total debt service for the second mortgage, then, is $4,335. In Example III, you'll notice that the debt service between first and second mortgages will cost $35,968. That's how much it costs for interest and principal to service these loans. The cash flow before taxes is $1,032. The investment in cash is only $40,000. There is a $225,000 first mortgage, and a $35,000 second mortgage. The cash flow before taxes on equity is 2.6 percent, but the total interest deduction has risen to $33,100. The buyer in Example III has $35,000 more cash to invest in other properties than the buyer in Example II, and $260,000 more cash left to invest than the buyer in Example I.

Other Benefits to Point Out. It just starts here, because you are servicing debt. You're paying back money that's loaned to you. So on top of the cash return on your equity, you're receiving the benefits of amortization of the mortgage (reduction of your debt), and an interest deduction that, when combined with your depreciation deduction, creates a tax shelter.

However, these examples must be considered from the standpoint of the investor in order fully to appreciate their implications. The investor does not want to tie up all her money in one parcel. She usually wants to buy as much property as she can with as little outlay of her cash as possible. This is why leverage permits her to multiply her investing power.

How to Explain Leverage to Your Prospect: An Action Dialogue. Using the preceding example, your conversation with a prospect might sound like this:

Broker: "Without financing, you would have to lay out $300,000 in cash. Although the *gross* income might be $60,000, you would enjoy $37,000 in cash flow before taxes, or 12.3 percent on your down payment. This isn't a bad return, considering how much less a return you'd get from investing $300,000 in stocks, a savings certificate, or a money market fund. But, surely you don't want to tie up all that cash. You could do almost as well—and at the same time increase the tax shelter benefits of this property—through mortgaging, which would also allow you to keep a great deal of this cash for other investments."

Investor: "How can I do that?"

Broker: "If you finance the acquisition with a $225,000 first mortgage, your cash outlay will be one fourth as much, and your cash return on equity will be 7.2 percent. By mortgaging the property, your equity in it will be less than it would had you bought it outright with all cash. However, you're interested in results by *total return* on equity, which in this case should substantially increase since you will have a $29,250 interest deduction. To top it off, we can carry this a step further."

Investor: "I'm interested. Go ahead."

Broker: "The seller has indicated that he will take back a purchase money mortgage at less than current bank rates. Because of this, you can acquire this property by investing only $40,000 and your cash return will be 2.6 percent at the time of purchase. But by acquiring the property this way, you'll have $260,000 still available to acquire several other similar buildings and will have picked up even more interest deduction."

Investor: I'll be damned."

A Word of Caution: Earlier you saw how leverage increases the potential for equity growth in an area of increasing values; however, it also can work in reverse in an area of decreasing values. A second caution regarding the abuse of leverage is in order here. Remember that you can from time to time arrange 100 percent financing for an investor, under normal conditions, but be careful to keep the financing down to a level where the property will realistically support the debt service.

However, there are two exceptions to this rule:

1. If a prospect is willing to speculate, and understands the risks and rewards, and is prepared to expend his energy and time to improve the property, then by all means arrange as much financing as the property and his ability can support.

2. If a prospect is in a tax bracket where maximum financing is desirable to create tax shelter (as explained later in this chapter), and if he is willing and able to invest whatever infusion of capital the property requires monthly to carry the expense, then maximum leverage may be called for. Mutual funds buyers many times invest $100, $500, or $1000+ per month to expand their portfolio—to increase their equity. By investing the same amount on highly leveraged income property, they are accomplishing the same result—but with the added advantage of exceptional tax and growth benefits.

Selling Point 2—High Return on Cash Invested

You won't have to spend too much time or effort explaining the big advantage real estate has over other forms of investment. Depending on the rate cycle you are operating in, compare the 7 to 14 percent return generated by an income property investment, with the 1 to 6 percent return savings banks pay; or with 2 to 6 percent from common stocks; or with the meager yield insurance for "investment's" sake returns. It becomes immediately obvious to the financially knowledgeable investor that real estate offers a much more attractive yield.

Selling Point 3—Tax Benefits

The tax benefits inherent to ownership of income property are more favorable than pertain to most other investment choices available.

However, the minute the word *taxation* is used, many otherwise intelligent beings shudder at the thought of complicated formulas and procedures, and reams and reams of paperwork and forms. Believe me, you can understand the basics with a bit of effort, and you can explain the benefits to a layman if you keep your explanation simple and uncluttered.

Initially, it is not essential that you know all the ins and outs of taxation as it applies to income property; however, the more you learn, the better you will be able to serve your clients. It is essential, however, that you understand some of the basic principles.

Most investors know that there are certain tax advantages to owning income property, but are not sure exactly how these work. You must be able to explain them in words that the investor will understand. Our goal here is to provide a simple guide to understanding and explaining these benefits.

The investor will (and should) rely on his accountant or lawyer to study the detailed tax ramifications of any real estate transaction. It is the tax adviser's duty to provide this expert counsel. And, it is your duty not to overstep your professional bounds and enter his domain. However, you must understand the basic advantages, in order to apply the techniques to creative brokerage. The pages that follow will help give you a better understanding of how to do this without overwhelming you with complicated formulas.

I must preface our discussion of tax benefits with one caution. In our examples, we will refer to a buyer's or a seller's tax bracket as 20, 30, 40, or whatever percent. It is a simplification to say that Mr. Seller, who is in the "40 percent bracket," is paying 40 cents on the dollar for taxes. He is actually paying 40 cents on the dollars he has earned over the amount that carried him into that bracket; below that, he is paying less. For simplicity's sake, however, we will assume that Mr. Seller in the "40 percent bracket" is paying 40 cents on the dollars in question for combined federal and state income taxes. This will enable us to present an easily understood, uncomplicated illustration of the types of tax savings afforded by real estate.

Making Depreciation Work for You. Uncle Sam, through the Internal Revenue Code, provides owners of income property with a novel and very lucrative way of saving tax dollars. Under our present tax laws, the federal government permits us to deduct from our income an amount to cover the "depreciation" of all the income property we own. The owner of an apartment building, for example, can deduct from his total income an allowance for the "wearing-out" of his building.

To understand fully why this is so advantageous, you must compare the effects of this same depreciation allowance on other business investments and observe how the end results compare to income property.

For example, a business can depreciate its equipment, such as its fleet of automobiles. The XYZ Manufacturing Corporation, say, will write off a truck in five years. However, when the truck is fully depreciated and its cost deducted from the net profit of the corporation, the similarity to the application of depreciation to income property ends. Why? Because at the end of five years, the truck is virtually valueless; it may be worth 20 percent or less of its original sales price. At the end of the same period, the reasonably well-maintained apartment building in a 6 percent growth area, will be worth 130 percent of its original cost (which will represent a five-year equity increase of 300 percent on a 10 percent-down purchase).

So then, Uncle Sam has allowed us to deduct a fictitious loss from our net return. How big of an advantage can you ask for?

Also, consider the fact that when XYZ Manufacturing Corporation pays its stockholders a dividend of, say, 4 percent at the end of the year, the depreciation has already been used by the corporation and is not available to the individual investor. So that the 4 percent—which is cited as return—cannot be improved by the application of depreciation. Our return on income property then is further enhanced by our ability to offset a portion or *all* of our return by applying depreciation.

Excited about the great investment you have to sell? Hold your breath; we haven't even scratched the surface yet!

How to Figure Depreciation for Your Prospect. To demonstrate how depreciation will save your prospect tax dollars, you must be familiar with some of the basics of determining the depreciation deduction.

Land is not a wasting asset, so it cannot be depreciated. Your first step is to determine what portion of the purchase price you can depreciate. By removing that portion of the purchase price attributable to land, the remaining balance is obviously the cost of the building, which can be depreciated.

How to Determine the Depreciable Amount. Although the following is not always the overriding consideration in determining how much of the purchase price is for the building, exclusive of land (i.e., "the improvement"), it is a good guide for roughing out your presentation. Take the percentage of the total tax assessment arrived at by the city, town, or county officials that is allocated to the building, and apply the same percentage to the purchase price.

For example: Mr. A. buys a five-unit apartment house which is assessed by the city for $180,000 (land and building). The building is valued by the city, for tax assessment purposes, at $162,000, the land at $18,000. The city then says that the building is worth 90 percent of the total. Mr. A. pays $250,000 for the property. How much is depreciable? Here's the solution:

$$\frac{\$162,000 \text{ (building assessment)}}{\$180,000 \text{ (total assessment)}} = .90$$

Then $250,000 (purchase price)
$\times$ .90 (building ratio)
$225,000 depreciable amount (building base)

Use the same procedure for arriving at the depreciable amount in other types of income property. You will generally find, however, that commercial property such as store blocks, shopping centers, and office buildings are located on more valuable land than the average apartment building. For this reason, you will not normally obtain so high a depreciable amount in commercial properties as you will in apartment buildings.

How to Determine "Useful Life". Before you can arrive at the amount of depreciation you can deduct, you must determine the "useful life" of the property. Any haggling between investors and the IRS was resolved with passage of the Economic Recovery Tax Act (ERTA) of 1981. ERTA simplified and redesigned the depreciation system to allow all buildings purchased after January 1, 1981 to be written off using methods and periods specified by the IRS. Since 1981 there have been numerous changes to these methods and periods such that you may find buildings being depreciated over periods of anywhere from 15 years to 40 years. Without going into the entire history of depreciation changes since 1981, suffice it to say that a building purchased in 2005 will be depreciated using the straight line method commencing with the month the property is "placed in service." If the property is residential rental property, the life will be 27.5 years. If it is not residential, the life will almost certainly be 39 years (there are some special types of property, such as farm buildings, that get different lives, but you can get your accountant to help you out if you are dealing with such a property).

Finally, based on past history, you should expect that Congress may at some point readjust useful life. Forecasting Washington's actions runs the same risk of fallibility as forecasting Wall Street's. However, if you understand how depreciation is calculated after studying the next few pages, you should have little difficulty in readjusting the math when any changes occur in the future.

Keep in mind that useful life for tax purposes may have little relation to how long the building will be standing. There are properties in my town as well as yours that were built 100 years ago, and will still be standing 100 years from now. Over the years they will be owned by dozens of different individuals, and each one will take a new tax base, based on his acquisition cost when he acquires the property. Each in turn may depreciate it "to the ground."

The Modified Accelerated Cost Recovery System (MACRS). The current depreciation system is an outgrowth of the ACRS system first introduced in 1981. It is now called Modified ACRS (MACRS), pronounced "makers." Under this system buildings are generally depreciated using the straight line method and a life of 27.5 years (residential) or 39 years (nonresidential). In the first and last years of ownership you only get depreciation for the number of months that you own the property.

Conveniently, the IRS has published tables that lay out the depreciation percentage for each year of building ownership based on the type of property and the month placed in service. (See Tables 7.1 and 7.2.)

To illustrate how the tables work, remember our Mr. A who bought a 10-unit apartment building. Earlier we calculated his depreciable basis in the property to be $225,000. Assuming he bought the property in July, you would figure his depreciation for the year of purchase by consulting Table 7.1 and finding row 1, column 7. There you would discover that Mr. A is allowed to claim 1.667 percent of the cost basis of his building as a depreciation deduction in his first year of ownership. Sticking with column 7, you would also note that in the second through ninth years Mr. A would claim a depreciation deduction of 3.636 percent each year. So, Mr. A's first year depreciation deduction would be:

$ 225,000 improvement
× .01667 July purchase, month 7
$3,750.75 depreciation

(For simplicity's sake, we'll assume that each property analyzed was acquired in the first month and utilize either 3.5 percent for the first year for residential properties or 2.5 percent for commercial buildings.)

How to Apply the Depreciation Deduction. Assuming that Mr. A. is using MACRS table, he will deduct $7,875 from his gross equity income, which is nothing more than his gross spendable income combined with his amortization accrued during that year. The result is the amount of income from the building that is *taxable.* In many cases, there may be no taxable income from the property (even after considering amortization) and the owner may have a tax loss.

Table 7.1.   Residential Rental Property Mid-month Convention Straight Line—27.5 Years

Year												

	Month Property Placed in Service											
Year	1	2	3	4	5	6	7	8	9	10	11	12
1	3.485%	3.182%	2.879%	2.576%	2.273%	1.970%	1.667%	1.364%	1.061%	0.758%	0.455%	0.152%
2–9	3.636	3.636	3.636	3.636	3.636	3.636	3.636	3.636	3.636	3.636	3.636	3.636
10	3.637	3.637	3.637	3.637	3.637	3.637	3.636	3.636	3.636	3.636	3.636	3.636
11	3.636	3.636	3.636	3.636	3.636	3.636	3.637	3.637	3.637	3.637	3.637	3.637
12	3.637	3.637	3.637	3.637	3.637	3.637	3.636	3.636	3.636	3.636	3.636	3.636
13	3.636	3.636	3.636	3.636	3.636	3.636	3.637	3.637	3.637	3.637	3.637	3.637
14	3.637	3.637	3.637	3.637	3.637	3.637	3.636	3.636	3.636	3.636	3.636	3.636
15	3.636	3.636	3.636	3.636	3.636	3.636	3.637	3.637	3.637	3.637	3.637	3.637
16	3.637	3.637	3.637	3.637	3.637	3.637	3.636	3.636	3.636	3.636	3.636	3.636
17	3.636	3.636	3.636	3.636	3.636	3.636	3.637	3.637	3.637	3.637	3.637	3.637
18	3.637	3.637	3.637	3.637	3.637	3.637	3.636	3.636	3.636	3.636	3.636	3.636
19	3.636	3.636	3.636	3.636	3.636	3.636	3.637	3.637	3.637	3.637	3.637	3.637
20	3.637	3.637	3.637	3.637	3.637	3.637	3.636	3.636	3.636	3.636	3.636	3.636
21	3.636	3.636	3.636	3.636	3.636	3.636	3.637	3.637	3.637	3.637	3.637	3.637
22	3.637	3.637	3.637	3.637	3.637	3.637	3.636	3.636	3.636	3.636	3.636	3.636
23	3.636	3.636	3.636	3.636	3.636	3.636	3.637	3.637	3.637	3.637	3.637	3.637
24	3.637	3.637	3.637	3.637	3.637	3.637	3.636	3.636	3.636	3.636	3.636	3.636
25	3.636	3.636	3.636	3.636	3.636	3.636	3.637	3.637	3.637	3.637	3.637	3.637
26	3.637	3.637	3.637	3.637	3.637	3.637	3.636	3.636	3.636	3.636	3.636	3.636
27	3.636	3.636	3.636	3.636	3.636	3.636	3.637	3.637	3.637	3.637	3.637	3.637
28	1.970	2.273	2.576	2.879	3.182	3.485	3.636	3.636	3.636	3.636	3.636	3.636
29	0.000	0.000	0.000	0.000	0.000	0.000	0.152	0.455	0.758	1.061	1.364	1.667

Table 7.2   Nonresidential Real Property Mid-month Convention Straight Line—39 Years

	Month Property Placed in Service											
Year	1	2	3	4	5	6	7	8	9	10	11	12
1	2.461%	2.247%	2.033%	1.819%	1.605%	1.391%	1.177%	0.963%	0.749%	0.535%	0.321%	0.107%
2–39	2.564	2.564	2.564	2.564	2.564	2.564	2.564	2.564	2.564	2.564	2.564	2.564
40	0.107	0.321	0.535	0.749	0.963	1.177	1.391	1.605	1.819	2.033	2.247	2.461

How to Demonstrate All This to Your Prospect. In Chapters 4 and 5 you were introduced to two sections of the Peckham Boston Analysis Worksheet. You are now prepared to use the third section of this worksheet, to demonstrate what your investor's net *spendable* income will be on a property after depreciation deductions and after income tax considerations. Lines 12 to 18 of the worksheet make up the tax analysis section.

Armed with the preceding information on depreciation, you should have no trouble in completing this section:

TAX ANALYSIS

Straight-Line

Depreciable Improvements _____   ____ %

Depreciation _____ Years

12. Net operating income (line 5)   _____

13. Less interest (line 6)   – _____

14. Less depreciation   – _____

15. Taxable income/Tax loss   = _____

Cash flow after taxes

16. Cash flow before taxes (line 9)   _____

17. Less estimated tax (line 15 × tax bracket)   – _____

18. Net cash flow after taxes   = _____

Here is a line by line explanation of how to use the Tax Analysis section.

Depreciable Improvements: Enter the portion of the purchase price attributable to the building (excluding the portion attributable to the land).

Depreciation Method: Enter the useful life available to the buyer—for example: 27.5 years.

Line 12—Net operating income: In Chapter 6 you converted seller's net to net operating income. The result appeared on line 5. Simply enter that figure on line 12. This represents the cash profit from the building's operation before tax implications and financing.

Line 13—Less interest: Enter the total amount of mortgage interest from line 6 of the financing section.

Line 14—Depreciation: Enter the amount of depreciation you have calculated for the property. Remember that this figure is arrived at by multiplying your improvement by the percentage of depreciation arrived at by consulting the table.

Line 15—Taxable income/or Tax loss: By subtracting lines 13 and 14 from line 12, net operating income, you arrive at either the taxable income or the amount of tax loss. Enter your result, and circle whether it is a taxable amount or a tax loss. If your depreciation and interest exceed your net operating income, then you have a tax loss. If they are less, then the difference is taxable.

Lines 16–18 will help you to show your prospect what his cash flow will be after tax implications.

Line 16—Enter the cash flow before taxes from line 9.

Line 17—Enter the estimated tax, by multiplying your prospect's "tax bracket" by the taxable income on line 15. The result is the estimated tax he will have to pay.

Line 18—Simply subtract line 17 (estimated tax) from line 16 (cash flow before taxes). The result is the amount your investor will have left over to spend after he pays his income tax on the taxable income from this building.

In Chapter 15, you will see how this Tax Analysis Section ties in with all other sections to form a powerful closing tool. When you see all these sections tied together, you will also see a general caution, which is reproduced below. Here, we again warn the prospect that he should check with his own tax counsel concerning the income tax implications of the contemplated transaction. We also point out that for demonstration's sake certain tax bracket assumptions are simplifications:

Note

The information on this Income Analysis Worksheet is intended as an EXAMPLE ONLY, to demonstrate estimated net cash flow after taxes, percentage returns, possible income tax consequences, and growth potential. All figures and percentages shown in this analysis are estimates. All information, allocations, and projections shown here, while based upon information supplied by the owner or from other sources deemed to be reliable, are not, in any way, warranted by The Peckham Boston Company. Tax bracket computations are assumed to be applied against the last dollars of taxable income. This is a simplification in most cases; however, the results projected will give a reasonable indication of possible tax savings. Independent tax counsel should be obtained concerning all income tax considerations involved.

An Example of Depreciation in Action. Dr. D., a prospect, is in the 40 percent tax bracket. She is considering the purchase of a suburban, 80-unit garden apartment complex. It was constructed by a builder who has asked you to sell it for him. You have the following facts in hand:

1. Purchase price $4,000,000
2. Improvement allocation: Purchase price, $4,000,000 less land value, $500,000 = $3,500,000
3. Depreciation method 27.5 year, straight line
4. Financing $3,200,000 @ 8% constant, 6% interest
5. Scheduled gross income $550,000
6. Net operating income: $310,000

You have completed the Income Analysis section of your worksheet, and you continue on and complete the Tax Analysis section. Your completed figures look like this:

INCOME ANALYSIS

1. Seller's net before financing   + _____
2. Rent stabilization   − _____
3. V & R allowance   − _____
4. Expense adjustment   + _____
5. Net operating income   = _____ $310,000.00

FINANCING

6. Interest (total) $192,000
7. Principal (total)   + _____64,000_____
8. Total   256,000   − _____256,000_____
9. Cash flow before taxes   = _____54,000_____
10. Cash down payment   800,000
11. % return on equity   6.75%

TAX ANALYSIS

Depreciable Improvements _____$3,500,000.00_____

Depreciation: 27.5 years   St. Line method

                            3.636 %

12. Net operating income (line 5) $310,000.00
13. Less interest (line 6)   − _____192,000_____
14. Less depreciation .03636 ×
     $3,500,000   − _____127,260_____
15. Taxable income/Tax loss   = _____<9,260.00>_____

Cash flow after taxes

16. Cash flow before taxes (line 9)   = _____$54,000_____
17. Less estimated tax (line 15 × tax
     bracket)   − _____<9,260>_____
18. Net cash flow after taxes   = _____$54,000_____

Keep in mind that the preceding example is computed for demonstration purposes only, and each building may vary widely as to the tax consequences and other benefits to the buyer.

Thus, there is *no* current tax due on income from this building. There's also a $9,200 *paper loss.* This means Doctor D. saves in taxes she would otherwise have been required to pay during her first full year of ownership and in addition has a loss carry forward, which we will discuss in the next section.

Understanding the basic principle of depreciation, and providing the investment by which all of this comes about, means that investors with tax problems will consider you a valued ally!

The Passive Activity Loss Rules. In general, unless you work full time in some aspect of the real estate business, your ownership of rental property subjects you to the "Passive Activity Loss Rules." What these rules are designed to do is prevent individuals from using losses from businesses in which they are not active participants against their other kinds of income—their wages, interest, dividend income, and so on. How the IRS does this is to group all the income or loss from all the passive activities together for the year. If the result is a net profit, it's taxed along with the rest of the person's income for the year. But if the net is a loss, the loss can't be deducted. It isn't lost, it just carries over to the next year and every succeeding year until the person either has a net profit from their passive activities or gets rid of the property that was the source of the loss.

So, in our previous example, Doctor D. had a tax loss from the initial years of ownership of her rental property but we didn't "do" anything with the loss because she couldn't use it against her hospital salary. Instead, the loss will carry over until she either sells the building or has a tax profit to soak up the loss. Confused? Consider—in confusion there is opportunity. Down the road, our doctor has another potential problem—taxable income, maybe even phantom income. With your help, the doctor has bought a good quality apartment building—rents have gone up, vacancy is low, operating expenses are under control. The net result is a profit from the property. Depending on the terms of the mortgage, principal payments may even start to exceed the shelter from depreciation resulting in phantom income. Now it's time for the doctor to either sell this property (thus freeing up any remaining passive loss carryover) or invest in a second property. In either case, the doctor needs your help and expertise.

How Long-term Capital Gains Treatment Can Save You Thousands. Uncle Sam also gives your investor a big break when he taxes the profit on the sale of a real estate investment.

To qualify for this favorable taxation on a profit, known as a long-term capital gain, your investor must have owned his investment for more than one year, and cannot be classified as a "dealer." There are many other ramifications and "twists"; however, for our basic understanding of the principles involved, these are sufficient.

When our investor's profit qualifies as a long-term capital gain, the IRS says that some of that gain will be taxed at a maximum rate of 25 percent and the remainder will be subject to a 15 percent rate.

Here's how it works:

1. Take the original purchase price;
2. Subtract any depreciation taken;
3. Add the cost of any capital improvements;
4. The result is your adjusted cost basis;
5. Subtract your adjusted cost basis from your net (after transaction costs) sales price;
6. This is your gain;
7. You then tax the gain at a 25 percent rate to the extent of depreciation claimed (item 2) and at a 15 percent rate on any remaining gain.

To keep the basic understanding of capital gains treatment as uncluttered as possible, the following example has been simplified, but, it is sufficient for a working understanding of the principles involved.

Capital Gains Illustrated

Purchase price	$ 400,000
Depreciation taken	– 40,000
Capital improvements	None
Adjusted cost basis	$ 360,000
Net sale price	$ 500,000
Less adjusted cost basis	– 360,000
Gain	$ 140,000

The $140,000 gain is taxed as follows:

$40,000 @ 25% = $	10,000
$100,000 @ 15% = $	15,000
Total tax on gain $	25,000

A Case in Point: Charlie Investor bought a property a few years ago for $400,000. He has taken $40,000 in depreciation during the course of his ownership. He has made no capital improvements. His adjusted cost basis is now $360,000. A good offer comes his way, and Charlie decides to sell the property for $500,000. The gain is $140,000 (the difference between his adjusted cost basis and the sale price).

Capital gains treatment is extremely valuable to all investors. But it's *spectacularly* valuable to investors in the high tax brackets. Reason: The dollar savings increase as the tax bracket gets higher.

Here's how the figures shape up: Charlie enjoys a capital gain of $140,000. If this was taxed as ordinary income in the 35% tax bracket, Charlie would pay Uncle Sam $49,000 in taxes. Because it is a long-term capital gain, Charlie pays only $25,000 in taxes—a $24,000 tax savings.

With such powerful tax factors at work for us, it's amazing that we even have to advertise our product. It's astounding that investors aren't lined up outside our door each morning when we open shop!

The Tax-Free Exchange. In Chapter 3 we briefly discussed the tax-free exchange, which is more accurately described as the tax "deferred" exchange.

Exchanging investment property is a highly specialized field and one that has been covered in depth by many publications. For now, study the following information and examples, and keep alert to special situations which call for the application of these principles. As we saw in the preceding section, when an investor sells a property at a gain they must pay a tax on that gain, even if they acquire another investment property immediately.

Learn this profitable exception: There is one exception to this rule, and it occurs when an investor exchanges his property for another "like kind" property—that is, one held for business use or for investment.

Section 1031 of the IRS Code provides that, if properly executed, there will be no tax due on this type of transaction. There are many "twists" to the tax-deferred exchange and the following facts are a necessary background before deciding whether you are ready for an exchange:

1. First and foremost, the exchanger must not be classified as a "dealer" in real property since dealers are not eligible to do exchanges.
2. As a general rule, an exchanger will completely avoid paying the tax only if they exchange for a larger property.
3. Many investors erroneously believe that they cannot exchange different types of property. Not so! Any property held for investment purposes is considered "like-kind" to any other investment property. For example, an apartment building can be exchanged for an office building or land for a shopping center or for a net leased retail building.
4. If an income property is sold on a non-installment basis and the proceeds reinvested, the gain cannot be deferred unless the exchange procedure is used.
5. Most exchanges involve at least three parties and are referred to as two-way exchanges with a cash out.

Here are some of the signals that indicate that you may be a prime candidate for a tax-deferred exchange:

- You have been approached by a buyer for your property but hesitate to sell because of the big potential capital gains tax.
- You would prefer to own relatively management-free property, such as a shopping center or a property net leased to a major tenant.
- You would prefer an income-producing property to your raw nonincome-producing land.
- You would prefer to own a property in a different geographical location.
- You would like to centralize your holdings by consolidating several smaller properties for one or two larger properties.
- Conversely, you would like to diversify your portfolio by divesting yourself of one or two major properties for several smaller properties.
- You would like to increase your tax advantage by exchanging for a larger, more highly leveraged property.
- Your estate-building plan has slowed because you have too much equity in your property.
- You may desire to exchange for a property that can be financed more readily than your present holdings.
- You may want to exchange for a property that is more readily salable.

There can be literally hundreds of reasons for using the exchange as a vehicle for accomplishing investment goals. The previous list outlines only a few possible motivating factors.

The Language of Exchanges. When arranging a Section 1031 exchange you will be working with, and relying on, accountants and attorneys that regularly deal with these exchanges. In working with these people self defense requires that you have some understanding of the buzz words they will be using. So, let's look at concise explanations of what some common exchange terms mean:

- *Exchange.* An exchange is the reciprocal transfer of properties.
- *Capital gain.* Simply stated, this is the taxable profit resulting from the sale of any capital asset, such as real estate.

- *Indicated gain.* This is the amount of gain that would be reported if a property were sold outright. In a sale, it's the difference between the basis (your book value for tax purposes) in the property and its sale price.

- *Recognized gain.* In an exchange, this is the amount that you will report as taxable gain in the year of the exchange. It will be the indicated gain or the total amount of what is commonly known as "unlike exchange," whichever is less.

- *Unlike property.* An unlike property in an exchange is anything that is not investment real estate. Unlike property is categorized as cash, boot, or net loan relief. Cash is easy enough to understand.

- *Boot.* Boot is the market value of any asset you receive other than real property in an exchange. For example, it could be an automobile or stocks.

- *Net loan relief.* In an exchange, this is the difference between your old loans and your new loans. If your old loans are greater than your new loans, you will be relieved of debt, and this difference will be included in unlike property along with any cash or boot you received. The total, if less than your indicated gain, will be your recognized gain and the amount you report.

- *Equity.* Equity is the difference between the market value of the property and the total existing loans. In an exchange, the equities are balanced by one party adding something of value, such as cash, boot, or a purchase money mortgage.

- *New adjusted cost basis.* In an exchange, the basis (book value) in the property acquired will usually differ from what it would be if it were purchased outright. It will be less by the amount of gain you defer. Your new adjusted cost basis is calculated by starting with the basis in your original property and adding any loans you assume, any cash or boot you pay, and any recognized gain you report. You must then deduct any cash or boot you receive and any loans you were relieved of from this amount. The net result is your new adjusted cost basis for tax purposes.

- *Deferred Exchange.* Also known as a delayed exchange or a forward exchange, it is the case where an owner gives up their property in exchange for replacement property to be received at a later date. As long as the exchange uses a "Qualified Intermediary" and completes the exchange within certain timeframes, it will meet the requirements for Section 1031 tax deferral. We'll discuss this type of exchange in more detail in the next section.

We don't in any way mean to overwhelm you with technical terminology. We simply set forth the previous as a primer on the language of exchanging with the recommendation that you consult your attorney or tax adviser for clarification before "making a swap"!

Tax-Deferred Exchange—Basic Case. Section 1031 of the Tax Code, which provides for the tax-deferred exchange of real estate investment property, was written into the Code over 80 years ago. In effect, Section 1031 says that real estate held for investment, for the production of income, or for use in trade or business may be exchanged for like kind property of equal or greater value. No gain or loss is recognized in connection with a properly structured exchange. This means that investors have been able to exchange properties and thereby avoid capital gains tax since the 1920s.

Behind the Reluctance to Do Tax-Deferred Exchanges. Despite the procedure's enduring proven value, many investors feel the tax-deferred exchange poses almost insurmountable difficulties. And they are deterred from using the procedure by their anxieties about its strange terms and multiple steps.

Terminology such as "like kind properties," "two-way exchanges with cash outs," the use of "leasehold interests" in property, and "deferred closings," makes many investors nervous. This is unfortunate because these same investors could profit immensely by using this magnificent tax-saving device.

The flexibility of the exchange procedure solves this problem for investors. A procedure known in the trade as a two-way exchange with a cash out, for example, has helped investors for decades.

A two-way exchange with a cash out takes place when Mr. A exchanges his property at 100 Main Street for Ms. B's property at 200 Main Street. Because Ms. B does not want to own Mr. A's property at 100 Main Street, and only desires to sell her property at 200 Main Street for cash, an investment broker prearranges for Ms. B to sell Mr. A's 100 Main Street property to a third party buyer for cash. The third party buyer located by the broker completes the two-way exchange and the cash out. Since a picture is worth a thousand words, here is what it looks like.

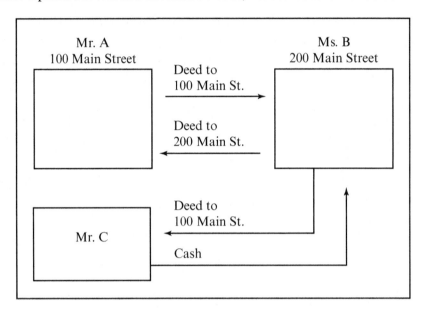

A variation of this procedure is for Mr. C., who desires to buy Mr. A's property, to purchase Ms. B's property for cash. To complete the tax-deferred exchange, Ms. B then exchanges the property she purchases for Mr. A's property.

These procedures are quite common and benefit each of the parties to the exchange: (1) Mr. A acquires property that is more suitable to his current investment objectives; (2) Ms. B disposes of a property she wants to sell; and (3) Mr. C acquires Mr. A's property. This property might not have been available without use of the tax-savings exchange technique.

The Delayed Exchange. Section 1031 exchanges are a terrific tax deferral opportunity. However, in the traditional exchange, it absolutely requires *that you find a property owner willing to exchange.* Many investors avoid tax-deferred exchanges because they think it is very difficult to locate a satisfactory exchange property. Their thinking goes like this: "First I have to find a property that I like. Then, that property has to be owned by someone who wants to own my property. It's like hunting for a needle in a haystack."

Often they are right! There may be no way to get all the pieces lined up to do a simultaneous 1031 exchange. Enter the Delayed Exchange. Let's go back to our previous example. We've got Mr. A who is ready to sell his property at 100 Main Street and Mr. C with a fistful of cash who wants the property and is ready to close. Mr. A's problem, as he has described it to you, is that he doesn't want to pay the tax on his gain and still wants to own some investment real estate—he just hasn't found the right property yet.

Big problem, simple solution. You bring in a Qualified Intermediary (QI). Don't worry, these people are easy to find. In fact, there is a whole industry built around being a QI. So now what happens? Instead of A selling to C, A transfers his 100 Main Street property to the QI in exchange for replacement property to be named later. The QI then sells 100 Main Street to Mr. C for cash. The cash sits in an account until you and Mr. A find the 200 Main Street replacement property. The QI buys that property from Ms. B and completes the exchange by transferring the title to Mr. A.

As with all things tax-related, there are some rules that need to be followed:

- *The 45-day rule:* This rule says that Mr. A has 45 days from the date of transfer of his 100 Main Street property to the QI in which to either close on the replacement property or at least identify one or more potential replacement properties. The properties identified must be specific—no "something in Missouri" or "an apartment building in Chicago." But you can say that it will be one or more of up to three specific buildings, such as "either 200, 300, or 400 Main Street." Also keep in mind that this identification must be in writing, delivered to the QI, and you must close on one of these specific properties.
- *The 180-day rule:* This rule says that the exchange with one of the properties identified in the 45-day letter must be completed by the earlier of the due date (with extensions, if necessary) of Mr. A's tax return for the year of the exchange or 180 days. See the tax "trap" here? Depending on when during the year Mr. A transfers his building to the QI, the tax return due date may be *earlier* than the 180-day clock. Of course this problem can be cured if Mr.

A extends his tax return—if he knows about the problem. Make sure the QI spells out exactly when the exchange period is up!

That's all there is to it—find the replacement property within 45 days and complete the exchange within 180 days. This is a lot more flexible than setting up a simultaneous exchange!

The Forward Exchange. So far, we've talked about a Delayed Exchange that follows a specific series of steps—find a buyer for your property, transfer the property to the QI, then find the replacement property you want the QI to buy for you to complete the exchange. But, you say, life is not always that neat. What happens if you first find the replacement property you want to own? You don't have a buyer for your current property and you'll lose the replacement property if you don't act fast. Are you knocked out of doing a tax free exchange? NO! The series of steps we just laid out is sometimes called a Forward Exchange. This is to distinguish it from, you guessed it, a *Reverse Exchange.*

Selling Point 6—Unrivaled Growth

We have talked about the effect of leverage in magnifying the growth of income-producing real estate. This, combined with the fact that our tenants are, in effect, paying off our mortgages with their rental payments, gives well selected real estate an unrivaled growth factor. No other safe investment available can match real estate for growth of owner's equity.

Some Investment Disadvantages—And How to Overcome Them. It appears that we have almost no competition at all, and we wouldn't, if it weren't for the fact that there are a few disadvantages inherent in ownership of income-producing real estate. Some of these disadvantages, as cited by proponents of competing investment vehicles, are partly valid—some are not. You must understand what holds investors back and be able to counteract their objections to real estate as an investment vehicle. Examine the two most important disadvantages.

1. The Problem—Lack of Liquidity

The most frequently cited drawback of income-property investment is that you can't call your broker and effect an immediate sale. There is no instantaneous marketplace such as the New York or American Stock Exchange. The advocates of competing forms of investment say that real estate owners are locked in, and that it is impossible to free cash because of the time element involved in effecting a sale.

Actually, as was noted earlier, with all of real estate's advantages, it's a wonder investors aren't lined up outside our doors. If it weren't for the impression of lack of liquidity, and the necessity for management (which we will discuss next) investors would be lined up. As it stands, even with these two major "drawbacks," there is a significant demand for our product! And with a broker who knows his product inside and out, the demand becomes even greater.

The Solution—How to Achieve Liquidity by Using Financing

One of the best ways to free cash quickly is by refinancing mortgage indebtedness. The owner, if he isn't mortgaged to the hilt, may refinance his mortgage (or if it is paid off, by arranging a first mortgage loan on his property). This can usually be done without much delay. And any capital obtained through financing or refinancing (hold your breath) is *tax-free* until the building is sold! This is because no taxable event (sale) has taken place.

In my opinion, the argument that the real estate owner is not liquid doesn't hold much water! If he wants to sell, he can sell tomorrow. Granted, he will most likely obtain a higher price if he waits longer and thoroughly exposes his property to the market. But by way of contrast, let's look at the stock investor, with all of his highly touted liquidity. If he needs capital tomorrow, he can sell. He can pick up the phone and sell but at what the market will pay, which could be well below what he paid for the stock or what he could obtain if he waited for a more "favorable" time. For goodness' sake, we can do the same thing with real estate—sell at what the market will pay!

2. The Problem—Necessity for Management

This disadvantage is the one that keeps many investors out of the income property market. Investors often feel that they are going to get phone calls complaining about plugged-up toilets, lights that are broken, refrigerators that aren't working, or disposals that aren't disposing. They fear the necessity to take time from an already crammed schedule to make minor irritating decisions. They know that stocks require no management—but forget the hours they spend each week studying the market pages in the paper and the condition reports in their expensive newsletters. They also forget the inflamed ulcers from the erratic performance of the market and from the realization, at a later date, that they sold low or bought high!

The Solution—Management by Professionals

Explain to your investors that you can arrange professional management for their building; and that by placing the management of their property in these well-trained hands, they will receive a statement at the end of each month showing how much came in, how much went out, and an enclosed check for the difference. The fee for professional management is quite reasonable in relation to the service obtained. Even after paying for this service, your investor will realize a much higher return on his investment than in other investment vehicles. When married to professional management, real estate becomes highly competitive with all other forms of investment. Overlook this arrangement where required, and you overlook many sales that would otherwise have been made—and commissions earned.

CHAPTER 8

Thirteen Immediate Sources of Buyers—And How to Approach Them

By now you have stocked your shelves with salable listings, and you understand how to finance your investments and prepare an operating statement. You say, "This is all fine, but I need some investors."

As is common with a high percent of the real estate people who add an income line to their regular business, your biggest fear is that all this time preparing to come face-to-face with a prospective investor will be wasted because you will be unable to find any buyers for your offerings.

Please be reassured by those of us who work full time selling income property, and set your fears aside. If you have the listings, you have the magnet to attract as many buyers as you can handle. Your biggest problem in time will not be finding the buyers, but will be qualifying them and reducing the hundreds (even thousands) of them to a few dozen who are "ready, willing, and able" to invest in and take advantage of the unique benefits of your product.

Spare yourself this anxiety. To set your mind at ease, let me point out that in my Boston area, any time a "red-hot" listing is distributed in our office, the place clears out. After several hurried phone calls, there is usually a crush at the exit door by the brokers, anxiously rushing out to submit the investment offering to an equally anxious investor.

I can't recall that these rushes have ever resulted in broken shoulders, a la Knute Rockne days; but you can be sure that there is no lack of customers when a 14-broker office clears out in ten minutes!

How to Amass a Huge File of Ready Investors

It will take you a short while to build up a list of qualified buyers; however, by using the following sources you will quickly assemble a huge list.

Most of the following sources will look familiar, as they are similar to the sources of sellers that we explored in Chapter 2. But here we will give some variations as to practical application and approach.

1. Newspapers
2. Local trade journals
3. Local financial reporting papers
4. Membership in organizations
5. Joint ventures and partnerships
6. Owner lists
7. Telephone books
8. Tax rolls
9. Published lists and directories
10. Advertisements
11. Blabbermouths
12. Blitzing
13. Writing a regular column

(In reviewing these 13 sources of buyers, it may be helpful to review Chapter 2 for additional detail and descriptive information regarding these sources.)

Buyer Source 1. Newspapers

As you discovered in Chapter 2, newspaper accounts of recent sales lead you immediately to a possible seller. Remember, too, that the previous owner is a very logical buyer at this point; now he probably has cash and time available to invest in a new property. Don't overlook the reported purchaser as a potential buyer for a similar type of property in your listing files.

Buyer Source 2. Local Trade Journals

In Chapter 2, we mentioned the *New England Real Estate Journal* as a fine example of a local trade journal. Within the pages of this weekly publication are found dozens of potential buyers. These leads are similar to those uncovered in Source 1, and there are usually more of them.

For example: Look at the text of this release in the *New England Real Estate Journal:*

> "John M. Peckham III, President of The Peckham Boston Company, the Boston income property firm, has announced the sale of a modernized five-story brick building containing ten apartments. The property located at 376 Boynton Street in the Back Bay has been sold for Robert Huron to Samuel Notice for $840,000. The sale was negotiated by Sam Smullin and Leonard Ross, who represented Peckham Boston."

Buyer Source 3. Local Financial Reporting Papers

In the Boston area, the *Banker and Tradesman* reports every real estate transaction in the state each week. Both the buyer and seller of each income property are very logical buyers of your wares. This source is the most prolific of all, with the exception of advertising. Everyone involved in income brokerage should read the reporting paper in their area as avidly as they do a novel.

How to Approach Leads Developed from Buyer Sources 1 to 3. In each of the preceding sources we have uncovered either (1) a new owner; or (2) a recent seller. Approaching these individuals is merely a matter of common sense. The straightforward manner is always best.

For example—to a new owner:

> Mr. New Owner, I noticed that you just purchased 10 Main Street. I'm John Jones with XYZ Realty. We have several fine apartment buildings available in that area, and we get new offerings each week. The reason for my call is to introduce myself and ask if you would like to have me keep an eye open for any exceptional investments that turn up in your area.

From this point on, John Jones will proceed with questions designed to qualify the prospect and determine his objectives; more on this in Chapter 9.

As you recall from Chapter 2, he will also attempt to list 10 Main Street from the new owner in this way: "Thank you for your time, Mr. New Owner; by the way, our office has many sincere buyers looking to invest in your area. Would you consider the possibility of a quick profit on your new acquisition?"

How to Approach a Recent Seller. "Mr. Recent Seller, my name is John Jones from XYZ Realty, I noticed that you just sold 10 Main Street. Our office has dozens of listings available in that area and in other areas within a 30-mile radius of your town. I'm calling to see when you could spend a few minutes with me to go over these offerings?" (Of course, the broker would also determine whether the seller has any other properties he might list.)

The preceding are merely examples of lead-in questions to introduce yourself and your objective. The specific details of qualifying the buyer follow in Chapter 9.

Buyer Source 4. Membership in Organizations

In Chapter 2, we explored the benefits of active participation in:

1. Local and regional Realtor organizations
2. Apartment owner organizations
3. Fraternal organizations and women's leagues

Everything we said about active participation in these groups in our discussion of how to generate listings is equally true for developing an active clientele of buyers. Many of the people you meet through your participation in these groups will someday buy or sell through you.

How to Approach Organization Members. Membership in organizations will afford you access to the members in person at the organization's various functions, and it will generally provide you with a membership list.

The In-Person Approach. If you have ever observed an alert income broker at an organization function (for example, a Rental Housing Association dinner dance), you probably noticed that he separates himself from his fellow brokers and friends, and makes an attempt to meet new clients. He talks to as many potential new buyers as possible at the cocktail party, and always manages to sit with an active buyer at dinner. His initial comments on meeting a new person might sound like this: "It's a pleasure to meet you, Mr. Investor. My name is John Broker from XYZ Realty, which is very active in apartment house sales. Are you actively seeking new investments now?" or, "Do you concentrate on apartment house investments, or do you prefer commercial properties?"

The income broker will always come to these functions well supplied with business cards, and always goes home with a list of names and notes as to investment preferences. The following day he calls his newly met investors to submit specific offerings and to qualify his new contacts further.

How to Operate with a Membership List. Most organizations have an alphabetical list of members that gives their names, addresses, and very often, telephone numbers. In the course of building up a list of clients, most new brokers will start at the beginning of the list and set aside several days for phone calls to members. These calls might start something like this:

> Mr. Investor, this is John Broker from XYZ Realty. We specialize in income property sales. As a fellow member of the Rental Housing Association, I wanted to ask if I might keep my eye open for some attractive investments for you, and get in touch when something exciting comes in.

As we mentioned in Chapter 2, this source alone will give you hundreds of leads to fatten your files. Your approach to leads set forward in Sources 5 and 6, which follow, should be essentially the same.

Buyer Source 5. Joint Ventures and Partnerships

Fractionalization is the future of real estate investment. As we have seen with condominiums, it is possible to divide almost any property into its physical components and market the individual parts. It is also possible to fractionalize almost any property through joint venturing, and allocate the risks and rewards of ownership to more than one party.

The terms *joint venture* and *partnership* are not synonymous. The term joint venture usually refers to a situation where two or more people join together to achieve a specific objective—not a continuing association.

The term partnership, on the other hand, often connotes a more permanent relationship between two or more parties.

Example of a Joint Venture. A developer and a group of investors wish to build an office building and sell it upon completion. The investors supply 100 percent of the working capital. The developer supplies 100 percent of the skill and time to construct the building. When the building is completed and sold, the developer receives 50 percent of the net profit and the investors share 50 percent of the net profit. This is a joint venture.

The joint venture began with the signing of a joint venture agreement; it ended with the distribution of the sales proceeds. The joint venture, then, is a temporary association formed for a single purpose.

Example of a Partnership. Two brothers decide to invest in real estate. They divide the acquisition costs and operating expenses. One brother handles the on-site management, and the other one handles the office responsibilities. They divide the cash flow and tax benefits, and—at a future date—will divide any net sales proceeds. As partners, they may be purchasing one property or several properties. Their partnership is intended to be an ongoing relationship.

All conditions, responsibilities, risks, and rewards of participation in either a joint venture or a partnership are negotiable. So it is conceivable that a joint venture agreement could be drafted with one party receiving most or all of the cash generated, and another party receiving most or all of the tax benefits of ownership. It is also conceivable that a partnership agreement could be drafted with one party receiving 95 percent of all the benefits, and another party receiving five percent.

In general, if we speak of a joint venture as a short-term or special-purpose association, and a partnership as a long-term association, we may think of the joint venture as a first step. That step, if successful, may lead to a second joint venture—or to a partnership.

The joint venture, then, can be utilized both for its own benefits and as a preliminary testing tool for an eventual partnership association.

Example: At a party, you are approached by a physician with the usual complaint of having to work half of each week for Uncle Sam. This doctor has money but no time and no expertise in real estate investment. You have another client who has time, expertise and a successful track record, but who is currently not maximizing his talent because of a lack of operating capital.

The doctor and your experienced client should, through your skilled and diplomatic intervention, be able to find common investment ground to explore. Since the parties had not met up to the point of your introduction, they might be justifiably reluctant to commit money and time for the long term. But you, of course, have a solution: to have each party agree to a trial association through a joint venture agreement. They'll engage in one transaction as joint venturists, and if successful, will be back to your office for their next cooperative opportunity—another joint venture, or a partnership. Keep in mind that you can supply the expertise and become one of the venturists.

How to Play the Match Game. You already play the *match* game as an investment broker, and the concept of joint venturing simply asks you to expand the parameters.

Here is how many of us in income property brokerage currently play the game: We take a listing on a property. We mentally run through a list of active clients hoping for a match. We hope to make a match from a list of clients with whom we have already dealt successfully. We have experience with them. We know them to be decision makers. Likewise, and equally important, they know us. You may have one or more clients who, if given the right circumstances, will make a commitment to you for a joint venture over the telephone.

Example: "Phil, I took a listing today on a 20-unit garden apartment building in Greenville. The numbers seem comparable to the Riverside conversion we did last year."

"Great, Jack; you know I've been waiting for this call. Let's go through with it. If you're free for lunch, I can meet you at the Hilton at two o'clock."

Keeping the Match Game Simple. The above dialogue is simple but realistic. It is conceivable that you have a client, Phil, with whom you have had a previously successful relationship. You know Phil, you've worked with him, and you know what he wants. You take a listing and, instantly and instinctively, you think of matching Phil with this new listing.

If it's a solid listing, you probably have several other established clients who would buy the building. You probably have several dozen cards on prospective buyers who have expressed an interest in this type of property. You probably could attract many additional parties through advertising. But why deal in probabilities? The answer is, of course, that you wouldn't. Phil is a known quantity. You match with Phil.

The simplicity comes *not* from the mechanics of the transaction. Phil, for instance, may expect a great deal of assistance and service from you. The simplicity, instead, comes from being able to see a beginning, the listing, and at the same time being able to see an end to a successful transaction—resulting in your commission.

In matching with Phil, you may already know and concede to yourself that months of hard work lie ahead, but the hard work isn't painful when you can see the end. In working with Phil, no matter how long the plan, you can see it in your mind with a successful and lucrative ending. In dealing with prospective clients or clients who walk in off the street from an ad, you can never be quite as sure about the fruits of your labor as you can be in making the match with Phil.

As a real estate investment broker, a vast majority of your time will be spent on activities for which you will receive no compensation. You might show a property ten times before a buyer is found. Assuming you are the selling broker, you have probably had nine misses to make one hit. If you are not the selling broker, all of your efforts, outside of possible future good will, have been for nil. Naturally, if you follow the guidelines in Chapter 10, you will keep your use of time in this regard much more productive.

So, you make your business life simple and your time as financially productive as possible by matching with the Phils, the known quantities, first. Hypothetically, if Phil will purchase every good investment property you can find, my advice would be to forget everybody else and say, "I work for Phil." Let's see how joint venturing can give you a new perspective on the income property business.

How Joint Venturing Can Give You a Fresh Perspective on Income Property Broker-age. Joint venturing gives you a chance to look at the income property brokerage business from a fresh philosophical perspective. Ordinarily, as brokers, we think in terms of listings. The more solid listings we have, the more successful we expect to become. We work at obtaining listings. Our thinking becomes property—or *thing*—oriented. There is nothing wrong with this perspective, but it does have some limitations. Right now, how many great listings are in your books? Honestly, most listings aren't great. Initially, most listings carry high seller expectations and become great—if ever—only through activity and negotiation.

In joint venturing, your emphasis is placed on buyers, *people,* rather than on list-ings, *things.* You study Phil. You know what Phil wants. In thinking about your pre-vious successes, you'll find there are many other clients like Phil. You have worked successfully with Dave, Roger, Jane, Arnold, and Steve. You have kept in touch with them. You know, right now, today, what Dave, Roger, Jane, Arnold, and Steve want in terms of real estate investment performance. Rather than conducting your busi-ness in search of the Holy Grail, the Great Listing, take it for granted that most listings will be ordinary until negotiation and compromise are completed at the bar-gaining table. Your real work is based upon finding the combination of people who, when brought together, will provide a new and productive source of sales.

Buyer Source 6. Owner Lists

The *Book of Assessed Values* (BOAV), which was mentioned in Chapter 2, is equally effective as a source of buyers. This publication and those similar to it in your area show who owns the property at such and such an address. Obviously, if he already owns an income property, he might be persuaded to add to his portfolio, and be-comes a powerful prospect for new listings located near his existing holdings.

Buyer Source 7. Telephone Book, Yellow Pages

So obvious, this source is often overlooked. Many active buyers and trusts let the public know that they want to buy income property, and even spend advertising and listing charges to help you locate them. For example:

> John Smith Realty Trust
> 50 Main Street, Boston, 555-8161
> Owners—Managers
> Real Estate Investments Wanted

Buyer Source 8. Tax Rolls

(See Chapter 2, page 18.) Again we note that present owners of income property are often interested in expanding their portfolios.

After you have assembled a list of owners in a particular area, you should select from your file a listing that is located in the same general area. When you call an owner, your approach might sound like this:

> Mr. Investor, I noticed that you own 100 Main Street in Smallville. We have just received an excellent offering in the next town (or next block). I'd like very much to sit down with you and explain the unique advantages of this investment.

Buyer Source 9. Published Lists and Directories

There are several nationally published lists of directories of buyers and sources of financing (possible joint venture buyers) which can be extremely helpful in the income property brokerage field. Here's an example of one I have used over the years and that I have found to be quite comprehensive:

"The Crittenden Real Estate Newsletters," published by Crittenden Publishing, Inc., P.O. Box 1150, Novato, CA 94949. Web: www.crittendennews.com

This publication is simply an example of many fine publications that list those institutions and companies involved in the ownership, purchasing, and financing of income properties. As pointed out in other sections of this Guide, sellers are often buyers, buyers are often sellers, and financiers and lending institutions are quite often potential buyers—through their various subsidiaries and through the potential for joint venturing.

Buyer Source 10. Advertisements

Advertising is often the most productive source of buyers. It is also the most expensive—but the dollar cost is easily outweighed by the return in earned commissions.

Because this source will be so important to you in your initial search for investors, it will be covered in detail in the following chapter.

Advertising by others, however, is another source of leads that costs you nothing and will generate dozens of buyers for your offerings.

Earlier, we mentioned that income brokers are "wined and dined" by the active investors. They want the broker to call them first, and call them quickly when a red-hot listing is published. With this in mind, it is certainly not unbelievable that active investors spend significant sums to urge all brokers to submit their latest offerings to them. Some of their ads will look like this:

PRINCIPAL WANTS
TO BUY INCOME PROPERTY

■ All replies promptly acknowledged
■ Quick action
■ All replies kept confidential

Call Mr. Buyer, 888-555-8161, or send details
to 200 Main Street, YourTown, Mass. 02614

How to Approach Buyers Who Advertise. While you are building your buyer files, follow up on these religiously. It is not considered good practice simply to mail a batch of operating statements to Mr. Buyer. You should first call or write the investor, asking what, where, how much, and why. He or she should be qualified as to objective just as all your clients are. We will explore these techniques later in Chapter 9.

Quite often you will see a similar ad, but with one of the following expressions:

■ "Wants to Buy Direct from Owner"
■ "Principals Only"
■ "No Brokers"

If you are in the process of building your buyer files, then by all means call Mr. Buyer, anyhow. But, as pointed out in Chapter 2, if his name is not mentioned in the ad, separate yourself from the rest of the crowd by obtaining his name from the telephone business office or from your reverse telephone directory.

Generally, the buyer who indicates that he wants to buy direct from the owner will nevertheless be delighted to hear from you if you have an offering that makes financial sense to him.

Buyer Source 11. Blabbermouths

Shop talk will often reveal that Bill Buyer and Doctor Smith are actively seeking income property. By all means, contact these individuals, qualify them, and submit your offerings that match their requirements.

Buyer Source 12. Blitzing

The term *blitzing* is generally applied to the process of seeking out listings that are not now on the market. If you have done your listing job well, you have found that in five out of ten cases, whether the owner has given you a listing or not, he has said, "When you find a property in this area (and of this type), please let me know." Or he may say, "I'm not a seller—I'm a buyer."

As soon as you hear these words, you should immediately find out what, where, how much and why, and card this information for later reference.

Buyer Source 13. Writing a Regular Column

One of the best ways to get your message across—to get free advertising, in effect—is to have a regular column appear in a local newspaper, under your own byline. You can write it yourself, or have someone write it for you. But the dividends it pays can be tremendous. (For further information on the special uses of writing a column, see the discussion in Chapter 2.) Do not overlook the power of reaching prospective buyers on the Internet with a regular e-letter.

Handling Buyers as Business Groups

You will use all of the preceding sources extensively when you first start to work in this exciting specialty; however, as you accumulate files of active investors, you will find that you become so familiar with the names you can reduce the time you spend in developing leads to a minimum. In time, you will rely almost exclusively on your advertising for leads. In further time, you will enjoy the most valuable of leads—referrals.

It is considered good practice, however, to maintain your contact with the other leads—to keep your ear to the ground by setting aside time each week to read your newspapers, trade journals, and reporting papers, and to remain active in various organizations.

Once your list is accumulated, and your initial contacts are made, you will find yourself trying to reduce your list of buyers to a manageable size. You will be adding names to your list from calls on your ads, and you will be deleting the names of those buyers with whom you have spent considerable time, but who have never made an offer on a property. We will cover prospect file maintenance in depth in Chapter 9.

Finding Buyers at Cyberspace Speed—The Huge Potential

As you will see in Chapter 14 the Cyber Age has augmented many of the techniques descried in this Guide. Finding buyers is no exception and may be the most exciting tool in the income property brokers arsenal.

In courses conducted by the Real Estate CyberSpace Society, we take on one of the students' active income property listings and promote it on the Internet at around 11:00 A.M. By 2:00 P.M. we check to see how many buyers we have and without exception we find responses from over 50 potential buyers for the property (or brokers representing those buyers). In three hours we have ferreted out as many buyers as we could locate in three weeks without the Internet.

Here's an example of an e-mail promotion for a property from an actual seminar in Ohio:

Subject: OHIO ESTATE SALE—208 APARTMENTS!

I'm here in Columbus with the CCIMs from the great state of Ohio doing the Society's one day RECS designation seminar, "Selling in CyberSpace."

John Aubry CCIM (about to become: John Aubry CCIM, RECS) is here with me and has a substantial apartment complex to sell.

John represents the trustees of a deceased manufacturing executive's estate who want to sell the estate's 208 unit, 10 building apartment complex, located on 14.76 acres of attractive landscaped grounds with every amenity imaginable.

This gem is over 95% rented and offered for only $4,950,000.

John said that he will show you how your buyer can create a huge increase in value with a discrete upgrade. Please get back to me post haste. John has promised to get all of the details back to you pronto!

This e-mail message went out at 9:42 A.M. and within 15 minutes we had 14 responses. And by the time the seminar adjourned at 4:00 P.M. we had received 118 responses. Not bad for a few hours' work.

Finding Buyers In Cyberspace

So you have a hot listing—or you own a unique property and you want to reach tens of thousands of buyers in the next hour. Finding buyers is a key element in any sales campaign. Where do you start? Here are the three steps to reaching and motivating action buyers in cyberspace:

1. Identify the most logical place to locate the buyer or someone representing the buyer.
2. Design a message which will get a favorable response.
3. Convey the information to the leads generated in a way that leads to a meeting, a showing of the property, or a letter of intent.

For now let's take a look at Step 1—locating buyers in cyberspace. We will continue with steps 2 and 3 in Chapter 14, where we will pull together a complete marketing campaign.

Identifying Buyer Hangouts—Two Examples

Walk with me through two recent quick searches to see where we might find buyers for two offerings: one an airport and the other a bed and breakfast.

A while back I listed an airport for sale. First I posted it to my web page and a few other web sites that allow the posting of information on properties for sale. Then I did an e-mail to 7,000 of my favorite investors and commercial brokers.

I then began to search around in places where people interested in aviation and airports might hang out. Using Alta Vista search engine, I entered "airport owners" and did a web search. This resulted in 73 hits (locations on the World Wide Web) that contained a reference to the search phrase "airport owners." One of these referred to the "Airport Owners and Operators Association"—a pretty good lead!

The next property on my desk was a really neat bed and breakfast. To find out where buyers for this kind of property hang out I did a similar search on the key words "bed and breakfast owners." This resulted in 22 hits, including the "Lanier Travel Guide." Next I did a search on the words "bed and breakfast and Massachusetts" and came up with 500 hits. Similarly a search on "guest houses and Massachusetts" yielded 57 hits, including a directory of "B&B's, country inns and guest houses."

I then found a newsgroup that concerns itself with "Hotels, Motels, Inns and Bed and Breakfasts."

While there I decided to make another search for people who might buy my airport. Shazam! Up popped a newsgroup called "misc.transport.air-industry."

Pleasant Surprises In Cyberspace

In the course of searching for airport buyers I ran into another airport listed by a broker in Connecticut. I quickly e-mailed him asking if there might be some synergism between his efforts and mine. A short while later he called and in the course of the conversation he provided me with a lead to federal grant money to help cities and towns buy private airports and convert them for municipal use. With up to 95 percent of the acquisition cost funded by the grant this information certainly made this broker's job more interesting!

Integrating the *Buyer Finding* Process

With these examples in hand, we will discuss integrating the *buyer finding* process into an overall cyber marketing campaign in depth in Chapter 14 to help you get significant results with a fraction of the effort you are probably using today.

CHAPTER 9

Proven Techniques for Qualifying Buyers

By now you are ready to sit down face-to-face with an investor. You're almost ready to submit investments and to analyze how these investments will benefit the potential buyer financially. I say almost ready, because one more step is necessary before you submit properties to your prospective investor—you must qualify your prospect. You must find out why he wants to invest before you can advise him regarding the availability of a property that will meet his requirements.

After you finish reading this chapter, contrast the highly effective techniques shown with those of the broker who rushes a new-found client out the door, and wastes the client's time and his own time showing properties without any real knowledge of the client's motivations!

In order to earn your keep in this business, you must be able to analyze your client's financial needs and emotional limitations, before you can accurately and quickly find the one or two properties among your listings that will best suit these characteristics.

You might not have the right property for him at this time. You might have to wait and get back to him as soon as an investment becomes available which meets his needs. If his demands are unrealistic, you will have to advise him on the current yields on various types of properties in your area. If he still insists on unrealistic yields, then you have saved hours of running time by uncovering this fact now, and not after three days of showing properties. Let your unrealistic buyer waste your competitors' time. Understanding the vital need for a system of qualifying your buyers, you are ready to study their needs and limitations in depth.

Remember that you are not selling real estate—you are selling *money* in the form of present cash flow or in the form of future benefits. Your buyers, whether they know it or not, want to invest in real estate for the same basic reasons they have invested in the stock market. But the benefits accruing to the real estate investor are far greater. This is what makes your investors so different from the real estate buyer who wants a house to shelter his family, and even different from the business or corporation in need of shelter in a commercial or an industrial property. The prime concern for these prospects is adequate shelter at an acceptable price. Shelter is not normally a factor in your negotiations. Your investors are motivated by the desire or need for one or all of the following:

1. Income
2. Growth
3. Speculation (a quick profit)

Generally there is some degree of overlapping, and some investors can be driven by a desire for all three. There is almost always one primary need, however, and the sooner you find it, the closer you will be to a sale.

Who Buys for Income?

A good example of the buyer motivated by the promise of increased income is the older couple, perhaps retired, who are now receiving a relatively low return from their present investments. Generally, they are not moved much by the promise of long-range growth potential, or by the prospects of the tenants paying off the mortgages over a 20- to 30-year period. They want *cash flow.* They want a relatively stable monthly income, but they want a higher income than they are currently receiving from other forms of investment. So they turn to income property. They are buying, then, primarily for income. If your buyer is close to or of retirement age, he is usually best served by a safe steady income in a well maintained, well located property.

Who Buys for Growth?

On the other hand, the young couple with an infant or young child, and a sufficient income from their primary jobs, are not so much motivated by the income aspects of our offerings. Of course, additional income is nice for everyone, but they are buying with an eye to the future. They want a building that will *grow in value,* so that when their children are ready for college, or when they, themselves, are ready to retire, they will have created an estate that will support these needs.

Many young couples will forego all cash flow in order to *leverage* their purchases, thus accumulating large holdings more rapidly. (See Chapter 7.)

Who Is the Speculator?

The speculator wants a relatively quick profit. His income is generally derived from resale. He wants to turn over his capital as quickly and as frequently as possible, each time selling for more than he paid. To do this, he will assume a larger-than-average risk.

The speculator has a particular knack for buying problem properties where certain improvements are necessary. He might buy an apartment building that needs modernization, or one that needs the hand of an expert to manage it properly, or possibly a property that needs refinancing of the existing debt (mortgage) structure to improve cash flow.

The speculator serves a definite function in our market. He will buy a property that the "income" or "growth" buyer would not touch. He will then get it into shape, either through physical, managerial or financial improvement, and offer it for sale to the less stout-hearted investor. Once the property has been improved and put into proper physical and financial order, the non-speculator buys it and has a trouble-free building. The speculator has his due profit, which has been earned by his entrepreneurship.

The young investor who is short on cash and long on courage, ability, and time can still create a fortune in real estate, providing he has established a good credit rating. Put the courageous young investor in the speculator's category. The condominium converter would also fit into this category.

Don't Underestimate Pride of Ownership as a Motive

Intertwined with these three primary objectives is one powerful underlying motivation not directly related to making money. This motivation does not have such an impact in other investment fields, but it's one that must be recognized in income brokerage—*pride of ownership*. The stock market investor can't readily pull his certificates out of the vault and display them to the world. But the income property owner can easily drive by his handsome brick building and casually tell his friends, "1041 is right over there. All filled up. Best investment I ever made." You won't even have to dig out this motivating factor because it's there, and don't forget it!

How to Classify Your Investors

It is helpful to recognize some of the classic types of buyers. When income brokers consult with each other within an office, they must be able to categorize an investor quickly. For brevity's sake, they cannot go into a historical and financial background on each investor. For this reason, a broker will generally refer to a prospect as a "young renovator" or as "a novice engineer," etc.

Generally the investor's primary profession—if it is outside real estate—is of interest, because it gives some indication of his background. Aside from his profession, the other descriptive terms are even more revealing. Here are a few descriptive words and phrases sometimes used, which will help you understand some of the general types of clients you will be dealing with:

The Active Investor

The active investor can own millions in income property and be a rock of substance, or can range all the way down to the struggling young speculator who is just getting started. Usually the larger the active investor becomes, the less he speculates. The smaller active investor is generally, very, very active buying and selling; he has to be—that's usually the way he feeds himself.

The Novice

A large portion of your prospective buyers will be relative newcomers to the real estate investment field. Many of them have become disenchanted with the stock market. Many of them are sick of seeing inflation "steal" their savings dollars and their insurance equities. The novice buyer will tax your patience, because before you can find him a proper investment you must educate him and gain his respect and confidence.

The Pro

The pro is a buyer who owns or has owned income property before and knows what it's all about. You don't have to educate him, and he won't have to check with "Uncle Elmer" to see if your proposal makes sense. He need not be a speculator, but he can be. He may well be, for example, a doctor who has invested in real estate in the past and is continuing to do so.

The Tax-Motivated Buyer

The tax-motivated buyer is upset because he has a large income and must *shelter* a portion of it to avoid paying too much in income taxes. He may also have had a property taken by eminent domain, and may be "under the gun" to reinvest or pay his capital gains tax. Work closely with your tax-motivated buyer—you can perform miracles for him. Tell him to ask his accountant how your offering will affect his income from a tax standpoint. Be sure to provide him with an after-tax analysis form. (See Chapter 7.)

The Low-Cash Buyer

The low-cash buyer is of necessity a speculator. He is usually a young investor who wants to create an estate through hard work—and he can with your assistance. If he is willing to move quickly and stick with his program, then by all means spend some time with his problems. You will be rewarded not only in commissions earned, but in the satisfaction of seeing your client create "something from nothing," using only his courage and ability and your creative brokerage. The low-cash-down buyer may also be a middle-aged man who has time available outside his normal job to devote to creating and overseeing a growing portfolio of real estate. In some cases, you must be willing to defer all or a portion of your commission in the form of a note and mortgage—particularly when your low-cash-down buyer is getting started. If he is sincere and you have faith in his ability and if he is a loyal client, then by all means help him as much as you can.

The Time-Available Buyer

The time-available buyer is looking for property where he can use his own talents to develop the existing potential. An example might be a schoolteacher who has time in the late afternoons to rent vacant apartments in a high-turnover-type building, or a painter or plumber or carpenter who has the ability and time to upgrade a run-down but otherwise sound property.

The Owner-Occupant

This owner-occupant type buyer will tax your income brokerage abilities, plus your ability to understand and appreciate the art of residential brokerage. The owner-occupant wants a building where he can move into one of the units and derive the investment benefits of the balance. You must be sure of what his own apartment needs are, as a suitable apartment for him and for his family is of utmost importance. Many owner-occupant type buyers will knowingly pay the "long dollar" for a property if the apartment is suitable.

The Renovator

The renovator is a special type of speculator: He specializes in buying properties that are run-down or are in need of repairs. Although the risk is high, there is usually great profit waiting for the renovator when he completes his project and rents the refurbished apartments at a commensurately higher rental. Renovators range from those who just "splash a little paint around" to the remodelers who go into a building and knock down walls, put up walls, rearrange room layouts, split up large apartments, and generally go all out to rebuild a property like new. Properties that are basically sound, but that are either in poor repair or in need of conversion to a better economic use, are the gems that move your renovator. There are many properties in this category and many talented renovators who will tackle the job to reap the potential profits.

The Converter

The converter, as noted earlier, is an investor who purchases an existing income property (generally apartments), and proceeds to convert the property to condominiums or cooperatives. (See Chapter 13.) The converter is generally in the position of reporting ordinary income rather than capital gains. But he can still come out extremely well. One of our favorite converters, when asked the question, "Don't you hate to pay ordinary income taxes?" responded by saying, "If there's enough income, it doesn't bother me at all!"

In submitting properties to the converter, keep in mind that he or she will be interested not only in the income and expense information generally produced for regular investors, but will be particularly interested in the financing arrangements which can be made during the conversion period. In addition, the converter will be particularly grateful for information relating to square footage contained in each of the rental units being submitted, and additionally, comparable sales prices on a square-foot basis for similar properties in the area.

The Bargain Hunter

The bargain hunter generally waits for an unusual opportunity such as a distress sale. He presents a difficult task for the broker, because the property he is looking for is not generally "in stock" and when one is available, it does not last long because of the distress nature of the offering. A distress situation develops when a builder, renovator, or converter completes a portion of his project and runs out of capital or credit. A distress situation can also often develop when an investor has leveraged his holdings to the hilt and runs into extraordinary expenses. The bargain hunter, if he is ever going to find his pot of gold, must be prepared to act quickly. He must be ready to sign agreements immediately and take title within a week or two—often within a few days.

The Waste-of-Time Buyer

The W.O.T. buyer is a lot like the bargain hunter; he wants a true bargain but he is not prepared to act quickly. He wants all the benefits that go with a firm and quick decision, but he lacks the courage or knowledge to make such a decision. The W.O.T. buyer generally wants maximum income, top growth potential, and the opportunity for a quick profit. He wants to accomplish all three in a high-demand area, with maximum financing at minimum rates. He wants several weeks to investigate the situation and to prove "beyond all shadow of a doubt" that he is buying well below the market, that his annual return will be "20 percent after vacancies and repairs," and that, if he desires, he can sell his agreement (contract) for a $200,000 profit. He wants statements mailed to him and demands addresses on the telephone. He is a very busy man and never has time to inspect new listings. "Send me the information and I'll look it over," he says.

At the end of this chapter, you'll see how you can keep your client files current and packed with *action buyers*—this procedure involves purging your files of the W.O.T.

Why It Pays to Write Off the Waste-Of-Time Prospect. Don't ever worry about losing a big sale by neglecting the W.O.T. Sure, out of every 100 W.O.T.'s there may be one who will eventually purchase a property from you (or from another broker—or on his own). Never shed tears when he does, because in order to uncover that one W.O.T. who will eventually buy, you must spend many irritating hours with the other 99. Look at the W.O.T. this way:

- It will take you 20 working hours to sell the W.O.T. a building, but—
- You will have to spend 20 hours with 100 W.O.T. buyers to make *one* sale.
- 20 hours × 100 buyers = 2,000 hours.
- With a $50,000 average commission, your hourly wage is $50,000 ÷ 2,000 hours, or $25.00.

Now, by contrast, consider what you are likely to earn working with a well-qualified prospect.

- It will take you the same 20 working hours to find the qualified buyer a proper investment.
- Your work with 10 well-qualified investors will result in one sale.
- 20 hours × 10 investors = 200 hours.
- With the same $50,000 average commission, your hourly wage is $50,000 ÷ 200 hours, or $250.00 per hour!

Why bother with 100 W.O.T. buyers to find the one who will eventually buy?

How to Handle Your Initial Interview

Your first contact with a potential investor, whether he has called on an ad or whether you have uncovered him through one of your other sources, will normally be by telephone.

Make an appointment to meet the buyer in your office. Don't make an appointment to meet two miles from the property at a local landmark, unless you already know your client very well. Early in my career, I spent many an hour cooling my heels waiting for a prospect to meet me at a specified location. Do your best to have him come into your office. If this is impossible, then go to his office. In Chapter 10, you'll learn how to handle the frequent request of "Give me the address and I'll swing by the property and save you some time."

At your first face-to-face meeting with the client, the first thing you must do is to determine his objectives. Why is he buying? We are not really in the real estate business; we are not selling real estate per se. Real estate is the vehicle by which you will solve the investment problems of the people with whom you are dealing. Real estate happens to be the vehicle that carries the income, the growth, the depreciation, and all the rest of the tax advantages inherent in the commodity we sell.

If you don't know and understand your client's objectives, you can show him buildings till the cows come home and, not knowing why he is buying, you are wasting your time (and his). Is he buying for return? Is he buying for certain combinations of these elements? Let's see exactly how to uncover this information.

How to Qualify Your Buyer for Best Results

There have been many systems devised for qualifying residential buyers, but in the past, the gathering of essential data concerning real estate investors has often taken the form of notes on paper napkins that have been re-entered on four-by-six file cards. Usually these carding systems have no uniformity and there is no set place to record all the vital data required.

With computers we can easily categorize this important information. Look at the following client data card pictured. Not only does this card have spaces laid out in each category, but it is presented so that you can merely circle most of the essential data without wasting time to write out each piece of information in longhand.

Additionally, this card provides, from beginning to end, the logical sequence of questioning that you must follow to gather the information you will need to assist your buyer. When I originally designed this card for my brokers at Peckham Boston, it was for use with installed data-processing equipment. My brokers, who are all experienced in real estate investment, are not the type who are easily impressed, and generally when they are, they hide their enthusiasm. When the illustrated form was initially distributed, they were not able to disguise their enthusiasm. Their comments indicated that "with a qualifying card like this, we can scrap the expensive electronic gear, because this card is so complete and easy to use." With their non-technical mindset and acceptance, the job of data entry became easier.

Name _____					Tel. No. _____					
Street No. _____					Down payment _____					
City, State, Zip _____					Profession _____					
Type Bldg. _____					Objective _____					
Pref. Loc. _____					Owns what _____					

THE ORIGINAL PECKHAM CLIENT QUALIFIER

The Peckham Boston Company Confidential Client Data

Objective				Cash Down		Type Investment				
Fixed Income	1	Growth	3	50—	(10)	Apts.	16	Hotel	22	
High Income	2	Est. Building	4	100—	(11)	Stores	17	Motel	23	
Safety	5			200—	(12)	Offices	18	Ind. Bldg.	24	
Depreciation	6			500—	(13)	Shop Ctrs.	19	Land	25	
Non-Mgt	7			1 million	(14)	Net Net L.	20	Conversion	26	
Resale	8	Upgrade	9	1 million +	(15)	Guest H.	21		27	

Profession				General Location		Specific Location			
						Town		State	
Doctor	28	Engineer	34	U.S.	40	1. _____		_____	
Lawyer	29	Self Employed	35	East	41	2. _____		_____	
Accountant	30	Gov't. Employed	36	North	42	3. _____		_____	
Educator	31	Businessman	37	West	43	4. _____		_____	
Crafts	32	R.E. Investor	38	South	44	5. _____		_____	
Securities	33		39	Central	45	6. _____ 7. _____		_____ _____	

Broker # _____ **Source** _____ **Date** _____

Additional Broker Notes—Over

How to Use the Client Qualifier

The top block has blanks to enter such basic information as name, address, and telephone number. The other blanks in the top block are self-explanatory. There is a small block titled *owns what.* Here you can insert "46 apts Back Bay" or any brief description of the type of property your client already owns (if any). You will find that this information will be helpful in analyzing your client as a potential buyer, and that it will be invaluable when you go on a listing binge.

When you first sit down with your investor, just enter his name, address, and telephone number and then, as your interview continues, jot in the additional data such as objective, cash down, and so on. Before moving down to the qualifying blocks, note that other information, such as addresses of property owned, partners' names, or any additional data, may be entered on the back of the card. (Additional blank cards may be attached, if necessary.) The back of the card also serves as a handy spot to record any properties submitted to your client, the date of such submission, and the result.

After recording the information in the upper block, you are ready to interrogate your client as to his needs and ability to invest in real estate. The word "interrogate" is used advisedly, since your tone in gathering the needed information must be one of firm, polite interrogation. The sincere investor will appreciate the thoroughness of your preparation, and will mentally compare your approach to the approach of other brokers who have chatted for a couple of minutes and then have crammed him in a car to show a dozen buildings.

How to Determine an Investor's Objective for Buying

The most important thing for you to uncover in your interrogations is *why* your investor wants to buy—*what* he wants to accomplish—in other words, his investment objective.

Earlier in this chapter, we found out that real estate buyers invest for the same reasons that stock market investors do: for income, for growth, and for quick profit through speculation. We also saw that there is considerable overlapping among these categories.

The first block in the "Client Qualifier" sets forth several objectives, which your buyer will give you. He might not state them in as many words, but through skillful interrogation you will uncover them.

How to Make a Client Examine His Own Motives. The qualifier is particularly useful when the buyer really doesn't know why he wants to invest. He walks in knowing that real estate is a great investment, but not knowing exactly why. Your opening remarks might go like this:

> Mr. Investor, before we go through our available investments, I can save you a great
> deal of time by analyzing your requirements. After all, it is your cash we are about to

invest, and we must be sure that we find a property that meets your objectives. A little time spent now will save us a great deal of time later, and will help us find the building which will fulfill your financial needs.

Mr. Investor will then either quickly outline his objectives, or will say:

> Mr. Broker, I'm not really too sure why I want to invest. I just want to make money.

At this point, you will explain what real estate can do for Mr. Investor. As outlined in Chapter 7, there are many special benefits that will accrue to the investor facing you. Don't ever assume that he is aware of all of the benefits. Explain also that most investors fall generally into the income/growth/speculation categories. With this background, you are now ready to discuss the specific items outlined on the qualifier.

Nine Basic Buyer Objectives

Objective 1. Fixed Income.

> Mr. Investor, many of our clients are preparing to retire or are retired, and have considerable equities in other forms of investment which do not yield the high returns available in real estate. For example, a client may have $200,000 in the bank drawing 2% interest, or $4,000 annually. He wants a higher income without depleting his capital, but he wants a relatively fixed, steady, safe return that he can count on. He has no desire to speculate, and he doesn't necessarily give a hoot about amortization or capital growth. Knowing his objectives, we can find him a building with relatively low amortization, made up for by good, steady income.

If your client falls into this category, he will let you know. If he's looking for growth or wants to speculate, he will indicate that these are his goals.

Objective 2. High Income. This category generally goes hand in hand with the income-oriented buyer—but keep in mind that the speculative buyer wants the property with high income, and wants to buy it at a price low enough to allow for resale at a quick profit.

Objective 3. Growth.

Mr. Investor, many of our younger clients are looking to invest in a property that will grow in value over the years. They are willing to invest on the basis of a lower return, but know that even a reduced immediate cash flow in real estate will greatly exceed the return from other forms of investment. Some of these investors have no immediate need for additional income. We have several investors such as engineers who are earning $80,000–$120,000 per year, who are living comfortably within their means, and in some cases are willing to forego all cash flow as long as the property safely carries all expenses and will increase steadily in value over the next few years. This type of client usually invests in a building with a conservative cash flow, but one which will appreciate in value because of its construction, location, or because of certain trends in the area. He looks to the continuing growth in real estate values plus reduction of his debt through amortization of his mortgage or mortgages.

Objective 4. Estate Building. This category goes hand in hand with GROWTH, and is another easily understood way of expressing this objective: both are concerned with increasing one's net worth.

You'll note that categories 5, 6, and 7, which follow, are centered in the objective section of the qualifier. The reason for this is that these three objectives can exist for either the income buyer or the growth buyer, but rarely exist for the speculative buyer. Let's examine them.

Objective 5. Safety. All investors except for the speculator will be looking for a high degree of safety, so that by circling this item on the client card you are not indicating anything too unusual. When reviewing your cards, the absence of this factor will be an indicator that your buyer has strong speculative instincts.

Objective 6. Depreciation. This category can apply equally to income and growth investors. Many times we will interview an investor who has worked himself up to a top tax bracket. He has a real problem. He has been in the stock market and he cannot depreciate his stock. He has a lot of life insurance, but the only thing this gives him is peace of mind. So we suggest a property that will shelter some of his income. If he is in the 50 percent bracket and we can shelter $200,000 of his income, even a property that just breaks even is worth $100,000 in current income to him.

How to Interview the Depreciation-Minded Buyer. Let's suppose you are interviewing an investor who has worked his way up to a top tax bracket. In the course of conversation he tells you:

> I've been doing most of my investing in the stock market. I've done very well, but I just keep paying more and more taxes. Naturally, I've got a lot of life insurance, but all that gives me is peace of mind. I wondered if real estate might give me something more.

You tell him:

> Mr. Jones, I'm sure it will. I've got several properties that should provide excellent shelter for some of your income.
> Let's see. For a man in the 50 percent bracket, I have one listing that could shelter about $200,000. So if you only broke even—and I'm sure you'd do better than that— you'd be some $100,000 ahead.

When you uncover an investor whose objective is to shelter income, circle depreciation on the Qualifier and give this individual a great deal of attention. Through income property you can work tax miracles for him!

Objective 7. Non-Management. Many investors have hesitated to enter the real estate field because they have no desire to become involved in managing an income property. Then you might ask your client:

> Mr. Investor, will you have some time available to manage the property? By this I don't mean cleaning halls or painting walls—you will have a janitor to take care of these tasks for you. I mean taking care of the books and processing tenant matters.

Your investor might indicate that he is willing to spend some time watching over the financial and physical aspects of the property, or he may say:

Mr. Broker, one of the reasons I haven't invested in real estate is the fact that I do not have the time or the inclination to receive calls from tenants and listen to their problems.

To which you counter:

Fine, I will mark non-management as one of your primary objectives, and we will look for a property which can be managed for a fee and still leave a very attractive return. This will allow you to enjoy all of the advantages of real estate investment and avoid the management problems. Your management specialist will collect the rents, pay the bills, and send you a monthly statement and check.

An alternative of course, is to locate and acquire a property leased on a net basis to a credit tenant.

Objective 8. Resale. If your investor indicates that he would resell a newly acquired property as a whole or as condominiums if a respectable profit is offered him, then circle *Resale.* This indicates that your client has some degree of speculative objectives. He may not be a speculator pure and simple, but you know he has the speculative spirit.

The true speculator, as we have noted, wants to buy property on the most favorable terms and at the lowest price, so that he can resell it at a profit. He is willing to take chances that the ordinary investor would avoid, and he is willing to spend time correcting existing problems in order to gain his well-deserved profit.

Circle *Resale* for the speculator, and serve him well. You will be paid a commission when he buys, and he will usually give you a listing as soon as he buys. You may even earn a second commission by selling his agreement or, more specifically, selling the rights he is entitled to under the purchase and sale agreement (contract).

Objective 9. Upgrading. As we have already discussed, the remodeler, renovator, or the converter is the type of investor who makes his profit not necessarily from managing the property, but from upgrading rundown buildings, e.g., putting in modern kitchens and bathrooms, redecorating hallways, increasing the rents and reselling at a profit. His profit is primarily derived from increasing the income of the property, through upgrading or converting.

If your investor indicates that his objective is to purchase a building that he wants to improve physically, then circle Objective 9 and put him in the speculator category; but keep in mind that once he upgrades the property, he might well hold it for future income and growth. Most renovators, however, will take a short-term profit so that they can move on to bigger and better renovation jobs.

How to Review and Summarize the Interrogation

After discussing all of these specific objectives with your client, review his card. Checks on items 1 and 2 indicate an income buyer. Items 3 and 4 indicate a growth buyer. Items 8 and 9 indicate a speculative buyer. Item 5 (safety) indicates that the client is not speculation-oriented. Items 6 (depreciation) and 7 (non-management) also indicate a non-speculative attitude, but can apply equally to income and growth buyers.

At this point, summarize his objectives into income/growth/or speculative, and enter your estimate of his main objective in the top block in the space opposite *objective*.

There are hundreds of combinations of objectives. Combining the Qualifier with a normal degree of common sense, you should uncover your buyer's objectives. Remember that the real estate you have for sale is the vehicle by which your client's problem may be solved. Without understanding your client's objectives and problems you can show an endless number of buildings, but the odds of stumbling on a suitable property will be heavily weighted against you. Take the time to interrogate. Time spent here will pay big commission dividends and will save you valuable time to work with additional qualified buyers.

Determining How Much the Buyer Can Invest

You must determine how much cash the buyer desires to invest. This must be handled discreetly in the interview. Don't ask, "How much do you want to *spend?*" but, "At this time how much would you care to *invest?*" Invest is the big word in selling income property—not spend. The classic answer is usually, "Any amount." But this does not help you at all.

My favorite method of determining an accurate figure when someone says "any amount," is to smile and go into my listing book and say, "I think I have just the thing for you then. I have a brand-new office building complex, which is lovely and generates a solid cash flow. It requires $3.5 million down and the entire price is. . . ." Usually, your "any amount down" buyer will interrupt, "Wait a minute. When I said any amount, I meant $100,000 to $150,000 down." Thus, very quickly without wasting your time, you are able to get a quick expression of how much cash he can invest.

Many times an investor will come in and say "I can invest $500,000." He is anticipating putting a second or third mortgage on the property to raise $400,000 of the $500,000. From studying operating statements in Chapter 6, you noticed that we often negotiate a purchase-money mortgage and take into consideration all of the financing. You must find out how much your buyer can invest *without encumbering* the proposed purchase. If he is a speculator and he is intending to obtain commercial financing to provide part of his equity money, he will understand the question and will probably level with you. If he is not an expert, not a wheeler-dealer, he probably won't know what you are talking about and just say, "I don't know. I have $100,000 in the bank, and I want to invest it." Then you know the actual amount of cash available.

It is always helpful to know where the money is now and the source of the buyer's equity. A subtle way to find out is to ask, "Have you been investing in the stock market prior to your interest in real estate?" or, "Are you receiving a two percent return in the bank?" Many times with such subtle questioning, you will determine where and how readily available the investment funds are.

The main sources of real estate equity capital are often the stock market, savings accounts, and proceeds from the refinancing of homes. Many people have mortgages that are paid down to the point that they are able to raise $200,000 to $500,000 just by refinancing a home mortgage which through the years has appreciated in value.

The Qualifier is set up so that you can circle any figure under *cash down.* It is a good idea to circle not only the highest amount which your client will invest, but also the lowest amount that he will invest in any one property (plus all of those in between).

For example, if your buyer says, "I can invest up to $75,000," you will circle

"100–" which indicates his down payment is under $100,000. You should then ask him, "Mr. Investor, if an attractive smaller investment becomes available, what is the minimum amount of cash you would put down on any one investment?" He might reply, "I don't want anything which requires less than $15,000." At this point, you would circle "50–." Notice that there is a space at the top of the card to write in his target down payment. In the space provided, write down his maximum cash down payment, in this case $75,000. You can also enter his minimum, and your entry would then appear: $25,000 to $75,000.

How to Determine What Type of Property the Buyer Wants

Ask your investor what type of investment he feels would suit his requirements. The average investor wants apartment houses. He can understand them better, and many times shies away from other forms of income property. No matter what type of property he expresses an interest in, you should explore the possibility of his investing in any of the other types set forth on the Qualifier.

Your conversation with an apartment buyer might go like this: "Mr. Investor, if we find a small office building located in your area that otherwise meets all of your requirements including cash down, would you want us to notify you?" This same approach should be used with all types listed on the Qualifier—don't let your buyer severely limit himself. Spaces 26 and 27 provide you with two blanks to write in any special requirements that are not covered elsewhere in that section.

When you complete your interrogation, write in the main type of investment your investor wants in the top block in the space provided after *type building*.

While you are interrogating your client, remember that if he is a new investor you may have to advise him about what types of building will fill his needs and still be within his financial and professional capabilities. Refer back to Chapter 1 for an analysis of which types of property best meet specific requirements.

Notice that several types of income properties are listed on the Qualifier. Throughout this Guide, our examples have been based primarily on apartment house investments. This is because these are the most easily understood and make the simplest demonstrations. Keep in mind that the principles and practices contained in this Guide apply equally to all forms of income property. Where there are any special problems in handling the other types of income property, these have been noted in the appropriate section.

How to Find Out What the Buyer's Capabilities Are

Your investor may wonder why his profession is important. An investor's profession to a great degree determines how much time he has available to manage the property. It also gives you a pretty good indicator of his professional abilities, his background, his problems, and sometimes his financial wherewithal.

For example—if your buyer is an engineer, he might have some time available in the evening or on the weekends. On the other hand, a doctor is not likely to be able to spend a lot of time chasing around after rents or taking calls about clogged toilets. The type of property you submit to your buyer depends somewhat on what his profession is. If he is a young workman, a plumber or a carpenter, you would submit an entirely different type of property from what would be right for a doctor. Talented craftsmen can *create* value with their own hands, where a doctor probably can't and doesn't have the time to.

Look again to the Qualifier. There are several general categories enumerated. Your client may fall into several of these. Circle as many as apply. For example, your client may be a self-employed accountant. If there is a word that more vividly describes his profession, write it in Block 39. When you have finished, write down the word or words that best describe your client's profession in the space provided in the top block near the client's name and address.

How to Discover Where the Buyer Wants to Buy

The next category on the Qualifier deals with location. Your buyer may prefer to invest near where he lives, where he works, or where he already owns property. He may have a real "bug" about certain towns or areas. Many times we will encounter an investor who states flatly that he will buy only in Brookline. Sometimes the area he picks is one where the demand is so great that property seldom comes on the market and when it does, it is priced so high (because of the demand) that it rarely leaves an adequate return. You must explain to your client that if he severely limits his choice of location or town, his chances of finding an investment that will meet his other requirements will be very slim.

Your advice might go like this, "Mr. Investor, I can appreciate your desire to invest in Brookline. It's a fine town; however, property so seldom comes available and is priced so high that it might take us years to get you started on your investment program. We certainly will submit all properties in Brookline that come available; however, I would suggest that you consider Brighton or one of the prime suburban towns near Brookline."

How to Indicate Location on the Qualifier. The Qualifier is set up so that you can simply check a block or blocks for general location in relation to your office. Let's say your office is in Philadelphia and your client wants towns only north and west of Philadelphia. Then circle *North* and *West*. If he wants to buy in the city itself, then circle *Central.* Use the *U.S.* block for any client who will buy out of state.

Now go directly to the *specific location* section of the Qualifier. Here you can itemize the names of specific towns, or even favored neighborhoods of larger cities. For example, in Boston, you might enter, "Back Bay, Beacon Hill, and Dorchester." For data entry these locations will be converted using zip codes.

When you have completed these sections of the Qualifier, abbreviate the top three location choices in the *pref. loc.* section at the top of the Qualifier.

If you have followed the Qualifier carefully, you now have the basic information necessary to find your client a property that will fit his needs. If his requirements are unrealistic, you must educate him at this point as to what you can and what you cannot accomplish under prevailing market conditions.

Determining Whether Your Client Is Ready to Act

Once you have accumulated this basic information, you must take one more step before submitting properties to the buyer. You must try to determine that he is ready to act, if the right investment is available. The following checklist will help you. If at the appropriate stage you can answer "Yes" to each question, then your buyer is certainly well worth the investment of your time and your utmost effort.

An Eight-Point Action Checklist

☐ 1. Will the prospect meet with you at your office (preferably), or at least at his office or home?

☐ 2. Does the prospect cooperate during the qualifying interview?

☐ 3. Will the prospect invest *now* if the right investment is offered?

☐ 4. Are the prospect's expectations realistic under current market conditions?

☐ 5. Can your prospect make the decision to invest in a specific property without consulting with a special "board of experts"?

☐ 6. Is the prospect prepared to inspect properties selected for his approval, and do it promptly?

☐ 7. After inspecting no more than six well selected investments, does he make an offer?

☐ 8. After negotiating his offer, does he counter with a *realistic* price and terms?

Action checks 1 to 6 can be explored immediately before inspecting properties, and can be re-evaluated throughout your dealings with your investor. Action checks 7 and 8 can be explored only after you have spent some time with your prospect.

If you use this checklist effectively, you will conserve your most valuable commodity—time—and the result will be more time available to invest with action buyers.

Action Check 1. *Will the prospect meet with you in person?* If you receive a call from an ad reader who is willing to meet with you in person—in your office, in his office, in his home—this is your first indication that he is sincerely seeking assistance in finding a proper investment. Remember that in time you will accumulate many—perhaps hundreds—of investors for each good salable investment offering. If a prospect will not sit down face to face with you to outline his needs and expectations, then your time is better spent with those who will.

The prospect might say, "Mr. Broker, mail me a statement or give me the address—I'm a busy man and this is the only way I operate." Your reply should go like this, "Mr. Prospect, if it is inconvenient for you to stop by the office, I would be most happy to meet you at your office or at a place that is convenient to you. However, here at the office I have access to many current investment offerings. So if this particular property doesn't meet your needs, I am quite certain that from our other offerings, I can find a property that does."

If your caller refuses to meet with you and you have no concrete knowledge of his ability, then ask him to watch your ads and keep in touch. Take as much qualifying information as possible over the phone, and tell him that you will get back to him if something comes in that might warrant his personal attention. Explain that your company advertises its most attractive offerings each week, and that if he is actively seeking income property, he should watch your ads, keep in touch, and plan to sit down with you as soon as possible. If you call him back two or three times and he is never available for a personal meeting, move this prospect's card from your active file to your incidental information file—which you can refer to on rainy days when all your more likely buyers are out of town.

Action Check 2. *Does the prospect cooperate during the qualifying interview?* When you systematically run through your Qualifier checklist, most buyers who have taken the trouble to meet with you will be happy to explain their financial goals and expectations. Occasionally you will run into the prospect who says, "Look, Buddy, you just find me something that makes sense and I'll buy it—never mind with all these questions. I'll decide what I should or shouldn't buy!"

The first time a new broker meets this approach, he is usually taken back by the apparent lack of cooperation on the part of his prospect. A sincere and forthright explanation of the need for such information will generally soften up such a reaction. You might say:

> Mr. Prospect, I can appreciate your ability to decide which property to buy and on what terms, and I'm sure that with your knowledge of income property you hardly need me to help you evaluate any offering. There is one area where I can be most helpful, however. My office obtains and prepares complete operating statements on hundreds (or thousands) of offerings each year. In addition we network electronically with a significant number of affiliate brokers. We are currently processing over 30 new offerings every week. Our staff of 12 (or 24) is constantly scouring the countryside and coming up with properties for sale which most investors would never hear about. If a person decided to try to uncover all the offerings we process in one month, he'd have to leave

his present endeavors and just spend full time looking for investments. Even at that, he wouldn't keep up with them.

Now, if I know what you want to accomplish, I can easily supply you with many offerings each month that might well fill your needs. Then, it's up to you to decide which of these you should consider. For us to rush around looking at properties without some knowledge of your goals and criteria would be like a surgeon opening you up to see what the problem is, without even knowing the symptoms of your distress.

If your prospect remains uncooperative at this stage, move his card to your incidental information file.

Action Check 3. *Will the prospect invest now if the right investment is offered?* As in residential brokerage, there are some prospects who want a two-year education in real estate investing, and then they might make a move. Many times the "student" client will bluff his qualifications and spend several months with you and then, after gaining his education, be embarrassed to level with you as to his real needs and abilities. Armed with your education, he will go to a competitor and invest. If your prospect will not invest now, let your competitor educate Mr. Student.

A Case in Point: Early in my career, I spent three solid working days (and several hours each evening selecting property investments) with two young investors who had formed a partnership with some money from their parents. They were most happy to meet with me, and were most cooperative in qualifying their needs. We inspected several properties and analyzed many more operating statements. On my third day with the young partners, we drove to Springfield, Mass. (three hours out and three hours back) to inspect a small office building that seemed to meet their needs. When we got there, one of my young prospects pulled a camera from his brief case and took several shots of the building. They were both enthusiastic about the prospects of acquiring the building, but had to "do some more research."

After several follow-up phone calls, which were never returned, I learned that I had been dealing with two students from Harvard Business School! I'm sure that my operating statements and photographs ended up in a thesis on the exciting field of real estate investing!

Try this direct approach: How do you determine whether your prospect will invest if the right property becomes available? *Ask him*—it's as simple as that. Your question might be preceded by a dialogue like this: "Mr. Prospect, I have several hundred fine investments to select from. Six months from now, I will have an equal or larger number of fine investments; however, they will be different ones. All of the information we have now will be obsolete. If we were to inspect several properties today and have to wait to make a decision, then our time will be wasted. We should wait until you can make your move and then spend as much time as possible to make a very careful well-thought-out selection. Are you in a position to invest right now if the right property is available?"

If there is any doubt in your mind as to the availability of funds, you can discreetly inquire as to what form the investment funds take now. You might find that Mr. Prospect expects to save $250,000 in the next two years for investment. Or that when he sells his business he will have $400,000. Or that he will have a lot of time to manage his acquisition about this time next year when he gets a promotion.

How to Put Off, Tactfully, the Prospect Who Is Not Ready. If you determine through tactful questioning that Mr. Prospect cannot or will not make his move for several months, then explain, "Mr. Prospect, when the time comes I'm sure that we can find the proper investment for you. I'm more than happy to spend some time this morning answering some questions on how you should proceed when the proper time comes, and I'd be delighted to have you call me in the interim if you have any further questions. Why don't you send away for Jack Peckham's Guide on income property, and study it in the interim?"

Give Mr. Prospect your card and any literature you have available regarding your office. Make a note on his card as to when he can make his move. Ask him to follow your ads every Sunday in the local paper, and encourage him to call you when the time is right. Move his card to a dated "tickler file" and get back in touch with him on "D Day." He will appreciate your straightforward approach and your follow-up call.

Action Check 4. *Are the prospect's expectations realistic under current market conditions?* Once you have determined your prospect's ability to invest now if the right investment is available, you must find out what the *right* investment is for him. By this time you have completed the Qualifier, and your prospect's comments during your qualifying interrogation should give you a clue as to whether his expectations are *realistic*.

A few strategic questions at this stage will assist you in your evaluation of the reasonableness of these expectations. You might ask, "Mr. Prospect, how long have you been looking for a real estate investment?" Or, "Mr. Prospect, do you currently own income property?" The answer to either question may be "Well, no, but I've been looking for a couple of years."

It does not take a couple of years to find a suitable real estate investment. If a serious buyer has been dealing with an astute broker with an adequate portfolio of listings, he should be able to negotiate an attractive acquisition in a couple of months.

How to Handle the "I-Remember-When" Prospect. If your prospect has been looking for quite a while, the reason is very vividly spelled out when the prospect rants and raves about how he could have "bought 10 Main Street for one-third the price fifteen years ago!" You must remember (and sometimes tactfully point out) that Mr. Prospect could have bought a brand-new automobile for one-third the price then too.

Some oldtimers have seen property appreciate over the years and remember when prices were relatively low. Unless you can update their thinking to current market conditions when submitting property to them that they could once have bought for half its present value, they may prove to be a waste of time. If you don't get some activity out of an oldtimer within 3 or 4 showings, put his card in the incidental information file.

One of my salesmen composed the gem that follows: Longfellow it's not, but his work vividly portrays the "I remember when" attitude.

Real Estate Turtles Lose Races
If I could just turn back the clock
What real estate I'd have in stock!
But I could never make a deal
Nothing showed me had appeal.

Lousy areas offered by the hour
Good for nothing—(But the Hancock Tower)!
Brokers advised—This land will be great.
I passed it up—Now it's Route 128!

Build in Framingham?—I don't like the "sticks"
No future there—I'll be in a helluva fix
I'll go slow and I'll do just fine.
D'ya know I could have owned Route 9?

Well maybe I do have special yearnings
I want to buy less than six times earnings
Other buyers were just stupid guys
They now hold deeds to a lush high-rise.

I frown at stuff I've seen before
Don't understand why it *now* costs more
I take no stock in a high growth rate
I'll just sit tight and procrastinate!

So I keep on looking with a negative view
And nothing I see will ever do
My buying power gets ever smaller
As I lose pace with the inflated dollar!

(His epitaph will read I'll bet
"He hasn't seen a good deal yet.
Played the role of a real slow-poker
May be missed—but not by his broker!")

You will find this poem effective in adjusting a prospect's outmoded expectations. Simply have your printer set up the poem on a 4 × 6 white card and keep a stock of these handy. Reproduce your business card on the back. When you encounter a prospect who complains about today's high prices, hand him a copy of the poem. The effect is sometimes startling. It's a great ice-breaker, and the usual reaction is a hearty laugh or at least a knowing smile. If this sales aid doesn't break the ice and provoke at least a grin, then you're probably dealing with a tough, closed-minded prospect.

Of course, you must always watch for the profitable exception.

A Case in Point: A few years ago, an old gent walked in looking for a sizable office building investment. He was wheezing and coughing while smoking up a storm. We discovered he was 74 years old and had owned some small six-family dwellings many years back. His objective? From the best we could determine, he just wanted one last fling at ownership and management. He had no family to build an estate for, did not necessarily need a steady income—he needed an *ego booster.* We found his ego booster in the form of an ultra-luxurious office building, rented to a major insurance company. He was delighted with the building, and we put it under agreement immediately.

At the signing of purchase and sales agreements, the oldtimer wheezed and coughed so that the salesman representing our office was sure the old man would never make it to the passing date some 30 days later. I had all I could do to keep my salesman from taking out a 30-day life insurance policy on him to cover the commission. The buyer made it to the passing (closing) and a year or so later we found a purchaser for the building and arranged a tax-deferred exchange for a garden apartment complex. He's still going strong! Because the broker understood his needs and didn't dismiss the prospect, he generated close to $10 million in sales! But there *is* a time to dismiss the prospect.

Finding Out What Return the Investor Expects. To determine if your prospect's expectations are reasonable, ask him what return he expects on his investment. Many times your prospect will indicate that he wants to invest cash equal to less than 10 percent of the purchase price, and experience a 20 to 30 percent return on that cash invested. The reason for such misguided expectations is either because he has been watching ads that cite such returns *before* vacancies and repairs, or he really doesn't know what real estate should return.

Many times when a novice begins to look for income property he has no real idea of what an adequate return should be, and as a defensive maneuver, he resorts to demanding extraordinary yields. This is your first clue that your prospect is not experienced in real estate investing. He feels that, like buying a car, where he is not sure of what price he can negotiate, if he demands a low enough price (providing a corresponding high return) he will not "get stung."

The experienced investor, on the other hand, will be able to tell you what return he expects, and his requirement will normally be within a point or two of what is feasible in the market. He does not have to resort to the novice's unrealistic defense mechanism, which is generated by uncertainty.

If you discover from your interrogation that your prospect's expectations are unrealistic, then go over the economic facts of life with him. Review recent sales and show him what can be accomplished. Go over the contents of Chapter 7 with him, and show him what can be done and what is not possible. Keep in mind that if your prospect is a particular type he might generate a 30 percent return—he might buy with no cash down—he might buy at a price considered below market—*but* he must have a special talent and be willing to use it. He must have an abundance of one or more of the following: money, courage, credit, time, or talent.

What to Tell a Novice Who Wants a Huge Return. Almost every week, some young prospective investor comes to me and says he has very little cash. He wants to know if he can start creating wealth through a real estate program.

My conversation with him usually goes like this, "Sure, it's possible to start with little or no cash and create great wealth by acquiring income property. However, you must have (and maintain) impeccable credit. You must have time available to maintain and improve the property you acquire, and you must plan to spend your time to do this. You must be willing to take calculated risks and be willing to acquire problem properties with a plan to solve the problems. You must understand the risks. You must understand that by acquiring property with maximum leverage (very little cash down) you should be satisfied with a property that will, at best, break even after financing and look to growth and amortization of your debt for your eventual profit—until you complete a program of improving the income. In this situation, you must have an adequate income from another source to provide for your personal needs. If you are willing to proceed, understanding the risks and the demands, then we are prepared to help you seek the rewards."

If your prospect insists on an unrealistic return, move his card to *incidental in-*

formation and let him come back to you next year after your competitor has spent many frustrating hours educating him.

Action Check 5. *Can your prospect make the decision to invest in a specific property without consulting with a special "board of experts"?* Many times, a novice investor will want to check with someone whose opinion he values before making the decision to make an offer on a specific property. In Chapter 12, you will learn what to do when your prospect brings in his expert later on in your negotiations. For now, however, you can save considerable time and effort by simply asking if he can make the decision on his own, or if there is someone he must consult with. Sometimes, your prospect is investing funds which must be released by family, friends, or business associates.

If you discover that Mr. Prospect will want to consult before acting, arrange to sit down with your prospect and his adviser before progressing with any property submissions. You must *qualify* the adviser and determine his interpretation of your prospect's needs.

Treat the adviser with utmost tact. Your diplomacy at this stage will pay great dividends.

Action Check 6. *Is the prospect prepared to inspect properties selected for his approval—and do it promptly?* If after proper qualification, your prospect does not show a willingness to inspect properties selected, this indicates either that he is not convinced that the properties are for him, or that he is not ready to act now and consequently, is not an action prospect.

As you will see, your qualifying continues throughout your negotiations with the prospect; but the time you spend actually inspecting properties is the most critical part of the qualification procedure.

If your prospect will not make time to inspect well selected investments, and if you contact your prospect two or three times with properties you are quite sure will fill his needs and he declines your invitations to visit the property—move him to your incidental information file. You will discover in Chapter 11 that you must physically inspect properties with your client before you can determine his real likes and dislikes. If he won't spend some time with you, invest your valuable time with those prospects who will.

Action Check 7. *After inspecting no more than six well selected investments, does he make an offer?* Assuming now that you have selected several properties which appear to meet your prospect's requirements, and have inspected them—has your prospect made some sort of an offer to purchase at least one of them? Has he expressed the desire at least to negotiate on price or terms? If your prospect doesn't make an offer after inspecting several (say about six) parcels, then one of three things is wrong:

1. You have not properly qualified your prospect.
2. You are not closing effectively.
3. He is not ready to invest, and consequently is not an action buyer.

When you have mastered the techniques in this Guide by actively applying them in the field, you will know how to qualify and how to close. Having confidence in your ability to do both, and having spent the proper time in phases 1 and 2, you can be quite sure that if over a period of time and after several property inspections your prospect has not expressed any desire to make an offer, you are not dealing with an action buyer.

What to Say to the Prospect Who Won't Act

Before moving a prospect's card to the incidental information file, pick up the phone and ask politely what the problem is. Your conversation might sound like this:

> Mr. Prospect, we have been looking for a property for you now for ten weeks. We have scanned hundreds of operating statements. We have been out three times and inspected a total of seven different buildings. Of these, I felt that at least three checked out very well and warranted an offer. Five of the properties have been bought by very knowledgeable investors. What can we do to find you a property to get you started with all the advantages of real estate ownership?

At this stage, Mr. Prospect will either modify his requirements or explain that for some reason his situation has changed and income property acquisition does not currently fit into his scheme of things. The earlier you elicit either type of information, the better off you are. If he modifies his requirements and they are reasonable modifications, he is ready to act. Then you can roll up your sleeves and find him that investment. On the other hand, if he is not an action buyer, then you have saved yourself and him a lot of annoyance by discovering the fact early in the game.

Action Check 8. *After negotiating his offer, does he counter with realistic price and terms?* Don't be dismayed if your prospect makes offers that are rejected on a few properties. The best prospect you can ask for is the one who makes a realistic offer on many properties with the hope of acquiring an occasional parcel. Beware, however, of the prospect who makes ridiculous offers and upon refusal of his offer by the owner, counters with equally unrealistic counteroffers or none at all. If this occurs, return to Action Check 4 and redetermine if your prospect's expectations are realistic. If not, you will save yourself some more valuable time by moving his card out of your action-buyer file.

How to Maintain Your Prospect Files

When you first begin developing a list of prospects, you will spend a great deal of time with *anyone* who expresses the slightest interest in investing. This is normal. Your first prospect constitutes 100 percent of your files. But as you accumulate more and more investors and qualify them, file maintenance becomes increasingly important.

A simple computer database with a system of categorizing becomes more and more important. Some brokers have devised prospect file systems that are so intricate as to defy description. In time, you will devise one that is comfortable for you to work with.

When in the Field, Write It Down!

When you are out of the office you can work with a 4 × 6 index card designed along the lines of The Original Qualifier on page 207 of this chapter. Remember a cardinal rule of prospect information accumulation—write it down! No matter how insignificant they seem, record all prospect data on your file card. This card can be paper based or an electronic file in a handheld device or notebook computer.

How to Handle More Than 100 Client Files

At this stage, maintain two files: (1) your action-buyers file; and (2) your incidental information file. Then add (3) your *tickler file,* which should be set up by month. If you discover that a prospect is not ready to invest now, but will probably be ready in November—then file his card with the rest of your prospects that you contact in November.

Whenever you move a prospect from your action buyer file to the incidental information file, you should ask Mr. Prospect to watch your ads and keep you informed as to any changes in his requirements. Many times your incidental information buyers will recontact you, and on the basis of new exploration you will move them back into your action buyer file.

If you were a "fly on the wall" in an active income office, you would see the top-notch broker regularly sorting his prospect files, thinning out his action file to keep it within manageable proportions. In addition, he will add fresh names to replace the old.

With today's searchable and programmable software programs you can quite easily program the equipment to do much of the tracking, matching, and scheduling work for you.

By investing the proper time to qualify the prospect as to requirements and his ability and capacity to act, and by dealing primarily with those who will act, the top-notch broker uses his time effectively.

And this is why the sales leader frequently earns more than the boss!

CHAPTER 10

How to Advertise Income Property— And Make It Pay Off Big

In Chapter 8, we investigated thirteen sources of buyers that you can find without advertising. If you don't have files with several hundred investors' names, you have to get them. You have to find out where they are. There are two ways to accomplish this: (1) contact buyers uncovered through the thirteen sources developed in Chapter 8; and (2) have the investors come to you.

One way to accomplish this initially is to advertise. As long as there are print media such as newspapers they will be an important vehicle for reaching buyers (and sellers). In this chapter we will explore the use of print advertising, press releases, and how to handle the response from these efforts. In Chapter 14 we will expand on the topic by outlining a complete online property marketing plan.

Your ads will result in calls from investors who will say in effect, "I saw your ad on a 12-unit apartment building. I'd like to hear more about it." Even some of the "old pros" will readily admit that preparing advertising presents a real mystery to them. They may be highly competent in all other phases of the business, but they have not mastered the art of creating powerful ads. It is important to understand that your ads should be designed to make the telephone ring and to create a favorable image.

Emphasize the Profit Factor In Your Ads

Although advertising homes often presents a problem to many brokers, it is not difficult to analyze advertising in our income brokerage field. In describing a private residence, one is dealing with the nebulous factor of "house and home," with all of its emotional implications. In income property, we are dealing primarily with one easily understood factor—P-R-O-F-I-T.

Remember, too, that the serious readers of residential ads are looking for a new home—a new place to live. The readers of your income property ads don't have to move their families and furniture to purchase an apartment house—so any of the hundreds of readers of income ads, if they are financially able, can call Monday morning, make a deposit Tuesday, put the building under agreement Wednesday, and take title within 30 days without upsetting their family routine one bit.

How to Write Ads That Build Sales

In order to write ads that ring the phone and consequently build sales, you must follow three basic rules:

Rule 1. Know your listings intimately.
Rule 2. Spend adequate time preparing your copy.
Rule 3. Understand what the investor looks for.

Know Your Listings Intimately

If yours is a small office or you are operating independently, then you should be very familiar with the listings you are about to write copy for. It is obviously considered poor practice to advertise a building you have not personally inspected—no matter how outstanding the figures appear.

If you operate an office with a large staff of brokers, it is likely that you are not personally able to inspect each listing. In this event, it is imperative that you obtain your selling staff's opinions as to which current listings are the best to advertise. You must also have them itemize some of the physical and locational details that make good copy. Then, combining this information with the dollars and cents in your operating statement, you are prepared to sit down and write your ads.

Spend Adequate Time Preparing Your Copy

As elementary as Rule 2 sounds, many brokers do not spend enough time writing their ads. In the rush of the business week, they leave their ad writing to the last possible minute, then dash off some scribbled copy and telephone it in to an equally rushed telephone "ad taker." The end result is usually a disastrous hodge-podge. Little wonder that the harried-hurried broker wonders why his advertising, which often accounts for 10 to 20 percent of his operating budget, doesn't draw an adequate response.

Depending on the size of your brokerage operation, the dollar waste, due to inadequate preparation time, can range from several thousand dollars yearly to *tens* of thousands!

A practice that I have found helpful is to conduct weekly sales meetings on Wednesday mornings. All of our brokers put their heads together and compile what we call our "Best Bets List." This list itemizes the 20 best listings in the office—the ones that should sell within seven days if the right buyers are uncovered. It is understood by our brokers that if they concentrate almost exclusively on the listings itemized on the Best Bets List, they will be using their time most effectively. It follows logically then, that over 90 percent of our ads come from this Best Bets List.

By using this system, I am able to operate comfortably within the guidelines of Rules 1 and 2. I know my merchandise from my brokers' comments, and I sit down immediately after our sales meeting, close my door to interruptions, and write our ads so that they can be typed, double-checked, and submitted to the newspapers to arrive well before the paper's deadline.

Understand What the Investor Looks For

Let's look at how an investor reads the ads. The first thing he will often do, if the ad provides him with the figures, is jot down the income and apply the gross multiplier—the magical gross multiplier that we discussed earlier. If you intend to advertise a building that is exceptionally salable but doesn't check out well when you apply a gross multiplier, don't give your readers the information that they will need to say arbitrarily that his offering is not good. As we have seen, the gross multiplier is by no means the only criterion in evaluating the potential income, profit, or benefits an investor can realize from his new acquisition. Remember that your objective is to *sell* the property, and if your ad can arbitrarily be dismissed, you will not receive calls and you will not sell the building.

You shouldn't advertise an offering if you don't feel it is salable to begin with.

You must put your best foot forward with the buildings you advertise. If you feel that your offering is salable, you should not present figures in such a way that your readers can arbitrarily eliminate the building from any further consideration. The dollars you spend on advertising are expended for one main reason: to prompt readers to call your office and introduce themselves to you or to your salespeople.

Some investors look for this. Another guide that an investor will apply to your ad is a "per-unit cost." You advertise 50 apartments in Yourville at $1,800,000, and your reader can immediately see it is priced just over $36,000 per unit. He thinks, "It looks like a pretty good deal; I'd better call them Monday morning."

Good ads should result in inquiries. Aim for an average of 10 to 20 calls a week on your ads. There is no reason why even the one-man office can't receive just as many calls as the larger office. Some of these small ads are just as intriguing as the big ones. If yours is a small office, keep your ads small. You certainly don't want to go over your budget for advertising. Even with small ads you'll get your calls if your ad is well written. Let's discuss the following example.

R
REALTOR®

30 NEW APTS.
WATERS EDGE

30 Luxurious apts. with WATERVIEW X Selling at around 7.5 TIMES GROSS X $80,000 (or less) down X 100% OCCUPANCY GUARANTEED By builder X will provide you with a steady and growing increase X for the LARGEST SELECTION OF NEW INCOME PROPERTIES. Call 523-4441, or stop by The Peckham Boston Company, 4 Longfellow Place, Boston.

Headline Your Ads with Trademarks and "Magic Words"

Writing effective headlines will draw readers to your ads. In every metropolitan area, there are certain single words or groups of words that hit home with your readers. Study your own market and determine what specific neighborhood, what property characteristics, or what end results are most likely to impress your investors. You can reduce these specifics to short descriptive words and phrases that are eye-catching. No matter how well written the body of the ad is, if there is nothing to catch the reader's eye, he won't even reach the *hard sell* delivered in the main portion.

There are two ways to catch the reader's eye. One is by repeated use of a trademark or symbol. Through its continuous exposure, reader's eyes will be automatically drawn to your ads. Investors unconsciously look for a repetitive mark.

The second way to catch the reader's eye is from the "display" section of your ad—the portion that is set forth in big, bold, black letters—the headlines.

Both the layout and contents of your ads must be designed to get a reader's attention and make him act. Since the headline often determines whether or not the rest of the copy will be read, it has a special importance. An extended list of headings that have helped us make many sales follows. Perhaps you can profit by them, too.

MAGIC WORDS	COMMENT
■ Condominium	Land is becoming very scarce in our area, and perhaps yours. By headlining this feature, you will draw the reader's eyes to the text or body of your ad. Although land sales are not generally within the scope of this work, there are many condominium complexes with additional land available for further construction.
■ Speculators	This draws the eyes of anyone with an ounce of speculative blood in his veins (and don't we all have a few ounces?)
■ Bargain	Everyone loves a bargain!
■ Investment	This is what our prospective purchasers are looking for, and it makes dollars and sense to sprinkle your headlines liberally with this word.
■ Waterview	Everybody wants to invest in property which enjoys a favorable view or location. A magic word in the Boston area is "waterside." Investors want property overlooking the Charles River and often push prices up to astronomical levels to acquire ownership of these prime properties. Obviously, in your city or town there are areas, streets, or landmarks that have great public acceptance. Use them to headline your ads whenever possible.
■ Estate	Everyone expects a bargain when an estate liquidates. Whether real bargains develop or not, the use of this magic word draws attention to your ads.

- Guaranteed income

  Many investors do not want to cope with the problems of turnover. A net lease situation, with one tenant responsible, on a long-term lease is always in great demand.

- AAA-1

  Implies solidity and steady uninterrupted income.

- Trouble free

  Wouldn't we all jump at an opportunity to rid ourselves of troubles?

- Back Bay

  Very similar in approach to the "waterside" headline above. In Boston, the Back Bay is a popular investment area, which most investors understand. This headline always catches the reader's eye and results in phone calls.

- $ $ $ $ + Gross

  An eye-catcher—and that's what headlines are all about!

- $20,000 down

  If you have a couple of slow weeks and have plenty of time, advertise a parcel with $15,000, $20,000, or $30,000 down, and believe me, you will receive 40 to 50 calls. It stands to reason that there are 50 times as many people with $25,000 or less to invest as there are with $100,000. So if it's a little slow, advertise low cash down and headline it. You'll be flooded with calls from investors with limited capital, and in many cases you will discover that your callers have substantially more cash to invest than the amount called for in your headline.

- Apartment remodelers/ Converters

  These magic words are aimed at a specific group. *Headline* the item that will appeal to this group. If it is a property that a remodeler or converter would be interested in, let him know that you have it. There are hundreds of investors in every area who are geared to upgrading rundown or antiquated properties or converting apartments into condominiums.

- Brand-new investment

  Many buyers, particularly the small investor, prefer a new apartment building and will invest on a lower net return for the prestige of owning a new property.

- Small apartment building

  This ad draws attention because there are thousands of small investors for each large investor.

- Not pretty

  We headlined a small ad on a terribly rundown property "not pretty" and received over 60 calls on Monday morning. Needless to say, when the occasion has presented it-self we have used this headline again and again!

A Checklist of Eye-Catching Words

Now you have the idea and reasoning behind creating eye-catching headlines. The following magic word checklist is offered without comment. You will be able to easily adapt many of these to your own area of operations:

- Investment!
- Small investment!
- AAA-1 investment!
- Money Maker!
- Huge cash flow!
- Trouble-free investment!
- View plus location!
- Huge profit!
- Investment bargain!
- $25,000 NET!
- Bread-and-butter investment!
- $15,000 down!
- 100% rented!

- Solid investment!
- Upgrade!
- $ $ $ $ $ $
- Choice investment!
- Speculators!
- Investment of the week!
- Invest $25,000—Net $3,000
- Apartment building foreclosure!
- Estate Liquidation!
- Forty apts—$30,000 down!
- Ugly investment!
- Panic priced!
- $8000 reward!

You can expand on this list and will, and you should keep good track of which magic words ring the bell in your area. Once you assemble a list of 15 or 20 key words and phrases which draw the reader's eyes, you are ready to write the body or text of your ad.

Put These Key Elements In All Your Ads

Look again at the sample ad. Obviously the text of each ad will differ in make-up. However, there are certain common elements in each of them. You should give the investor some of the following information:

A. What you have to sell—e.g., 30 new apartments with a waterview.
B. How much cash is required—e.g., $80,000 down.

C. Where the property is located—e.g., well located 20 miles north of Boston.

D. What the property will do for the investor—e.g., will provide a steady and growing income.

In many cases, some of the preceding information is not included. Always remember the old advertising phrase, "Sell the sizzle, not the steak." Remember that your objective is to make the phone ring—to have investors make themselves known to you. Combine your knowledge of what the investor looks for in an ad, discussed earlier in this chapter, with your ability to create eye-catching headlines, and you will be as busy as a one-armed paperhanger, answering calls from prospects who want more information on the property!

Avoid These Pitfalls

- *Pitfall 1* In some sections, such as my Boston area, brokers advertise net returns on equity before an allowance for vacancy and repairs. Be sure that your ads give the reader an opportunity to compare apples with apples. If the prevailing custom in your area is to advertise returns before these allowances, then it may be wise to advertise your net returns in a like manner; however, always be sure to inform the reader that the return cited is "before V & R."

- *Pitfall 2* Build a reputation for honest advertising. Remember that understatement is a powerful force, and that untrue overstatement may draw a reader's call once, but as soon as he uncovers the misstated truth, he will never call again on your ads.

- *Pitfall 3* Advertise properties that you are sure can be delivered on the terms and conditions set forth in your ad and on your operating statement. If you are in doubt as to the current status of an offering, call the owner before writing your ad copy.

- *Pitfall 4* Be sure that the owner does not object to your advertising his property for sale. If in doubt, make that call. (Remember that many income property owners do not want their tenants or others to know the property is on the market.)

- *Pitfall 5* Don't give your listings away to the competition. In Chapter 2, on sources of sellers, you noted that other brokers' ads will often give away an open listing by supplying enough detail to make the property identifiable. Never give the reader or a competitor enough information to identify your listing. Some brokers go to great lengths to disguise their ads.

Example: Broker A has a prime 23-unit apartment building on Commonwealth Avenue, Boston, to sell, but he knows that brokers B and C had the listing for sale from a previous owner and might recognize it from the ad. This is possible because there are not many buildings on this street with *exactly* 23 units. Broker A might advertise his merchandise as a 21 or 22 unit building to throw brokers B and C off the scent. Many brokers, not knowing of this technique, have driven themselves up a wall trying to find the 21 unit on Commonwealth Avenue! Brokers who use this technique almost always *understate* the number of units, so no one can point an accusing finger at them for exaggerating in their ads.

I point out this technique merely to show the extremes to which a broker will go to protect his merchandise. If you are going to advertise open listings, don't pay good money for your ads only to hand your competitor a free listing.

When to Use Institutional Ads

Most experts agree that the small office can realize a much better dollars-and-cents return by advertising specific buildings for sale. Institutional ads do not normally "pitch" specific listings, but are aimed at enhancing the image of the broker. Image-building ads are fine and are a *must* for the large office; they cannot be overlooked when setting up the annual advertising budget. But, because of the necessary lineage required, they are an expensive luxury for the small operation.

Institutional ads will generally return more income from listings gathered than from the buyers they unearth. After experimenting in the Boston area, I have found that institutional advertising has paid dividends when used in our trade journals. A constant campaign in these papers has assisted in creating a solid company image within the industry; however, I have avoided these costly large ads in the big metropolitan papers, preferring to advertise specific properties there.

Observe These Do's and Don'ts

When the time comes for you to plan an ad campaign that includes institutional ads, attack your project with the same enthusiasm you devote to your regular sizzle ads. Set aside enough time to prepare your ads and turn your creative streak loose. Don't fall victim to the one habit that wastes more advertising dollars than any other I know: don't design an institutional ad and let it run unchanged for weeks and weeks on end. Nothing is more easily overlooked than an unchanged ad—no matter how good or how big it is. After a few weeks the constantly repeated ad becomes transparent and makes about as much impact as the page number!

How to Capitalize On Free Ads

You may budget hundreds, even thousands of dollars for advertising each year, but unless you take advantage of *free* advertising, you are missing an opportunity to expose your name to thousands of readers who might never read your *bought* and paid-for ads.

If someone came to you and said, "Mister, I can get you 20,000 lines of advertising next year in newspapers read daily by hundreds of thousands of people, and your total cost will be less than $2000," you'd probably call the looney squad! Your tipster is right, though. Here's the breakdown:

For 52 weeks you send one release per week to the three major papers in your area—the cost:

Photographs @ $5 each × 156 (3 × 52)	$ 780.00
Stamps and stationery @ $1 × 156	+ 156.00
Secretary 1 hour/week @ $15	+ 780.00
Total	$1,716.00

Most brokers know that the newspapers will print newsworthy accounts of interesting recent real estate activity that is of general interest. Most brokers know that the papers don't have time to send reporters out to gather this information. Most brokers know that the majority of such accounts appear as a result of the broker writing an account and sending it in to the paper. Most brokers know all of this and know the value of such publicity—but most brokers don't take the time to capitalize on this form of advertising.

Real estate editors usually classify these releases as news and are happy to print well prepared releases because readers can look at a picture of the building, see the number of units and the sales price. It gives readers a guide to what people are paying for properties now. I consider each one of these "free ads" worth 100, perhaps 1,000 times more than what I pay for a conventional ad. The impression they make on the investor is amazing because he knows they are not paid for. He knows that they are news. Investors lend a lot more credibility to this type of information than to a paid ad.

Try doing this: If you make a sale, attend a real estate course, or are elected director of a local real estate board, whatever you do that is newsworthy—mail in a release. It isn't difficult. Send it to the paper or the papers with the largest circulation among investors. There is so much value in this type of press that if papers charged for printing these releases (which they don't), most brokers would gladly pay twice the rate per line that they pay for their classified advertising.

Consider how the investor thinks. Look for a minute at the illustration on page 241. There was a similar type of release in Chapter 2. We saw that when other brokers send out these releases they provide you with potential listings. And in Chapter 8, we saw that these same releases provide you with potential buyers. Why then do other brokers go to the trouble? Why should you?

Because investors are much more impressed with news articles than with paid for ads, they react with much less natural suspicion. If you could read the thoughts of an investor reading the release pictured on page 241, they might go something like this:

> How in the blazes did that lucky investor find a good-looking building like that in Malden for only $40,000 per unit? . . . Who was the broker? Oh, yeah—Peckham Boston. I think I've heard of them. Maybe I'd better give them a call.

And he does!

The Peckham Boston Company
Negotiates $1,800,000 Apt. Sale

MALDEN, MASS.—A brick 45-unit apartment building located at 155 Collingwood Ave. has been sold for N.O. Realty Trust to Chirp Realty Corp.
The purchase price was reported as $1,800,000.
The sale was negotiated through The Peckham Boston Company of Boston.

A Case in Point: When this release appeared in the local papers, one of my brokers received an angry call from one of his buyers who told him that he'd better get on the ball and find him a building like that for $40,000 per unit—and why in blazes didn't he submit the one pictured to him in the first place? My broker calmly checked his weekly reports and informed the caller that he had submitted the property to him on February 3. The caller sheepishly bought a similar property through us three weeks later!

Data Realty's Peckham
Forms Development Firm

John M. Peckham 3d, founder and long-time president of Data Realty Co. of Boston, a major real estate brokerage and consulting firm, has announced the formation of The Peckham Boston Co., headquartered at Four Longfellow Place at Charles River Park.

"For now," said Peckham, "we are resting our traditional brokerage hat and preparing to flex our muscles in the role of real estate developers and principals."

The new firm, said Peckham, is already involved in the marketing and development of more than $100 million worth of condominium projects and is actively seeking joint venture conversions with existing property owners.

Involved in the new venture with Peckham are Angela Bonin, who has been with the Data Realty Co. for several years, and Mark Grossman, a condominium expert and consultant.

The principals, said Peckham, have all been involved in the conversion and development of more than 3000 units of condominiums over the past few years which include such well known properties as Hammond Park, Newton; Glover Landing in Marblehead; Ferncroft Village in Danvers, The Somerset in Boston, and Cabot Estates in Chestnut Hill.

The newly formed firm also is prepared to handle all phases of marketing and will arrange for financing and equity capital in connection with joint ventures.

Peckham said that Peckham Boston will carry on all the previous functions of Data Realty companies except for its investment brokerage activity.

Peckham Boston will be the parent company of the existing Data Management and of its condominium functions, he said.

Peckham is a former president of the Mass. Assn. of Realtors and in

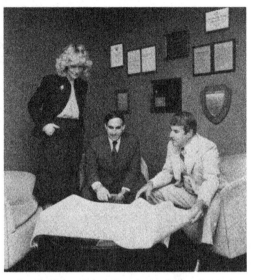

Principals of newly formed condominium development firm. The Peckham Boston Co., left to right, Angela Bonin, Mark Grossman and John M. Peckham 3d.

1980 served as a vice president of the 750,000 member National Assn. of Realtors. He has authored several real estate books and for many years ran a column in the *Boston Herald* on "Investing in Real Estate."

Grossman has served as a consultant to lenders, developers and condominium associations throughout New England and in other sections of the country.

Bonin has been involved in real estate brokerage and development more than 10 years. She has coordinated marketing of more than $140 million worth of commercial and investment property working with both local and national clients. She is a native of Houston and a graduate of the University of Houston.

John Peckham's Goal—the 'Merrill, Lynch' of Investment Property

Ever since World War II when the inflationary spiral started, economists have been saying well located real estate, both the single home and investment property, has been one of the soundest methods of protecting the value of the dollar.

Their statements, though, usually appear in business and professional publications unseen by the bulk of Americans.

So, John M. Peckham III, a young man (38) with an extraordinary capacity for running a business (Data Realty, Brookline), lecturing at seminars in the Greater Boston area and writing a column, Investing in Real Estate, that appears in these pages, assumed the responsibility of getting this message to investors.

This has been the word in his talks, his books, his investment newsletter and in his appearances at trade functions.

In eight years, he built a prosperous business from a two-desk, one-phone office to an organization of 45 in several divisions. The investment property division went from gross sales of $8 millions in 1988 to more than $40 million last year.

He set up a Real Estate Investment Service feeding 350 offices throughout the country Data's offerings each month. Two hundred of these offices are in Massachusetts. The network accounted for approximately 30 percent of his investment sales last year.

"Where else can an investment property owner put 350 offices with over 1000 salesmen to work on his property by making one phone call?" Jack asks.

A wholly-owned subsidiary, Data Real Estate Investment Corp., which forms limited partnerships for Massachusetts residents, through Peckham Investment Associates last year reached full capitalization of $800,000 after six months and acquired a 150-unit North Reading apartment complex. Second Peckham Investment Associates has completed capitalization of $850,000 and has acquired a shopping center west of Boston and is negotiating for additional income producing real estate.

Another subsidiary is Data Realty Management Corp. offering professional management to owners throughout New England. Last quarter's performance, Jack reported, showed vacancy and credit losses of less than one-half percent.

One of the first firms to enter the condominium field, Data has two divisions—Condominium Sales and Condominium Consulting. Among the projects added in the last month: Commonwealth Brockton, 317 units, $6,500,000 gross; Baycrest Towers, Revere, 72 units, $2,900,000 gross; and Charles Court East in Needham, 116 units, $4,500,000 gross.

His firm marketed the 116-unit Glover Landing conversion on Marblehead Harbor for 4.5 million and the water-side conversion of Beacon on the Charles. He is also broker for Ferncroft Village in Danvers, the recreational condominium complex around a golf course. More than $5 million of these units have been sold.

New projects are expected to include units in Weymouth, Brookline and on the Cape.

By November, Jack is projecting an organization of nine offices, a staff of 70 and a growth curve that will make him look like the Merrill, Lynch of the investment property field.

And Jack is not adverse to pointing out that real estate is a far better investment than common stocks, perhaps an unfair comparison in these days of Watergate.

In his books, published by Prentice Hall, "Master Guide to Income Property Brokerage" and "101 Questions and Answers on Investing in Real Estate" Jack has stressed the advantage of equity building through leverage (using borrowed funds), appreciation, almost constant since World War II, and tax advantages (depreciation) not aimed primarily at the sophisticated investor who can afford to buy major properties but to the modest investor who, he believes, should make a cautious start perhaps in a two-family house. With one successful venture behind him, Jack knows he has a client for more substantial properties.

These ideas, which he writes and preaches, earned him civic laurels as one of Greater Boston's 10 Outstanding Young Men and Realtor of the Year back in 1969 for the Massachusetts Association of Real Estate Boards and the Greater Boston Board.

How to Submit an Acceptable News Release

When you submit your releases to the real estate editor, give him the names of the buyer, the seller, the address, a brief description of the property, the selling price and, by all means, the name of the broker! Although it's not absolutely necessary, a good photograph is "worth a thousand words." See the illustration on page 241.

Unless you are a camera wiz spend a few dollars to have a professional photographer prepare the photos. These are dollars well spent. But watch out for this: The question is often raised that buyers might object to publicizing the amount of money they paid. Before sending out releases, you should clear this with your buyer and the seller. Most of the time there will be no objection.

Your releases don't necessarily have to be centered around a specific sale. A new idea or unique approach to brokerage—or a decision to branch out into some new area of real estate—can provide enough material for an informative and attention-grabbing newspaper story. See the article on page 242. This article reported a newsworthy development—and was of course a very helpful form of advertising.

The same is true of the article reproduced on page 243. This type of publicity can't be bought; and there's no way to put a dollar value on it!

A good approach is to invite your local real estate editor over for a visit. Before you do this, have a story for him. Don't waste his time—assemble some information that will be interesting to his readers, and then invite him over. You can do this on an individual basis or you can throw a full-fledged "press party" with the works! Either way you do it, be sure—and this bears repeating—that you give him a story. If you don't, forget any repeat visits.

How to Handle Answers to Your Ads

As a result of your sizzle ads, your institutional ads, or your free ads, you are going to receive telephone calls from potential investors who want more information on the property advertised. All of the well-known rules of salesmanship and courtesy on the phone apply equally to residential and income property.

There are two points that may appear elementary at any level of real estate selling, but are important enough to repeat: (1) screening phone calls is essential to the extent that if you choose to advertise open listings, they should not be compromised to an unknown voice on the other end of the line, and (2) as you get information about the caller, write it down and enter it into your computer database. Nothing is more necessary than assembling and recording data regarding your prospective buyer, for future use.

The following are examples of common problems that recur in our business, and the procedures and conversations you can customize for handling them.

An Example of How to Handle Phone Responses Most Effectively

If you run a multi salesperson office make sure that each salesperson gets an equal share of the calls. When a buyer calls a large office, have the telephone answered by a receptionist who will give the calls out on a "round-robin" basis. The salesperson should give very little information over the telephone until he has the caller's name, address, and phone number. The conversation might go something like this—

> *Caller:* I am calling about the 32 unit apartment building you had advertised in the Sunday paper. Where is that?
>
> *Salesperson:* I'm sorry, but I can't give you the address yet; however, it's well situated in the Back Bay area of Boston.
>
> *Caller:* Why don't you just give me the address and I'll drive by and take a look at it? That'll save us both a lot of time and aggravation.
>
> *Salesperson:* Could I ask who's calling, sir? My name is Jack Peckham.
>
> *Caller:* Well, what difference does it make? What do you care as long as you sell the building?
>
> *Salesperson:* Well, actually I'm not allowed to give out any information unless I know whom I'm talking to. So if I could just jot down your name . . .
>
> *Caller:* This is John Smith.
>
> *Salesperson:* And your address, sir?
>
> *Caller:* What do you need my address for?
>
> *Salesperson:* This is primarily for our mailing list. (Mailing list is a good term in selling this type of property. If an investor thinks you are going to mail him operating statements, he will give you his address in a flash. Assume this fellow does.) And your telephone number, sir?
>
> *Caller:* Well, let me see, its 934-uh, let's see, 25 uh 92.

How to Tell If the Caller Is Genuine

If there is any doubt in your mind as to whether the caller is legitimate, use an old gimmick. Tell him you have another call on the line, and that you will call him right back. Perhaps he will say that he is on a pay phone. Counter with: "Could I call you this evening or at your office later on?" You can normally tell whether or not the caller is legitimate. If he will not give you his office number or his home number, forget him. He is not worth the trouble.

There are enough legitimate buyers so that you don't have to waste your time with the people who are trying to steal listings. If this is happening, at least you are protecting yourself. If he sounds legitimate, give him the *basic* information he requires. Do your best to persuade him to come into the office, make an appointment to see the property, and go over the operating statement.

If there is any doubt as to the buyer's intentions, check the phone number. Occasionally you will reach the bird sanctuary!

How to Withhold Information Tactfully

Obviously it is very important to be pleasant on the phone. Occasionally, in this business, you will find some abusive and self-important people calling on ads. You should always maintain your composure, and explain that you cannot initially give addresses on the phone. Be honest with your caller, explain that you are merely complying with office policy or the *owner's request.* Many times I have told an insistent caller, "If I give you an address on the phone, you will have to find me a new job, because I won't be able to work here any more."

Another effective means of handling the insistent "address grabber" is to explain tactfully that the owner has specifically requested that you refrain from giving the address on the phone. You can continue by pointing out that "certainly Mr. Caller, you can appreciate that if you made such a request, you would expect us to honor your wishes."

The ultimate objective of advertising is to sit down face to face with new investors. Give your caller enough information to make him want to meet with you and learn more. Don't succumb to the lazy, non-productive habits of giving addresses over the phone. Don't stop your sizzle selling with your ad. You must continue to sell the sizzle on the phone. This is your chance to sit down with your next buyer. If you spend good money advertising your offering, you certainly must be convinced that it is an exceptional buy. Let your caller know that it is exceptional, and don't mince words. Try saying this:

> Mr. Caller, we selected this building to advertise from 40 (or 400) other available listings. I have seen this solid building. It is well located in the most valuable section of the city. The property is well maintained and is priced to sell this week. Let me sit down with you and go over the figures. Can you stop by around three-thirty this afternoon, or would tomorrow morning be more convenient?

Don't expect your caller to refuse a meeting. If he wasn't interested he wouldn't have called to begin with. If he refuses to get together in your office—or in his office—or in his home—after such a positive presentation, then either he isn't much of a prospect or the property advertised isn't his cup of tea. If the latter is true, then you must sit down together to qualify his goals further.

CHAPTER 11

How to Show Income Properties for Fast-Action Sales

You have advertised and received a response to your ads. A prospect has come into your office, and you have qualified him as to his preferences and objectives. You have selected two or three properties and have analyzed the operating statements with him. You are now ready to show him the buildings. Remember it's not all facts and figures.

How the Emotional Factor Can Make Sales

Up to now, very little emotion has entered the relationship between you and your prospect. All conversations have pretty much revolved around cold, impersonal figures and mathematical computations. Powerful emotions do become manifest, however, when you visit and inspect the property. Many a prospect has set aside all reason when he sets foot into a big luxury building. He starts thinking, "I sure would be proud to own this building." More sales resistance melts at the point of seeing the property than at any other stage—particularly if the building is good looking and well maintained.

I know this is true because as an investor I have done it myself. Many times I have worked an operating statement backward and forward and said to myself, "I won't pay a penny over $800,000 for this property." Once I see the building, however, and after driving by it again a few times, my tune changes to, "Well, I could probably pay $820,000 and make it work out." By the time the negotiations are complete, I pay $850,000!

The More You Show, the More Sales You'll Make

There is one absolute must for income brokers. You must show the property to make the sale—and the more you show, the more sales you will make. Take a 4 × 6 index card and print in big bold caps **THE MORE I SHOW, THE MORE I EARN.** Carry this card in your pocket, or prop it up on your desk. Look at it every chance you have. Believe it and show, show, show. If you do, you will be among the top producers in your area, despite any limitations in your financing or negotiating knowledge. You will accumulate the knowledge of all other phases through the activity you create by showing as many properties as is humanly possible.

Don't fall into the lazy habit of sending someone by to "see the outside." If the property is for him, pick him up, take his hand, and lead him to and through the property. This is the *only* way to sell income property!

Some Special Problems, and Strategies to Solve Them

Thousands of words have been written on showing residential homes but, to my knowledge, not a word has been printed on the unique problems of showing income properties. And, believe me, the problems are unique!

Residential brokers, beware! Remember, when you show a home, your seller is usually living there and obviously is on your side. The homeowner-seller often tries so hard to be helpful that his efforts hinder the progress of the sale. Entire chapters have been written on how to prevent the homeowner from being *too* helpful.

The unique problems involved in showing income property stem primarily from the fact that the owner does not live in the building, and it is usually tenanted by people who may be fearful of any possible sale, and in the vast majority of cases have no great love for the present landlord. Let's examine some of the special strategies which will be helpful in solving these problems.

Showing Strategy #1: How to Get Into the Building

In showing homes, there is generally no problem in getting in and inspecting the house from top to bottom. The only minor problem that may arise is in setting up an appointment time that does not seriously affect the routine of the owner. Many times he will alter his routine in order to help the sale.

The ideal way to get in to see the income-building is to obtain a complete set of keys (or a master key) when you list the property. Carefully tag and identify the keys, and make sure that all the brokers in your office know of their availability. With the keys to the building available, there is no trouble at all in getting in for inspection; however, as we shall see, getting in is only one-tenth of the battle.

Generally we hold the keys of 10 to 15 percent of our listings. Many owners will be reluctant to relinquish keys and will insist that they (or the janitor—or some other person) be contacted each time the property is to be shown. They will then meet you at the property with their keys and admit you to the building. This is a cumbersome procedure, because sometimes the owner cannot be reached while you are sitting in your office with a "red-hot" prospect. Often your prospect becomes lukewarm by the time you reach the owner 24 hours later. Of course, if there is a full-time janitor on the premises, who is authorized to show the building, then your entry problems are solved.

How "Inaccessible" Can Mean Unsalable. Let me give you an example of the adverse effect a lack of keys has on the broker's ability to make a satisfactory sale. We had a listing on a prime 16-unit Beacon Hill apartment building for about six months. The property was on our Best Bets list for months, which indicated that it was considered very salable by the majority of our brokers. But we had no keys and we were required to contact the owner each time we needed to show the building to a prospect. The owner was a very busy man and could not usually get away quickly to let us in. Even though the property was very salable, the brokers quickly tired of arousing their prospects' desire to purchase, and then seeing their efforts melt away due to inability to inspect the property. The building (although still very salable) was dropped from our Best Bets list.

Owners sometimes will not provide keys or cooperate in showing the property by appointment. Instead they will tell you to knock on the tenants' doors and ask them to allow you to inspect their apartments "for the purpose of assisting the owner in certain financial transactions."

A Way to Gain Entrance. In order to assist our brokers in gaining the cooperation of the tenants, we designed an official-looking I.D. card that identifies the broker and asks for the tenant's assistance. It looks like the one on this page.

We have the card laminated in heavy plastic to keep it from becoming "dog-eared," and also to give it an official appearance. By using this card, our brokers have raised the "open sesame" ratio from 33 percent to over 50 percent—that is, before the use of the card about one tenant in three would allow the brokers and their prospects to inspect the apartment. With the I.D. card, better than half of the tenants approached will cooperate by allowing the inspection.

THIS IS TO CERTIFY THAT

R
REALTOR®

_____

**Represents The Peckham Boston Company
as an Investment Broker**

and may from time to time be required to inspect certain buildings in order to assist the owner in connection with financial transactions.

Any courtesy you can afford this representative will be greatly appreciated. If there are any questions regarding his presence on the premises please call 523-4441.

_____

Investment Broker   Date   Authorized Signature

This method of showing the apartment house points out the fact that this is not a business for the bashful broker. You must show to sell. If you are reluctant to knock on a door and explain your presence and solicit the tenant's cooperation, then, by all means, you must overcome this reluctance or get out of the business.

Showing Strategy #2: How to Phrase a
True but Tactful "Cover Story"

In residential sales, there is rarely a problem arising out of the owner's desire to conceal the fact that his house is for sale. Usually all his neighbors know that he is being transferred, moving to a different neighborhood, or building a new house.

With income property, however, there are many legitimate reasons for not announcing to the world the fact that the building is for sale. The primary reason for the owner's desired secrecy is that he does not want the tenants to become aroused with fears (usually unfounded) that a sale of the property will upset their status quo with rent increases, policy changes, or tenancy terminations. For that reason, the owner will many times request that when inspecting the property you use a "cover story." Some brokers, upon a face-to-face confrontation with a tenant, will say they are from the "insurance company" or, even worse, from the "building department."

I believe that this is a grave error; the use of such obvious ruses has often proved very embarrassing to the users. The tenant, when offered such a story, will sometimes ask, "What company?" or "Let me see your identification"—and the broker is left with egg on his face and panic in his heart.

It is necessary, however, in most cases, to avoid telling the tenant that the property is for sale. In conjunction with our I.D. card, we explain that "the owner, Mr. Jones, has requested that we inspect the building for financing matters, and we would appreciate your cooperation in allowing us to inspect your apartment for layout and design." Obviously, it is important that you know the owner's name before arriving at the property. Check the listing sheet before leaving and jot down his name.

Many times a tenant will say, "Oh, the apartment is a horrible mess. Can you come back some other time?" You then must explain that you are not inspecting for cleanliness and that you won't even notice any housekeeping, as you are only interested in the general layout of the apartment. By combining the I.D. card with an effective truthful cover story, and by refusing to succumb to timidity, you will be able to inspect better than half of all apartments.

Showing Strategy #3: How to Soften the Impact of Tenant Complaints

As noted earlier, the homeowner is your ally when showing his home to a prospective buyer. The tenant in an income property is many times an arch foe! Remember that tenants very seldom have much good to say about the building, the apartment, the janitor, or (especially) the owner.

The Kind of Information You'll Hear from Tenants. Once you are inside an apartment and inspecting it, don't be surprised when the tenant *volunteers* little tidbits of information—all usually detrimental to your case. His (or her) comments might go something like this:

- "So Mr. Owner wants to get some financing. Yes, I'll be happy to show you my apartment, but I'm sure I should be honest and tell you a few of the problems."
- "This rat trap hasn't been painted in seven years. Look at the ceiling where the water came through six months ago."
- "You should hear these steam pipes bang when the heat comes on—if it comes on."
- "Perhaps you could speak to the owner and get me some screens, and also have him send an exterminator over to get rid of the roaches that are all over this building."
- "Look at this refrigerator—must be 25 years old. All the tenants are fed up with this joint."

Expect comments like these from some of the tenants you encounter. If your prospect is a "pro" or owns property of his own, he will easily understand that he is hearing human nature through the vocal chords of the tenant. However, if he is a novice prospect, you must prepare him for the shock by explaining the nature of tenants to him on your way to the property.

A straightforward approach to the problem is best. You might, for example, say: "Mr. Prospect, since you have not inspected income property before, I should explain one problem we may encounter. Quite often when tenants are in, they will complain at great length about the building or their apartments. It is very rare to find a completely satisfied tenant. I want to explain this because professional investors know this from experience, and the complaints don't upset them. Of course, if it sounds like there's a serious problem, I'll be glad to investigate. But I want you to know that we'll hear complaints of some sort in nearly any property we inspect." If no complaints arise when you arrive, you are that much better off.

Investigate Legitimate Complaints. Specific complaints that appear to have merit should be investigated, of course. The tenant who points out water stains on the ceiling many times does not add that this happened when Mrs. Smith, upstairs, let her sink overflow once. Unless the problem is investigated with the owner, the tenant will leave your buyer with the impression that water is flowing down the walls from the roof, and that this happens every time it rains. Nine out of ten complaints can be very satisfactorily explained by the owner or his janitor.

The most vociferous complaints usually come from the long-term or elderly tenant who has plenty of time to sit and dwell on these problems. She (or he) will finish a tirade about the peeling wallpaper, the cracking plaster, and the old appliances, and then feel very satisfied that she has gotten back at the landlord who has been taking her money for years.

The most effective means of turning these complaints to your advantage is by using six little words in a question to the tenant—"How long have you lived here?" The answer will many times be, "Oh, about 23 years." Turn and smile to your prospect, and move on to the next apartment.

Showing Strategy #4: The Janitor: How to Get Him On Your Side

The owner quite often will not want the janitor to know that the property is for sale, fearing that the janitor will start looking for another job or will gossip with the tenants and let them in on his secret. It is usually best for the owner to take the janitor aside and explain that he is considering a possible sale of the property, but that he is sure that any new owner would want to retain the janitor's services. The owner could even make it a contingency of the sale that the janitor stay on to assist the new owner for at least a minimum period. Many buyers will even insist on this provision.

How to Talk In Terms of the Janitor's Interest. Many owners go further and explain that if the property is sold within a certain period, the janitor will receive a significant bonus. If the janitor has been properly prepared in this way, you will find him very cooperative.

If, on the other hand, the janitor has not been informed of a potential sale but suspects it from the brokerage activity, he can be very uncooperative on your first meeting. If this occurs, you can help your cause by talking with the owner and encouraging him to sit down with his janitor to explain what is happening and reassure him that his job is secure. A properly oriented janitor can pave the way to a sale.

Showing Strategy #5: How to Control the Factor of Cleanliness

In residential sales, the owner of a property usually will have his property cleaned up and neat when you arrive to show his house. In selling income property, the owner should be encouraged to redouble his efforts to keep the building clean. No matter how hard he or his janitor try to keep the building clean, at times you will show the property when it is far from spotless. Even if the janitor has swept the halls thoroughly in the morning, a careless tenant can destroy the image by tracking in mud and dirt a moment before you come. A delivery man can accomplish the same. The owner has very little control over the housekeeping efforts of each individual tenant.

The pro who sees dirt or sloppy housekeeping won't bat an eyelash, but you must cater to the untrained eye of the novice buyer.

After you show a particular property a few times, you will find out what time of day is best for bringing prospects through. You'll discover that the tenants put their trash out on Tuesdays and Thursdays, or that the janitor cleans thoroughly on Monday, Wednesday, and Friday mornings. You may also discover that the tenants in apartments 1, 3, 9, and 12 are exceptionally cooperative and maintain neat apartments. Enter this information in the office "log book," if one of your fellow brokers has not already entered it. Then try to pattern your showings around the newly discovered cleanliness schedule.

You might call two or three of the tenants in advance of an important showing. Explain to them that the owner, Mr. Smith, wants you to inspect the building at 2:30 this afternoon, and that you are calling them in advance to let them know what time you will be by their apartment. Many brokers have found this technique very helpful. They are easily able to get the tenants' telephone numbers from the street address telephone directory mentioned in Chapter 2.

Case in Point: Why I Cleared Hallways to Earn a Commission. Cleanliness can be particularly vital if a novice investor decides that his wife should see the property. Early in my career, another broker and I made a sale by literally cleaning up a front hallway. I was the selling broker and a very dignified gentleman and friend, Sam, was the listing broker; but on this day we were both janitors.

I had shown a solid brick apartment building on Bay State Road in Boston to a young novice investor, and he was quite impressed with the location and the potential profit. He was ready to buy, but at the last minute decided that his wife should see the building. Although the investor did not object to the state of cleanliness, I knew that his wife would be revolted and would most likely veto the purchase.

The foyer of this building had once been beautiful—a work of art. But now the gorgeous paneling was filthy. The owner had let this beautiful foyer deteriorate into a dust-collecting rubbish area. It was May and there was still a Christmas tree propped up against trash barrels, all scarcely hidden behind a crudely constructed partition. The place was thick with flies and the smell of decaying garbage.

Our buyer's wife was due to inspect the property at three o'clock that afternoon. Sam put in a rush call to the owner and pleaded with her to get down there to clean up the place. He made it frantically clear that the whole sale would go "up in smoke" if the buyer's wife saw the foyer in its present condition.

The owner told Sam that she couldn't get a janitor on this short notice, and that she couldn't be bothered. Sam said, "Well, I can get a kid in there to clean it up but it'll probably cost you 30 bucks." Naturally, we couldn't find anyone to do the job on such short notice, so we transformed Sam's shiny Cadillac to a garbage wagon. We bought cleaning supplies and disinfectant. We swept the place out. We emptied the trash barrels, hauling them off in Sam's trunk. Finally, with the seams of Sam's tailor-made suit coming apart, we finished the job with generous amounts of sweet-smelling disinfectant.

Neither Sam nor I minded the effort of cleaning up the hallway. It was such a change of pace, we really enjoyed it—especially when the reward was a good commission (we made the sale). Incidentally, Sam and I split the $30 cleaning fee, too!

Showing Strategy #6: How to Capitalize on the "Traffic Jam" Problem

Many times when a red-hot listing is distributed to the brokers, several of them will get on the phone and immediately bring their favorite prospects out to see the building—resulting in a "traffic jam." This problem is peculiar to income property, because the astute buyer will drop everything when he receives a rush call from his broker to view an exceptional listing.

Some brokers panic on the sight of one or more other brokers and their clients at the scene. The polished broker, however, will readily admit to his client that the other brokers and their prospects also know a good thing when they see it, and if it weren't for the fact that this is such an exceptional listing, they would not have rushed out so quickly. The broker will thus capitalize on the traffic jam problem by encouraging a quick offer.

Showing Strategy #7: How to Sell the Profit Potential of a "Rough" Building

At the beginning of this chapter we mentioned that upon seeing a well maintained, good-looking building, a buyer will find it difficult to suppress his enthusiasm. Many times, however, a rough building may be just the buyer's cup of tea. It may give him a higher cash flow, and in some cases, more potential for profit through systematic upgrading.

The pros who upgrade run-down properties won't need any reassurance in seeing the condition of the property. They will see the potential created through previous neglect. The novice, however, may be horrified at the neglect and, without realizing the potential for profit, he may think as most unsophisticated investors, "I certainly wouldn't want to live here."

What to say: You must point out, "This certainly isn't a building where you would want to live, but that isn't the reason we're considering it. The main reason for investing in income property is profit, and because this property has been neglected, the potential for profit is great. If this property were in top-notch condition, the price would be much higher. In effect, you have the opportunity to make repairs which put three to four dollars in your pocket for each dollar of outlay."

In showing the neglected property, you should point out the repairs that can be effected, and show that a little carpentry and some paint will go a long way in increasing the value of this property. Your strategy is to point out the defects before your prospect has the chance to. This will disarm him, and if this is truly the property for him, he will be most receptive to your projections of cost and the resulting increase in value.

Showing Strategy #8: How to Decide How Much You Should Show

In Chapter 9 on qualifying, we examined the question of how many different buildings to show a prospect before moving him to the incidental information file. Most new brokers ask, "How many apartments in a given building should I show the buyer?"

Most experienced investors will insist on seeing the exterior, the basement and the heating plant, the public hallways, and a reasonable sampling of apartments (or office suites, or stores). A reasonable sampling can vary greatly among building types.

If you are showing a new garden-type apartment building to a seasoned investor, he will want to see at least one of each type of apartment. If the building contains 40 two-bedroom apartments, all of similar design and with similar amenities, and 20 one-bedroom apartments, plus ten studio apartments, then he will want to see three apartments—one of each type. If he is inspecting an older property, he might want to see more of each type to check on the general state of repair of the various categories.

The novice, on the other hand, many times wants to inspect all 70 apartments! You must explain to him that you cannot disturb 70 tenants until negotiations have reached the stage where your prospect is quite certain that he can buy on terms acceptable to both him and to the owner. Explain that you can show him a good sampling, and that when he makes his offer he can contain a clause that his offer is contingent upon examination and approval of the balance of the apartments.

Showing Strategy #9: Your Best Pattern of Showing

As in residential brokerage, there is a pattern or ideal "road map" to showing income property. Keep in mind, however, that this road map must be flexible; try to follow it unless circumstances dictate the use of an alternate route. You should approach the building by the most scenic route. Show your prospect the most desirable aspects of the neighborhood in which the property is located. If there are some well known or high-rent structures in the area, point them out.

Upon arriving at the building, spend a few moments examining the exterior. If it is brick or an exceptionally impressive structure, let your prospect absorb the scenery.

Your next step is to enter the front door and inspect the front hall or lobby. From here it is a good idea to visit the basement and heating plant. From the basement, you should walk back up through the public hallways to the roof. Following inspection of the roof, you will inspect your sampling of apartments. Upon completion of the apartment inspection, it is always wise (especially if the building is impressive) to stop outside the property and again let the prospect view the exterior.

Let the Prospect Browse. A digital camera can help you make the sale. Take it along and get a couple of good shots of the exterior. E-mail one to your prospect, so he can show his family the handsome building he is going to buy. Go back to the office, print out a copy, and file it in the property folder, or post it on your picture display board.

While inspecting the property, allow your prospect to spend as much time as he wants poking around—the more time he spends, the more he will understand the property and the less doubt or confusion will exist in his mind. If you have a cooperative janitor, or tenant, or owner who can assist your sale, then by all means conclude your inspection by sitting down with your prospect and the janitor. Let your prospect ask any questions he feels he needs answered, to assist him in understanding the property better.

In showing other types of income property, you should follow the same general pattern of showing:

1. Exterior,
2. Lobbies,
3. Basement (including heating plant),
4. Public halls,
5. Roof,
6. Rental units (stores, offices, etc.), and
7. Exterior.

If the building possesses any exceptional features, by all means dramatize them. Don't assume that your prospect will see the good features without your help—he'll normally be too busy looking for the drawbacks or problems. The following section will help you to develop your ability to dramatize some selected features.

How to Appeal to a Buyer's Five Senses

There's an old saying that some brokers who claim "twenty years' experience in the business" actually have only one year's experience—repeated twenty times. Some brokers go on showing properties the same way they did twenty years ago, with no attempt to improve their presentations or to understand what motivates prospects when inspecting properties.

There is one sure way to get through to the mind of your buyer, and that is to appeal to all of his five senses. In order for your presentation to motivate him, he has to either *see* it, *hear* it, *taste* it, *touch* it, or *smell* it. Dramatize your showing, appealing to as many of the buyer's senses as possible so as to really impress on him the property's major features.

Some of the following examples may seem a bit extreme, but I use them to impress you with the importance of not becoming a tour guide. A tour guide does nothing but walk into an apartment and display the obvious, for example, dragging a buyer into a small room equipped with a tub, sink, and toilet and dramatically pointing out, "This is a bathroom."

Following are some features that can be dramatized to appeal to and impress upon the senses of the buyer. You can impress these features on your prospect's mind by dramatizing them as described.

How to Appeal to the Sense of Sight

You must give your buyer enough time to view the property and its features in order to impress them indelibly on his sense of sight. Some sales aids that will help are:

- Photographs
- Aerial photographs
- Drawings
- Floor plans

- Street maps
- Manufacturers' brochures

Some features that particularly appeal to the sight senses are:

- Handsome buildings
- Redecorated apartments
- Clean public areas
- Nicely kept landscaping
- Impressive surroundings

Don't leave it to chance. Point out these features and make sure your prospect sees them. You might say, "Mr. Prospect, look at the manicured lawns and beautiful plantings around this building. There isn't a place in the city where you'll see a rhododendron to equal this. And have you ever seen such care and attention given to flower beds and shrubs? This property has obviously been given the best of attention. You will see the results of this attention as we inspect the inside of the building."

How to Appeal to the Sense of Hearing

Even the auditory nerves can be brought into play when selling income property. Features that might appeal to the sense of hearing are generally those that make the building quieter. For example, sound-proofing, carpeting, or quiet tenants.

These can be dramatized by stopping in a public hall and saying, "Mr. Prospect, let's be absolutely quiet. I want you to know that the builder spared no expense to make this property exceptionally quiet and comfortable for the tenants. Listen . . . not a sound. Listen while I run down this hallway . . . the deep pile carpeting absorbs the sound of my steps. The tenants have been selected and screened carefully to preserve peace and quiet. I think you will appreciate the advantage of owning such a well-conceived, well managed investment property."

How to Appeal to the Sense of Taste

To point out the extreme in appealing to the five senses, assume that you are showing a store block or a shopping center. A fine restaurant is located there. You can even appeal to your prospect's taste sense by having lunch in the restaurant and pointing out, "Mr. Prospect, before a restaurant of this quality picks a location, it makes extensive surveys to be sure that it is an area of stable and steady economic growth. Certainly, its decision to locate here indicates that this block will enjoy continuing prosperity."

Some may find this example a bit extreme, but it goes a lot further toward making the sale than an offhand comment that "This is the restaurant."

How to Appeal to the Sense of Touch

Very seldom will the average broker make his prospect touch or feel some of the features of the building. There are many features that can be dramatized to appeal to the touch sense:

- Sound construction
- Fine kitchen cabinets
- Fine finish trim
- Quality wallpaper
- Sound stair railings
- Good heating systems

This can be dramatized and impressed indelibly in the mind of the prospect. For example, "Mr. Prospect, feel the quality of this wallpaper. The present owner has not spared any expense in maintaining this fine property."

or

"Mr. Prospect, feel the marble on the countertops and the finish work on these kitchen cabinets. Look how this drawer rolls in and out easily. That's because the builder didn't skimp on any of the materials in constructing this building. For example, these drawers are on rollers, not just on slides. Flip that light switch. Notice, it's a mercury switch and doesn't click (hearing and touch). The builder could have saved thousands of dollars by using average materials on this apartment building. You will be investing in one of the best constructed properties in the area."

How to Appeal to the Sense of Smell

There are a few features that favor the olfactory nerve—in the sense that they don't offend it by objectionable odor.

- Suburban area (no factory fumes, etc.)
- Clean building
- Kitchen exhaust fans and range hoods

To dramatize these features you might say: "Mr. Prospect, because this solid building is in a quiet suburban town and surrounded by lots of open space, it is a very desirable place for tenants to live. Take a deep breath. Inhale that clean air. About all you can smell is the fragrance of those beautiful pine trees scattered about the lot."

or

"Mr. Prospect, did you notice that the builder has installed the finest quality range hoods in each kitchen? While we're standing here in the hallway, see if you can smell any cooking odors. (*pause*) None, and believe me, the tenants appreciate living in a building that was so well planned and well built. As owner of this property, you should enjoy a fine quality of tenant and exceptionally high occupancy."

The features cited in the preceding examples are by no means intended to be a complete list. Remember how important it is that you "get through" to your prospect. Appeal to his senses whenever possible, and never overlook the opportunity to dramatize each selling feature.

An Action Memo

By the way, if you didn't stop on page 249 and make a sign for yourself, do it now. Take a card and print in bold letters:

THE MORE I SHOW,
THE MORE I EARN (AND LEARN).

This simple message is one of the most important in this Guide!

CHAPTER 12

How to Master the Fine Points of Selling Income Property

All of your preparation has been building toward the day you sell your stock in trade—your income property listings. The preparation of these listings, which involved an understanding of listing techniques, financing, pricing, and operating statement structure, and your understanding of sources of buyers, advertising, and how to qualify your investors is about to pay off in commissions earned and in the satisfaction of an important job well done.

I must assume that you have either studied a course in general salesmanship, or are naturally endowed with a certain amount of sales ability. It is not the intention of this chapter to introduce you to any miraculous hocus-pocus which will make you a super salesman—you don't need any prestidigitational skills in the income brokerage field. By combining native ability with the solid practical techniques in this Guide and hard work, you will become the catalyst that creates income property sales.

At Peckham Boston, my "multi-million-dollar" brokers have been very normal individuals. Not one is a magician. They share two common traits: (1) they understand their business; and (2) they work their shirts off.

In the next chapter we will discuss the final presentation that makes the sale. Remember for now that you started to close the sale the moment you came face to face with your prospective investor, and have continued toward the close during your qualification interview and the physical showing of the property. In this chapter you will learn:

1. to anticipate some of the common questions which your investor will ask—and how to reply;
2. to anticipate some of the common objections which your investor will raise—and how to reply; and
3. some of the common plus features you can stress, and how to present them convincingly.

How to Answer Frequently Asked Questions

Your prospect's response to any investments submitted to him will normally come in the form of questions or objections. The questions he asks will help you to understand what motivates him, or what worries him, or what his real expectations are. Learn to be a good listener, and by all means allow your prospect to do most of the talking. The top-notch brokers in our field are the ones who allow the prospect to talk himself "blue in the face." The only way you can find out what your prospect really wants is to get him talking and then listen—really listen, and absorb what is said or left unsaid.

It is equally important that you learn to anticipate what questions to expect and that you have a realistic (and brief) answer to the prospect's questions. Notice also that most of the broker's replies end with a question or statement, which is intended further to draw out the prospect's motives or desires, or to motivate him to action. The questions that follow are a sampling of some of those most frequently asked of income property brokers, and some typical responses. The responses cannot be applied to all situations and, depending on the circumstances, you must alter the same response to fit the facts. You should also change the phraseology to suit your own personality.

Prospect Question 1: "Why Is the Owner Selling?"

This is the most common question raised by prospective investors. The question is usually fairly easy to answer in residential sales, because the owner is normally either moving to another area or into another house. In income property sales, the reasons are well spelled out in Chapter 3:

1. The owner wants to take a profit.
2. The owner has problems.
3. The owner wants larger property.

Usually the experienced investor will not ask this question, since he judges the investment on its own merits. However, it is sound brokerage to know why an owner is selling, and to be able to reply convincingly. Your reply could be:

1. "Mr. Prospect, the owner of this property is a builder, and his main talent lies in creating income properties, not primarily in owning and managing them. He can create more income for himself by building more or larger properties, and he is willing to sell at a fair price so that the investor can see a good return on a new property."

or

2. "Mr. Prospect, the owners of this property have decided to split up their assets and dissolve the partnership. If it weren't for this situation, Mr. Prospect, this fine property would not be available."

or

3. "Mr. Prospect, the owner of this property contacted us because he is preparing to invest in a much larger property. This fine building, although it is too small for the owner, is ideal for you because of its prime location, etc."

Prospect Question 2: "Has Anyone Else Made an Offer On This Property?"

This is a very proper question for an investor to ask. The question is two-pronged. If someone else has made an offer, the prospect wants to know what offer has been refused. This will give some idea of what price level is *not* acceptable to the owner. The second prong is a search for reassurance that someone else thought this was a good investment. Your reply could be:

1. "Mr. Prospect, we have had this property available for less than a week, and it has not been exposed to the market before that. No one has made an offer yet, and this gives you an opportunity to acquire this fine property before someone else buys it."

or

2. "Mr. Prospect, no one has made an offer. I think this is due to the fact that this property is located well out in the suburbs and has not been exposed to the general market. I feel that the time is right to get in there with an offer."

or

3. "Mr. Prospect, we have had two offers on this property, both of which were unacceptable to the seller. His price is firm, as indicated on the statement. Because this type of property is so hard to find, I am quite sure that it will sell very soon and that the seller will obtain his terms because it is realistically priced. I think that we should present an offer to the owner today."

Prospect Question 3: "How Long Has This Property Been On the Market?"

Again, this is a proper question. Of course, the buyer feels that if the offering has been on the market for an extended period of time, perhaps the owner may be thinking of dropping his price. In the income field, it is true that sometimes an owner will list his property at a price in excess of market value, looking for a larger profit than the market will bear. After a few frustrating months, he will then lower his sights. When your prospect asks you how long the property has been on the market, he may be saying in effect, "Do you think that because the property has not sold quickly, I might buy it at a lower price than the owner is asking?" Your reply could be:

1. "Mr. Prospect, this property was just put on the market a few days ago. I contacted you right away because I wanted you to be the first to know that it is available. Because this is just what you've been looking for and meets your requirements so well, I think we should act quickly on this offering."

or

2. "Mr. Prospect, we have had this property for about four months. Many times a property does not receive a tremendous amount of activity immediately, because it is one of hundreds available at any one time. I would say that the time is right to make an offer, as the owner has just recently lowered his asking price."

Prospect Question 4: "How Long Has the Seller Owned This Property?"

Your prospect wants to know if the seller is a short-term or long-term owner. Short-term ownership many times generates a suspicious attitude on the buyer's part. The investor usually thinks that there is something radically wrong with the property if it is being sold after only a short period of ownership. In residential brokerage this may sometimes be true; however, remember why our investors are in this business—P-R-O-F-I-T! There is nothing wrong with reselling an investment in a short time and generating a realistic profit. Stock market investors do it every day! Your reply could be:

1. "Mr. Prospect, the seller has owned this property for a short time. When he purchased it, he did so with the intention of reselling for a reasonable profit. He obtained it at a very favorable price and is entitled to a small profit. Under the circumstances, we should look primarily to the property itself and not to the seller's motives. This property is in outstanding condition and generates an excellent net return."

or

2. "Mr. Prospect, the seller has owned this property for over 20 years. If it were not for a tax problem, he probably would hold it for another 20 years; however, his accountants recommended that he sell and acquire a larger property to give him a larger tax base, so that he can gain more depreciation. I would suggest that we move quickly on this prime parcel."

Prospect Question 5: "Do You Have an Exclusive?"

Be careful with this one. The prospect reveals one of two motives by asking this question:

1. He wants to be assured that if he decides to buy, you can deliver the property without the pressure or worry of another broker "beating you to the punch" and thus losing control of the property.

or

2. He has ulterior motives that might involve trying to bypass you as the recognized broker.

Although there are very few buyers who would attempt to deceive the broker by using devious means to purchase a property introduced to him by the broker, you should be aware of the fact that this will occasionally happen—and be on guard when the fact that you do not have an exclusive becomes a big issue with the prospect. We have found these replies effective:

- *If you have an exclusive:* "Mr. Prospect, we do have an exclusive, and I feel that this property is fairly priced and should sell quite quickly. We should investigate this offering immediately."
- *If you do not have an exclusive:* "Mr. Prospect, we do not have an exclusive; however, we are quite close to the owner and feel that we can negotiate very attractive terms. Because the possibility exists that someone else could purchase this property, I would suggest that we investigate the merits of this offering without delay."

* * * * *

The five prospect questions listed in the preceding section are the most frequent ones you will encounter. There will be many more of a less frequent nature. Once you have mastered the art of answering convincingly the frequently asked questions, you will be able to apply the same technique to almost any general type question asked of you. Just remember to let your prospect talk. Remember to listen. The prospect will tell you as much about his motives with his questions as he will with his statements.

How to Answer Your Prospect's Objections

In *any* form of selling you must expect to encounter objections. Selling income property is no exception. You will find it very reassuring to remember that when a prospect raises objections, it shows her interest in the property submitted. You will occasionally run into the prospect who glances at your operating statement, inspects the property, and says, "That's nice, I'll look it over." At no time does the prospect raise any objections or find any fault. That's not a good sign. Unless you bring objections or fears out in the open, you cannot answer them or reassure your prospect.

Always remember that your prospect, no matter how sophisticated she is, wants reassurance. She wants to hear your convincing explanation of why she should invest in this particular property. You must (1) be convinced that this is a good investment for your prospect, and more important, you must (2) be able to convey your convictions to the prospect. To do this, you must bring her fears and objections out in the open and then reassure Ms. Prospect item by item.

Most prospects will bring their objections out of hiding with ease. Be thankful for the 80 percent plus who readily tell you, "I don't like the condition of this building." They have saved you a great deal of digging and probing to find out just why they won't act. The other 20 percent who don't raise objections must be handled so that they will tell you just why they are not ready to act. The magic word here is WHY.

How to Draw Out the Reticent Prospect

To draw out the silent prospect, you must use the word WHY.

"Mr. Prospect, we've been over the operating statement. We've seen the property, and apparently everything meets with your approval. *Why,* then, are you not ready to start negotiations to acquire this fine building?"

Your prospect might say, "I don't like it."

You say, "Why?"

This sounds like the little boy searching for an answer with repeated "Whys." It should. The little boy wants a specific, understandable answer—and so do you.

How to Assume the Role of Adviser, Rather Than Adversary

Assuming that you have now brought the prospect's objections to light, let's prepare to answer his questions. Notice, I said *questions* in the first part of this chapter. But you point out we are talking about *objections* now.

Whenever a prospect raises what he considers *objections,* it is always effective to approach your prospect not as an adversary but as an adviser. By referring to his objections as questions, you will be able to assume this stance.

Mr. Prospect says: "This building has too many vacancies. Something must be wrong here."

Your approach to his question:

> "Mr. Prospect, I'm glad you raised that QUESTION. The situation puzzled me at first, too, until I did some research and found that . . . "

How to Disagree Without Being Disagreeable

Also remember another basic approach to prospects' objections, the "Yes, but" approach. This is another way to answer your prospects' objections without taking the role of the antagonist. When Mr. Prospect says, "This price is much too high," the antagonist says, "Mr. Prospect, you're wrong; this is very realistically priced."

The master salesman uses the "Yes, but" approach as follows: "Mr. Prospect, I can understand why you might feel that way; however, comparing the merits of this fine property with many other recent sales, we have found that . . . "

Before analyzing the seven basic categories or questions a prospect may raise, remember that your prospect wants to buy. He wants reassurance, and he wants the answers you are preparing to give him. In short, the prospect really wants to be SOLD!

The Seven Basic Objection Categories

Objections that your prospects will raise fall into seven basic categories:

1. Price objections.
2. Condition objections.
3. Location objections.
4. Tenancy objections.
5. Dollar-and-cents objections.
6. Personal likes and dislikes objections.
7. Stalling objections.

You have already qualified your prospect and shown him a property, and he begins to raise objections. You are delighted that he is bringing his objections (concerns) out in the open. Here are suggestions for handling each of these objection categories.

Category 1: Price Objections

Price objections generally arise either because the property is, in fact, overpriced, or because the prospect is not really sure what price he should pay, and out of self-defense he objects. Price objections can be expressed in many ways. For example:

"The price is too high!"
"This is over eight times the gross!"
"The down payment is too high!"
"This is too big for me!"
"The seller must have overpaid!"
"The seller is out of his mind!"
"$70,000 per unit is too high!"

Assuming that, based on the offered terms, the price is in line with similar properties, your reply could be:

> Mr. Buyer, I can understand why you might feel this way. The price certainly would be lower if it were not for the superior construction and top-notch location of this building. This is an investment you will be proud to own, and its value should improve over the years. I'm glad you raised the question of price. Let me show you in dollars and cents what this building will do for you.

Category 2: Condition Objections

After viewing the property, your prospect should raise objections regarding the condition of the property. Don't be alarmed when he does; be thankful, because he's helping you to close. Condition objections sound like this:

"This building is in terrible shape!"
"The bathrooms are not modern."
"The hallways are filthy."
"The place hasn't been painted in years."
"The boiler looks terrible, etc."

Your reply could be:

Mr. Buyer, I can understand your concern. If this property were made neat and clean and if the halls were redecorated and sparkling, then the tenants would pay more rent, and this would increase your cash flow. This is just the type of situation the alert buyer looks for, because there is room for improvement. Let me also point out that the rents are well below the area market, and if these deficiencies were corrected, the property would not be available at such an attractive price. I would suggest that we make an immediate offer . . .

Category 3: Location Objections

Your prospect may object to the location of the property you have submitted to him. His objections will sound like this:

"I don't like the location!"
"It's not near my home."
"I won't buy in Greenville."
"I will buy only in Cambridge."
"It's next to a gas station."

Your reply could be:

Mr. Prospect, I can understand your position. This is not the best location; however, if this solid building were located in Bestville, it would be selling at a much higher price, and the return would be much lower. Let's look at how much cash this property will put in your pocket each year . . .

or

Mr. Prospect, I can understand your desire to own a property near your home; however, if you desire we can arrange professional management to take care of the property for you. Let's look at the fine return this solid building will give you . . .

or

Mr. Prospect, I wouldn't rule out Greenville so quickly. It is not very often that we obtain such a prime property that shows such a large return. Let's see what this investment will do for you . . .

or

Mr. Prospect, by limiting yourself to Cambridge, you are eliminating 95 percent of all the investment offerings that cross my desk. I can understand your desire to acquire

273

Cambridge property; however, the demand is so great for property in that area that thousands of investors have pushed the prices very high, leaving very few properties available at prices which leave a fair return. It might take years to find the right investment if you limit your choice to Cambridge. I would suggest that we also look in areas such as Brighton or Brookline. As a matter of fact, I have a beautiful twelve-unit on Commonwealth Avenue . . .

Category 4: Tenancy Objections

Many prospects will object to the existing type of tenancy or leasing arrangements. Usually these conditions are a matter of poor management and are correctable. You will hear the objection voiced as follows:

"The type of tenant here is unstable."
"I don't like buildings rented without leases."
"There are too many vacancies."
"There are too many leases expiring in three months."

Your reply could be:

Mr. Prospect, the owner admittedly has not given this property the right kind of management. He has had family difficulties and has been out of town a lot in the past year. With proper management, the unstable type of tenant can be replaced with excellent tenants. With proper screening you will get a high grade of tenant. The outstanding location of this solid building lends itself beautifully to a high grade of occupancy. The leases coming due and the apartments which are rented without leases afford you an opportunity to upgrade the caliber of occupant, and to write new leases on very favorable terms. I would suggest that we look at the potential here. I have some projections based on comparable rents in the area.

Category 5: Dollars-and-Cents Objections

Your prospect will quite frequently attack the dollars and cents of the proposed investment. His objections will sound like this:

"The expenses listed are too low."
"The rents are too high."

"The vacancy and repair allowance is too low."

"The return is too low."

"The financing is poor."

In the following chapter, you will see how to adjust all of the figures and consolidate the financial information into an accurate and convincing presentation. At that time, you will learn how to counter such objections, by showing your prospect just what the property will do for him.

Category 6: Personal Likes and Dislikes

This type of objection falls into two main subdivisions, either: (1) there is some characteristic of the property that your prospect dislikes, or (2) there is some characteristic of properties in general that your prospect likes and subject property lacks. His objections will sound like this:

Dislikes

"I don't like electric heat!"

"I don't like one-bedroom apartments."

"These apartments are furnished."

"I won't buy a building with luxury apartments."

"I hate frame buildings."

Likes

"I won't buy a building without air conditioning (or elevators, or incinerator drops, or laundry facilities or whatever)."

"This building is not close to transportation."

"There's no parking."

"There's not enough land."

Your approach to this type of objection must be to show your prospect that, to eliminate all buildings that do not conform exactly to his standards is to limit severely his chances of obtaining his financial objectives. Your reply could be:

Mr. Prospect, if we look only for investments which are close to transportation, we may well overlook an exceptional buy which meets all of your other requirements. Now, this property shows an exceptional return, and in all other respects has what you want. Let me show you what this building will do for you . . .

Category 7: Stalling Objections

Stalling objections are not usually specific as to the property itself, or what it will do for the prospect. Usually they will be used only when your prospect has run out of concrete reasons for not buying here and now.

They usually sound something like this:

"I can't buy it now because I want my friend, the expert, to go over it with me."
"I want to talk it over with my wife."
"I just made an offer on another building."
"I'm going away for two weeks."
"What else can you show me?"
"Don't pressure me."
"I don't have a check."
"There are no funds in my checking account."
"I need time to think it over."
"I won't sign anything without my lawyer."

Your approach to questions in this category must not sound like undue pressure on your part; however, it is essential for you to discover whether the objection is legitimate or merely a manifestation of your prospect's natural sales resistance. Your reply could be:

Fine, Mr. Prospect, I would be happy to meet with you and your expert (wife, lawyer, etc.) to review this fine investment, but I think that we should do it now. Can we call Mr. Expert now?

Expect your prospect to hedge. If you cannot reach the third party at once, set up a time to get together that evening or the following day. Be sure to set a definite time!

Mr. Prospect, we have reviewed dozens of available properties and narrowed them down to this one, which suits your needs better than any of the rest. I don't have anything as good to show you at this time, and I sincerely think that it would be very difficult to find an investment in the future that would be as ideally suited for you as this one.

Any objection of a stalling nature requires that you set a definite time to meet again to commence negotiations on the property. When Mr. Prospect says, "There are no funds in my checking account to make the deposit," you might reply, "Mr. Prospect, is that the only thing that stands in your way to making an offer on this prime investment?" To which he either answers "Yes" or brings out a heretofore hidden objection. If he answers "Yes," you ask him to transfer the funds and meet with you tomorrow.

The stalling objection is often used as a cover-up for a hidden, unexpressed objection. Many times, if you can eliminate the reason for the stall, you will "smoke out" the real unspoken objection and discover that the unspoken objection is easily countered and overcome.

How to Make These Techniques Work for You

Keep in mind that there is no *pat* answer to any objection. The objections we have covered are intended merely as a guide to help you anticipate the type of objections a prospect may raise. You will develop a technique of replying to objections that is most comfortable to you. After you have developed your replies "under fire," sit down and write them out in longhand. Polish them up and spend some time practicing your replies under various conditions with your fellow brokers (or with your spouse) or even out loud in front of a mirror.

A close friend of mine is a fine amateur magician, in addition to being a very astute businessman. When he was younger he used to practice his sleight of hand in front of a mirror for hours to perfect his every move. In a short time he became the best magician within 50 miles. If he and other hobbyists like him can find the time and expend the effort purely for the satisfaction of being tops at their hobbies, then certainly it is worth the effort for you to train yourself to excel in your vocation. A few extra hours of self-training will put many more dollars in your banking account, and additionally earn you the satisfaction of being the best real estate broker around!

Helping the Prospect Make a Decision

Once you have developed confidence in your approach to objections, apply your techniques sincerely to overcome your prospect's fears. This is salesmanship. Your prospect wants to buy—he wants to be convinced to buy. He will be disappointed if you don't make a genuine effort to sell him on the value of the property he is considering. If you are not convinced enough to show him why his fears and objections are unfounded, then why, for heaven's sake, did you submit the property to him in the first place? Remember, too, that there are many other legitimate fears and objections that will be expressed by your potential buyer.

Your job, as broker, is to separate legitimate objections from those expressed only because the prospect wants and needs to be convinced that he is buying the right investment. If the objection is legitimate and unsolvable, bypass the property under consideration and find a building that will suit his requirements (so long as they are reasonable).

If you are going to be a successful income property salesperson, you must never forget that the investor sitting in front of you wants to be sold. He raises the questions in order to hear what your answers are to his objections. It is your job to satisfy him.

How to Present the Plus Features Convincingly

In any property you submit to a prospect, there are certain features that outweigh others. Good salesmanship dictates that you should dwell on the *plus* features of any proposed investment. If you didn't think the property in question had some features to justify your proposal that Mr. Prospect consider it, obviously you would not have submitted the property to begin with.

Don't get into the sloppy habit of assuming that your prospect will recognize all of the good features and understand the benefit he will gain from them. To see an example of good salesmanship, spend a free lunch hour at a new car agency and find out who the top producer is on the sales floor. Ask to see the new Spitfire, and see how he puts you behind the wheel. Watch him point out how the steering wheel will adjust to any comfortable position. He will have you try the adjustable seat. He'll turn on the stereo system so you can hear the music. He'll have you smell the brand new top grain leather. He'll run through every feature of the Spitfire if you let him. Then he'll sit you down at his desk and show you why this car will have an extra high trade-in value. He'll point out that it is built to be maintenance-free. He'll even climb under the car with you to show you the super-duper suspension, which will give you the smoothest, most comfortable ride on the road. He knows that without his stressing these features, he doesn't have a sale. And he knows that he must present them convincingly and enthusiastically. You must too.

Twenty-Five Features to Stress

1. Good location.
2. Sound construction.
3. Good condition.
4. Professional management.
5. High return.
6. Solid leases.
7. Low cash down payment.
8. Swimming pool.
9. Public transportation.
10. Long-term tenants.
11. Parking.
12. Resident superintendent.
13. Laundry facilities.
14. Good financing.
15. Air-conditioning.
16. High occupancy rate.
17. Security deposits.
18. Elevator.
19. Brick construction.
20. Low rents.
21. Long-term owner.
22. View.
23. Incinerators.
24. Town sewage.
25. Covered parking.

Sample Sales Deliveries

Look at how the top-notch salesperson might present some of these features, and stresses why they will benefit the prospect:

Good Location

Mr. Prospect, because this building is in such a fine location, you should suffer very little rental loss. This is a building which any investor would be proud to own. If you should decide to sell in the future, you should have no trouble in selling quickly. This furnishes a safety cushion for you, and any buyer should appreciate the peace of mind this provides.

Sound Construction

Mr. Prospect, because of the solid construction of this fine building, you should have practically no major repairs. This soundproof building will have a very long useful life and a resulting *high resale value.* You will *save money* on repairs you would normally have to make on less solid buildings, and because of the continuing good condition of this property, you will maintain a very stable tenancy. This is a property that any investor would be proud to own.

Good Condition

Mr. Prospect, as you can see, this property is in excellent condition. Because it is spotless, it is a very desirable place to live, and there will be no immediate cash outlay required to put it into rentable condition. The fact that tenant turnover will be kept to a minimum will make your rental income secure and will leave you more time for leisure or other business matters. This is a building which not only should provide a good secure income, but should give you and your family a great deal of personal satisfaction.

Professional Management

Mr. Buyer, because we can arrange professional management for this building, you will be proud to own a clean, well-run income property with very little personal trouble, and with a high quality of tenancy. Because of this, your return will be very stable, your building will be well maintained, and you should suffer very little annoyance or loss due to slipshod management. In short, you will have all of the advantages of real estate ownership without any of the headaches.

You will observe that in the four preceding feature examples, each of the facts or features given is followed by a related benefit. There is no point in bringing up a feature unless it is followed by a benefit or benefits. Remember that the prospect buys benefits, not features. Make it a rule to always explain the benefits of any important feature you point out.

As with your reply to your prospect's questions and objections, you will develop a comfortable presentation for each feature. By all means develop these presentations and *use* them. When you do, you will be ready to move your prospect to action.

CHAPTER 13

Condominium Conversion: An Exciting Wealth-Builder

Condominium conversion can add a profitable dimension to the business of investment property brokerage. Your study of the material in this Guide, together with your own practical experiences, places you in a position to expand your reach into the condominium marketplace—while providing a valuable additional service to your clients.

This chapter will give you a familiarization with the condominium conversion process. It will also give you confidence in the transferability of your present investment brokerage expertise to the condominium conversion field. You will see that the best opportunities have not yet been skimmed off the top, but rather that they lie in the future awaiting your participation.

Condominium Marketing: A Case History

As far as we can tell, our firm handled the marketing of the first major condominium conversion (over 100 units) in the country. In the late 1960s, we were retained to market a lovely oceanside apartment complex of 114 units, known as Glover Landing, in Marblehead, Massachusetts. The profits from that project were staggering, and we were off on a cloud of euphoria. Following that experience, we have involved ourselves in the conversion and marketing of literally thousands of apartment units, ranging from high-rises to townhouses to suburban garden-type apartment complexes.

In the early years, we concentrated heavily on luxury-type units, but we have more recently found that "bread and butter" suburban garden-type apartment complexes with rather ordinary features have filled a big void in the market, caused by the lack of affordability of newly constructed condominiums and housing in general.

One of the procedures with which we have had great success is to arrange a tax-deferred exchange for the owner of a property who is interested in conversion to condominiums. On several occasions, we have arranged for the owner to exchange that property for a commercial or net leased property, and then purchased the conversion property from the owner of the commercial property—thus completing a two-way exchange with a cash-out. By saving the owner of the conversion property significant amounts of tax dollars, we are generally able to acquire the conversion property on relatively favorable terms. One of our more complex transactions involved the exchange of a Boston area high-rise for 31 net leased properties located in seven states, at a tax saving of approximately $1.5 million to the owner. The owner even smiled when he paid us our fee, which was well into six figures.

In the course of our involvement in the condominium marketing process, we have worked for many major developers and institutions. We have had the good fortune to work with such giants as the Mellon Bank, Royal Bank of Canada, Bank of New York, and many other institutions. In addition, one of the greatest satisfactions we've had is in traveling to other parts of the country and assisting real estate brokers to negotiate marketing contracts with owners who want to convert, and in setting up marketing organizations and procedures. Quite frequently, this has been accomplished with little or no cost to the real estate brokers—as the cost has been absorbed by the owner who wished to convert.

In addition to acting as marketing agent, we have on many occasions purchased properties and acted both as principal in the ownership of the property, and as marketing agent for the conversion. Many of these acquisitions have been done in conjunction with an institution such as a service corporation's subsidiary, or a lending institution.

Condominium Conversion is a Liquidation Decision

You would probably say that your primary function as an investment broker is to find a ready, willing, and able buyer for a property owner who has made a realistic liquidation decision. You're usually dealing with one seller and with one buyer. You negotiate and close one transaction. You collect one commission. Simple enough.

Now, what is different with condominium conversion? You still deal with one owner who has made a liquidation decision; but in this case, you are not dealing with a single buyer, but with 10, 50, or a 100 different buyers. More work, more time, more planning, more risk? Yes. One commission? No. You may be placing yourself in the advantageous position of collecting 10, 50, or 100 separate commissions! In addition, you may be collecting consulting and management fees.

Condominium Conversion Can Lead to Big Bulk Sales

Throughout this chapter, you will notice that the condominium conversion process has been approached generally through the eyes of the converter or the marketing agent for the individual condominium sales. So all of the information will be extremely helpful to you in analyzing existing apartment houses that are offered for sale for submission to a potential condominium converter.

The presentation process is quite similar to that which will be made to an *invest and hold* buyer. The operating statement will be similar in many respects to that presented in Chapter 6. However, the data analysis worksheet loses its significance when submitted to a condominium converter. More important than after-tax cash flows are the salable square-foot figures for the units being sold, along with comparable sales data encompassing recent sales for units that are similar to those being offered. Usually, these comparable sales are expressed in terms of square-foot pricing. Knowing the square footage of the property being offered, then, will give you a good indication of the potential gross sellout of the property you are brokering.

The brokerage of existing apartment buildings to converters is important business. And as an income property broker, you certainly should do everything you can to add this specialty to your repertoire.

For simplicity we have omitted income tax issues from the following discussion of profits. Always be sure to consult with a tax professional in connection with any contemplated conversions.

The Profits of Condominium Conversion

Why will many owners who are seeking to liquidate their properties consider condominium conversion? Take the following example:

Let's assume your client owns a well located and maintained, free and clear 40-unit apartment building. The building is worth $2,000,000. In other words, you could sell this building as is for your client for $2,000,000. You and your client presume from your experiences in the business that the building has conversion potential, and that an average unit could be sold for around $80,000. On the surface, the numbers look like this:

Gross Value as Condominiums	$3,200,000 (40 units × $80,000)
Gross Value as Apartments	–2,000,000
Gross Value Increase from Conversion	$1,200,000

Estimating Conversion Costs

Gross profit is *not* net profit. In selling an apartment building "as is," you can rely on previous experience. You can tell the owner with some degree of assurance that if his two million-dollar building is sold for that amount, the transaction costs (legal, escrow, commissions, etc.) would amount, to say, 7% or $140,000—leaving a net of $1,860,000.

Condominium conversion is much more complicated than a direct "as is" sale. Some capital improvements to the building will probably be necessary. Architects, engineers, and contractors must be consulted and employed. And since there will be many more people involved, each will be anxious to take at least a nibble from the extra $1,200,000.

You may already have some experience in estimating conversion costs. However, it may be beneficial to investigate previous successful conversions in your local area, and talk specifics with the principals involved.

In the following example, let's take 25% of gross sell out as a "ballpark" estimate of those costs. You must do your own research on a local level—remembering Murphy's Law: "If anything can go wrong, it probably will."

Gross Value as Condominiums	$3,200,000
Conversion Cost Rule of Thumb	× .25
Conversion Costs	$ 800,000

At this point, you may feel that I'm swinging between saying that condominium conversion is the best thing since sliced bread, and saying that it is the biggest pain in the neck you can imagine! Well, you're right. I'm showing you how to see the profits, but I want you to understand the risks.

Now, let's get back to profits. The $800,000 estimated for conversion costs may seem high, but remember that many conversion cost expenses are payable only on the sale of the individual units. The profit potential for the conversion of the example building more realistically becomes:

Increased Gross Value from Conversion	$1,200,000
Cost of Conversion	− 800,000
Net Increased Profit from Conversion	$ 400,000

Again, $400,000 net for a conversion liquidation over an "as is" liquidation certainly appears to be worth the effort. Your client will still probably insist, "Sure, let's go ahead. Not tomorrow; let's start right now. I'm leaving it all in your hands, Mr. Broker, just call me when the checks are printed. Thanks a lot; you're great!"

What's the fatal flaw in the figuring that we've just done? As you saw in Chapter 5 on *How to Price Income Property to Sell Quickly,* any broker who wishes to inflate property values can have his listing book overflowing. But how much of his time is being spent on fruitless effort?

With condominium conversion, you can forget everything you ever learned in grade school about fractions. The concept behind conversion is that the parts will always add up to more than the whole. Why shouldn't there be excitement for this process if you can look at any building on paper, fractionalize it, and give it a new enhanced value?

Understanding the Time Commitment

A real concern that you and your client must consider in determining whether the potential profits for either of you are justified is the time commitment. Consider how much time elapsed between the taking of a solid apartment building listing and the final passing of papers. It may have been two, four, or six months. You listed, advertised, showed, negotiated, sold, closed, and collected. You earned your commission and are now ready to move on to another exciting project. The seller has his profit too, and is ready to reinvest. Oh, how simple this option may look. But it's easy to make a mistake and become involved in the wrong conversion attempt.

In a carefully considered and conceived conversion attempt, two to six months may be required just for the exploratory and planning phases. The total conversion time for the best projects with a minimum of hitches may be 12 to 24 months. Yes, your client may be willing to commit this amount of time for $400,000 in additional profit. And you also may be willing to commit this amount of time as you eye a good share of the $800,000 in conversion costs. But everything hinges on converting the right property in the right market and at the right time.

The Mini-Checklist for Suitability

The world of real estate is waiting to be converted. The Mini-Checklist for Suitability used at Peckham Boston is not by any means a substitute for an in-depth feasibility study. It is a tool to help eliminate from consideration properties whose conversion time has not arrived yet. It lets you pick the winners for yourself and your clients. Remember that there usually is no perfect score.

The Checklist presumes a knowledge of your local market in a general real estate sense and the current position of condominiums within the local market. If you currently lack this expertise, the Checklist can be used as a guide to the type of knowledge you must acquire before you venture a step further into the condominium conversion field.

MINI-CHECKLIST FOR SUITABILITY

	Yes	No
1. Will 30 percent or more of the present tenants purchase?	☐	☐
2. Is the property located in a high-occupancy area?	☐	☐
3. Is the property located in an area that lends itself to individual ownership?	☐	☐
4. Is there high population influx?	☐	☐
5. Are the existing units of adequate size and equipped with sufficient amenities to warrant individual ownership?	☐	☐
6. Is the property located within a reasonable distance of the probable market?	☐	☐
7. Can the units be absorbed into the market in a reasonable period of time?	☐	☐

8. Can the units be priced competitively? ☐ ☐
9. Will the unit prices be less than the going prices of single-family houses in the area? ☐ ☐
10. Will the condominium offer a better value to the purchaser than a rental unit would? ☐ ☐
11. Is there a limited supply of new houses and condos on the market? ☐ ☐
12. Are resales in the area selling at top prices and moving expeditiously? ☐ ☐
13. Will at least 50 percent of the leases expire within six months? ☐ ☐
14. Is the property convenient to transportation? ☐ ☐
15. Do local and state laws support conversion? ☐ ☐
16. Is the property located near employment and shopping areas? ☐ ☐
17. Is there community support for conversion? ☐ ☐
18. Is the cost of construction of new homes and condominiums in the area high? ☐ ☐
19. Is interim financing available? ☐ ☐
20. Are end loans for buyers available at competitive rates? ☐ ☐

How to Evaluate a Property's Suitability for Conversion

A property suitable for conversion will run a fairly straight line down the *Yes* column of this checklist. Looking at each question should give you and your client a feeling for the relative strength of the particular property when evaluated against current offerings, local market conditions, and general economic conditions.

1. Will 30 percent or more of the present tenants purchase? As stated, time is of the essence in any conversion attempt. A property with a high tenant purchase ratio should "sell out" more quickly than a building where few tenants are willing (or able) to make the financial commitment to buy their units.

The present tenants live in the building and they know the building. They know if the heat and the air conditioning work. They know if the pipes rattle or leak. They know the area around the building. Most tenants probably would buy if the building is sound and the cash requirement is low. Additionally, price concessions are often made to present to tenants as an inducement to purchase. Further, in some instances, it may actually be cheaper to own than to rent. For these reasons, a majority of tenants should at the very least be willing to listen to a conversion plan before they reject the idea outright.

You, on the other hand, probably do not know the building as well as either the tenants or the owner. If an owner looks at this first question and says, "No, I don't think any of those people will buy. They haven't got any money, and they're always complaining," this should be a red flag warning sign to you. You certainly don't want to be the new fall guy who has to listen to all the complaints for the next year or two.

2. Is the property located in a high-occupancy area? Buyers will be persuaded to purchase their units or other units in the building if leasing comparable space in different buildings is not a real possibility. Often some areas of the country experience a close to zero-vacancy situation. The term *zero vacancy* applies to a market with a vacancy rate below 5 percent, since the remaining 5 percent of units are only vacant due to turnover or rehabilitation. The tighter the rental market, the stronger the conversion market.

3. Is the property located in an area that lends itself to individual ownership? As already mentioned, condominium conversion involves taking certain risks. If the conversion attempt can be characterized as bold, innovative, or creative, be aware of the additional risk factor. If the building in question is to be the first conversion in a particular area, there is extra risk involved since you will be setting, rather than relying on, precedent. If the building is a warehouse in an industrial area that your client wishes to convert to residential use, fine; just be sure that you can look beyond the numbers to the time and risks involved.

4. Is there high population influx? This question asks you to consider the strength of the real estate market in general. If there is a general housing shortage and subsequent demand, this should translate to a strong condominium market.

5. Are the existing units of adequate size and equipped with sufficient amenities to warrant individual ownership? Most apartments are leased on a yearly basis. This year-to-year tenancy gives occupants a great deal of flexibility in that if they make a lifestyle change, they can fairly easily change their rental apartments to accommodate it.

The ownership of a condominium involves a more permanent commitment to living space. A person contemplating change within a year or two will ordinarily decide to remain a renter, rather than to buy a unit—unless you can show them short-term profit potential.

The unit size with the most consumer appeal is the two-bedroom unit. The two-bedroom unit gives the single person a guest room or an office. It gives the young married couple a children's room. It gives two unmarried people the opportunity to buy and share expenses.

Larger one-bedroom apartments may appeal to the cost-conscious younger or older buyers. Three-bedroom units may require installation of a second full or half bath to be marketable. Buildings with a high percentage of studio apartments, or units larger than three bedrooms, may require special marketing techniques. For instance, in many conversions, a four-bedroom unit would be shown as a two-bedroom with a den and dining room, or as a two-bedroom with a guest room and library. The floor plan of the unit wouldn't change; but the marketing focus might be altered to attract more affluent buyers, rather than families with several children.

6. Is the property located within a reasonable distance of the probable market? The main appeal of the condominium is often in urban and other highly populated suburban areas. The greatest advertising campaign in the world may not spur the general market to drive, say, 50 miles. You certainly wouldn't want to be the sales agent who's alone day after day at the "Boondocks Swingin' Singles Condo."

7. Can the units be absorbed into the market in a reasonable period of time? Twelve months to two years is an average period of time for a conversion project. Some conversions have been accomplished in just a few months, and some have taken much longer. Your success may rely heavily upon your ability to study, understand, and predict such trends. If there are already a number of conversion projects struggling, you must realistically adjust your strategy.

8. Can the units be priced competitively? Again, you must be sensitive to the existing market and advise your client accordingly. As noted earlier in the Guide, it makes little sense to list an overpriced building. And it makes equally little sense to have any part in marketing overpriced condominiums.

9. Will the unit prices be less than the going prices of single-family houses in the area? A majority of recent studies have shown that while the condominium has gained buyer acceptance, in most areas, the single-family house is still the heavy favorite. People will choose condominiums over single-family houses either because they offer more amenities or convenience, or because they are more affordable. The condominium project under consideration must be a better dollar-for-dollar investment than the single-family house—from the buyer's perspective.

If there is a surplus of moderately priced single-family housing on the local market, any condominium conversion attempt is going to meet stiff competition. It is good news for converters when the economics of future residential development do not appear to lie with the single-family detached house.

10. Will the condominium offer a better value to the purchaser than a rental unit would? It is good when the financial future for the renter is not bright if there is a shortage of quality affordable rental housing. The ownership of a condominium unit does give buyer protection against escalating rents. A renter will always be subject to the whims of both owners and the marketplace. A condominium purchase, on the other hand, gives a former renter much greater control over future housing expenses, especially if fixed-rate financing is made available.

When a buyer is able to look at fixed-rate financing, coupled with the additional benefits of tax deductions, interest deductions, appreciation and the prestige of ownership, the logic should prevail that a rental apartment becomes a less attractive choice. In other words, an owner should be willing to spend more per month than a renter for comparable space, since ownership includes significant additional benefits.

11. Is there a limited supply of new houses and condos on the market? A buyer will choose an older property, house or condo, over a new house or condo because the older property offers one or more of the following: a better location, a lower price, superior construction, character, or more living space for the dollar. There is no competition between old and new, the older or converted property must offer the buyer something more for his housing investment.

12. Are resales in the area selling at top prices and moving expeditiously? A strong buyer demand market should signify a strong condo conversion market. If there is little general real estate activity, the conversion may have to wait for the market to recover.

If your brokerage business to date has been strictly investment-oriented, you will want to acquire additional expertise to be a successful condominium conversion agent. You must have experience in residential real estate sales or, at least, have access to someone who has this residential experience. You can't guess or assume you know the answer to many of the specialized residential questions. Answers must be derived from these efforts of thorough research—though some may be as close as several phone calls.

13. Will at least 50 percent of the leases expire within six months? Tenants who are not planning to purchase units in the converted building are normally worried. They are worried about their future housing plans. They are not worried about your plans or problems. They only recognize the fact that the owner is disrupting their living arrangement. Unless you are prepared to assume the burdensome task of relocation, expect little cooperation from non-buying present tenants.

To fall within the total conversion time frame, assume that you may not have access to a majority of the units for at least twelve months. Condominium conversion is like going to the dentist: You expect trouble, and if nothing happens, you feel great. However, be realistic. Some tenants may not be prepared to move out on the day their leases expire, and may even procrastinate for months. Your recourse is legal. The courts in conversion attempts often tend to sympathize with the disrupted tenants and allow liberal amounts of relocation time. A safe course would be allow at least two months after a lease expiration date before promising a prospective buyer a specific unit.

One strategy to mention now is the possibility of buying a tenant out of a lease. A lease has value both to you and the tenant. It is not beyond the realm of possibility that you may be able to free a unit by reaching a cash settlement with a tenant to vacate, especially if you have cash buyers waiting in the wings.

14. Is the property convenient to transportation? Many buyers choose the condominium living alternative to rid themselves of the ordinary hassles of life, such as home maintenance tasks. Many condominium owners have found it possible to enjoy life without complete dependence on the automobile. If your project is convenient to public transportation, you have an enticing marketing incentive appealing to many prospective buyers.

15. Do local and state laws support conversion? The "as is" apartment building is usually taxed once. One owner pays one tax bill. After the conversion, there may be 50, 100, or 200 owners who will each receive and pay a property tax bill. The "as is" property tax bill is not simply prorated among the new building owners. The paper value of the building has increased—perhaps substantially—through conversion, and it is this new larger appraisal figure that will be prorated among unit owners. In simple terms, government gains additional tax revenue through condominium conversion. (It also may be argued that government gains more permanent and civically responsible citizens through individual property ownership.)

Although, from a fiscal standpoint, local governments should enthusiastically support condominium conversions, support—for political reasons—may be lackluster, or even nonexistent. There may be a local history of condominium conversion that precedes your efforts—a history that may be good or bad. As a result of this history, tenant protective laws may have been enacted. You must, of course, be aware of any and all laws relative to condominium conversion, and how these regulations may impact on your project.

16. Is the property located near employment and shopping areas? You should be able to answer this question from your information obtained on the transportation question. If unit owners have the option of walking to work or shopping, you have a superior location. Older buildings often offer this alternative.

17. Is there community support for conversion? A successful conversion attempt in an area will quickly breed imitators. As soon as one building "goes condo," tenants in neighboring buildings will hope or fear that they are next. Whether they hope or fear for the conversion of their own building will determine whether they support or interfere in the conversion of your client's building.

Take this example: You dutifully fill out all of the appropriate forms for your client's conversion, and you receive a date to appear before the approval board. To your mind, it's all a formality. You are professionally organized, and you, your client, and a well paid attorney are confident. Only a few tenants have expressed strong opposition to the conversion. These few tenants, if they show up at all, should prove little challenge to you.

How wrong you can be! These few tenants have been busy organizing while you and your client have been mapping a marketing strategy. They have formed a "Tenants Against Conversion" association, and are linked to 25 other similar organizations statewide. They have also written and widely distributed their newsletter called "Save Our Homes." You have a lawyer. They have a team of "socially conscious" lawyers. It is not easy for you to read your well written and documented speech over a chorus of hundreds, screaming and crying to the approval board, "Please don't let these outsiders drive us from our homes into the streets!"

The situation above is a worst-case scenario, but it can happen. Just remember the old Boy Scout motto, "Be Prepared." The concerns of all existing tenants, whether they are major or minor, justified or unjustified, must be addressed. One tenant who feels that he or she has been treated with indifference can make a mountain out of a molehill. So, during your planning stage, you must allocate sufficient time to meet with existing tenants individually. By helping them, you may avoid later grief. This will be time well spent. One tenant can hold up a conversion for months. And in condominium conversion, time is of the essence.

If you have the support of the existing tenants in a conversion attempt, you should have community support. If you have one or more tenants fighting your conversion, you may be arousing a community's strong negative reaction.

18. Is the cost of construction of new homes and condominiums in the area high? This is another research question. The answer may seem obvious; but make a few calls and verify your assumption. You may be on safe ground if your converted units are low- or medium-priced. However, you may be competing against new construction if your units are higher priced.

19. Is interim financing available? Some lenders have progressive lending policies, while others treat any mortgage request for multi-unit buildings as speculative. If you're an experienced investment broker, you already know the area lenders that are willing to listen to reasonable mortgaging requests for income properties. Although they may be few in number, these lenders are probably your best bet when it comes time to talk about interim and end-loan financing for your client's conversion.

The time to talk about financing is from the date of the project's inception. Once you have your proposal on paper, solicit the advice and support of the lenders. A lender can be considered a partner in the project and, as such, involved in all decisions and revisions regarding the master conversion plan. Let the lenders feel informed and involved. They want to believe in you. They want to lend you money for this project. Mortgage money of all types is always available to the broker willing to put in the time to find it.

20. Are end loans for buyers available at competitive rates? Mortgage money is almost always available. The question is at what rate and on what terms. During some years, mortgage money demand is slack when rates approach higher levels. Demand rebounds, however, when rates fall to more comfortable levels. During the time frame of your conversion, interest rates will probably fluctuate and your marketing strategy must be flexible enough to adapt to changing rates. If interest rates for residential loans rise significantly you must react. You may react by lowering the price of the units, or you may offer an extra amenity, or you may "buy down" the rate to a lower level.

Once you have committed yourself and your firm to a conversion, you should be prepared to adjust and readjust to changing market conditions. You can only pity the poor broker and client who, when times get tough, sit twiddling their thumbs while philosophizing about the restrictive monetary practices of the Federal Reserve Board. Be prepared to take the immediate steps necessary to bring buyers in to see your project, regardless of the prevailing economic conditions. Every month, every day, between inception and completion of a condominium project, costs money.

Establishing a Conversion Team

A primary objective of any investment broker involved in condominium conversion is to analyze the conversion potential of a given building. As already mentioned, get this part right, and the rest is relatively easy. The Mini-Checklist got you started in the right direction. Picking the right projects is of such importance to your firm, your client, and yourself, that it would be foolish to consider acting independently. But, as an investment property broker—even if you are a one-person shop—you can't act completely independently. You are an adviser who in turn needs many advisers.

In answering the Mini-Checklist questions, you relied first upon your own experiences, knowledge, and instincts. You also had the input of your client. Then, if there was any doubt, you had:

- Other brokers, if any, in your firm.
- Other clients who may have condo experience.
- Other consulting professionals, such as your attorney, banker, accountant, architect, and engineer.
- Other investment firms with whom you have a cooperative understanding.
- Other members of trade groups to which you or your firm may belong.

All of the above people may become, at some point, part of your condominium conversion team. Therefore, it is often beneficial to think of yourself not as an individual working alone, but rather as the leader of an organized team.

Your condominium conversion team can be either formally or informally organized. With a formal team, each person is aware of being a part of the team and having a formal role in the decision-making process. All will have been given specific responsibilities and will receive commensurate compensation. They may be salaried employees. They may be paid a fee for their services. Or they may be working for a percentage of the commission. A formally organized team will probably hold regularly scheduled reporting and brainstorming meetings.

With an informal conversion team, only you are aware of the organizational structure. Everyone else is consulted only as needed, and compensation, if any, is on a fee-per-service basis.

There are advantages and disadvantages to using either a formal or an informal structural format for your conversion team. The main point is that *you* know the plan to be implemented, and that you have ready access to personnel capable of providing information and solving problems.

The following Condominium Conversion Support Team chart is provided to give you a general idea of the type of support personnel that may be utilized at various points in the conversion process. You may fill out the chart yourself, or seek recommendations from others; for example, who is a reliable electrical contractor? The time to organize your team, in any event, is now—before questions or problems arise. If you don't know any reliable electricians, you can pick up the phone and get recommendations, rather than wait for a "lights out" emergency.

This chart is not static, but rather it evolves with time and circumstance. You will make changes as necessary, as you are the team leader.

THE CONDOMINIUM CONVERSION SUPPORT TEAM

Attorney _____   Telephone Number _____
Accountant _____   Telephone Number _____
Banker _____   Telephone Number _____
Property Manager _____   Telephone Number _____
Architect _____   Telephone Number _____
Insurance Agent _____   Telephone Number _____
Engineer _____   Telephone Number _____
Carpenter _____   Telephone Number _____
Painter _____   Telephone Number _____
Landscaper _____   Telephone Number _____
Electrician _____   Telephone Number _____
Handyman _____   Telephone Number _____
Plasterer _____   Telephone Number _____
Exterminator _____   Telephone Number _____
Plumber _____   Telephone Number _____
HVAC Contractor _____   Telephone Number _____
Copywriter _____   Telephone Number _____
Sales Manager _____   Telephone Number _____
Advertising Agency _____   Telephone Number _____
_____   Telephone Number _____
_____   Telephone Number _____

Remember: Before you dare venture forth proclaiming your expertise as a condominium conversion specialist, you must:

1. Recognize which buildings are convertible given numerous variables. (Use the Mini-Checklist to help.)
2. Have access to personnel to get the job done professionally. (Use the Condominium Conversion Support Team chart for this purpose.)

The Condominium Conversion Process

The condominium conversion process can be divided into three distinct and separate phases:

1. The mini-feasibility phase,
2. The pre-marketing phase, and
3. The marketing phase.

Assuming you have completed and have familiarized yourself with the Mini-Checklist and the Condominium Conversion Support Team chart, you shouldn't have any trouble moving through the various steps of each phase.

In marketing the "as is" building for investment, rather than conversion, you move through a series of steps: you list, advertise, show, negotiate, sell, close, and collect. If you have a good listing, the rest is easy—almost mechanical.

In converting and marketing condominiums, you also move through a series of steps—and if you have a good listing, the rest is also easy. The steps are:

Mini-Feasibility Phase

_____ Will the property yield a higher net price as condominiums as opposed to an outright sale?

_____ What will the costs of marketing be (including advertising, promotion, rent loss, and sales commissions)?

_____ Can suitable financing be obtained?

_____ Do existing leases or state laws preclude delivering possession for an extended period of time?

Pre-Marketing Phase

Assuming that your mini-feasibility indicates that you should proceed, then these steps should be followed:

_____ Retain competent legal assistance to draft the necessary legal documents, including the master deed, individual deeds, purchase and sale agreements, and the condominium bylaws.

_____ Develop a marketing plan to include an advertising and promotion budget; the training of a sales force; the setting up of a sales office and model apartments; and the preparation of the sales brochures and auxiliary sales promotion literature.

_____ Conduct a formal appraisal and feasibility study. This study should include, at a minimum, the value of the property—both as an apartment property and as a completed condominium project. It should also indicate the estimated market value of each condominium unit, and the probable absorption rate of these units into the market.

_____ Arrange interim and permanent financing commitments.

Marketing Phase

Once the pre-marketing phase is completed, you are ready to enter the final and most satisfying phase, since you begin to enjoy the major financial rewards of your labor. The following checklist, although brief, gives a useful guideline to the steps involved.

_____ Commence marketing. You or your staff should be prepared to provide prospective purchasers with cost estimates indicating probable out-of-pocket costs of ownership, along with estimated tax savings and equity buildup due to mortgage and principal reduction and anticipated growth.

_____ Once a sufficient number of binding contracts to purchase have been executed, dedicate the condominium, deed out the initial units, and proceed with the marketing of the remaining units.

The name of the game in condominium conversion is simply to match yourself with the right property and with the right owner. Remember, you'll be living with both for a long time. If you make the right match, your general investment broker-age experience will carry you through smoothly, step by step to significant rewards.

The Future of Condominium Conversion

It never ceases to amaze me when people in our business speak of condominium conversion in the past tense. They seem to regard condominium conversion as a passing fad, as if it were a phenomenon like the hula-hoop or the pet rock. I wish I had a dollar for every time I've heard, "Come on, Jack, all the best proper-ties have already been converted." Then, these people go on to tell me about the great opportunities in modular stacked housing, life-care centers, or underwater farming.

Yes, I agree that there are many exciting investment opportunities outside con-dominium conversion. I will even agree that some of the cream has already been skimmed off the top—some of the easy buildings have already been converted.

So, where does that leave us? It leaves us with tens, maybe hundreds of thou-sands of apartment buildings which haven't been converted. It leaves us with mil-lions of first-time buyers who are frustrated by the high costs of ownership but who still desperately want a piece of the American dream. We have a product and we have a market. And, we're still just scratching the surface if we limit our thinking to only residential real estate.

Every store block, shopping center, office building, professional building, and industrial park is convertible. Young buyers want a shot at owning a home, and young investors want a shot at owning quality investment real estate. If they can't buy a whole apartment building, we'll sell them a unit or two. If they can't buy a whole group of stores, we'll sell them one or two stores. Conversion, fractionaliza-tion, makes real estate affordable.

Some will argue that investment property prices are rising to the point that the day of the individual investor is over. In the future, they say, our clientele will be limited to pension fund managers and insurance company executives. But I think to accept this logic is to make a big mistake. I think that the future condominium con-version of residential, commercial, and industrial real estate will open up a whole new market for individual investors.

How to Handle Commercial Condominiums

Many of the same caveats apply to the conversion of non-residential properties as apply to the conversion of residential properties. You must pick the right property to work with, and the right owner to work for. If you can do that, the job is relatively easy. If you have had experience and gained expertise in marketing commercial properties "as is," you can adapt these skills to marketing commercial condominiums. Here's a brief illustration of how a transaction might evolve:

Example: You are approached by an owner who wishes to convert an 8-store strip center into commercial condominiums. Your research of the market and of this particular property lead you to an estimated "as is" sale's value of $1,600,000. The numbers:

Gross Value as Condominiums	$2,400,000
Gross Value "as is"	−1,600,000
Gross Profit from Conversion	$800,000

Again, we must figure a conversion cost factor to arrive at a net figure. Using 20 percent, yields—

Gross Value as Condominiums	$2,400,000
Estimated Conversion Cost Factor	× .20
Conversion Cost	$ 480,000

The profit potential for the conversion of this building becomes—

Gross Increased Profit from Conversion	$800,000
Estimated Conversion Cost Factor	−480,000
Conversion Cost	$320,000

At first blush this net profit from conversion may not appear to justify the time and risk involved. But suppose that, in contacting the existing merchants, you find that all but one would be interested in purchasing its space. Now the conversion takes on a new look, and all that will be left for you and the owner to do is to find either another merchant to buy the one space available, or one investor to buy and lease the one space available. This deal can be a quick in-and-out transaction with additional profits both to you and the owner.

Expanding the Condominium Concept

There are residential buildings to divide and sell. They can be two units, or two thousand units. Every manner, shape, and form of commercial, office, and industrial building is available to divide and sell. But don't rest yet. Instead, expand your thinking on the total condominium fractionalization concept.

Let's say you are hired to convert an apartment building. The building and the owner pass your qualification tests. It looks like a nice, clean, simple transaction. You sell the individual units. But are there other options? You could sell the units, sell enclosed garage spaces, sell outside parking spaces, sell mini-warehouse bins in the basement, sell workshop space in the basement, and sell cabanas by the pool. You could sell the land under the building using a ground sale-leaseback. By expanding the condominium concept, you could turn one condominium project into six-plus condominium projects. Whether the end result of all this dicing is justifiable is what your job is all about.

When Not to Advise Conversion

I have tried to show you the many available opportunities in the field of condominium conversion. There are many possibilities, and you should research them carefully before you commit yourself to any owner or any property. As previously mentioned, if the property doesn't pass the Mini-Checklist or the Mini-Feasibility Phase, or if you can't see yourself working with this owner for the duration of the conversion, say, "No, thank you." If you believe in the condominium concept, you can sell your belief to many owners and buyers; and you'll never want for the next chance.

Cyberspace Marketing Tips

Search Terms. The Internet is a fertile ground for gathering additional information to inform and support condominium conversion efforts. For example, a word search on the Internet, at this writing, on the following subjects, yields the following volume of resources:

"condominium conversion"	47,200
"condominium conversion information"	25

"condominium conversion checklist"	11
"condominium conversion potential"	31
"condominium conversion financing"	14

Comparable Sales. The Internet can be very helpful in researching the information you need to document the feasibility of the project. A search for the following terms at this writing yields the following volume of sales price resources:

"home sales price information"	766
"condominium for sale"	21,000
"condominium for sale" + Boston	830
"condominium for sale" + Chicago	3590
"condominium for sale" + Memphis	736

Researching Your Conversion Team. One of many search engines may be used to round out your conversion team. For example a word search on the Internet, at this writing, on the following subject, yields the following volume of resources:

"condominium lawyers"	258

CHAPTER 14

How to Sell Like a Giant Using Cyberspace Tools

There is significant power for you when you combine the good solid basics in the other chapters of this Guide with the powerful Internet and technology tools and techniques available today. We will review these in this chapter.

A Vision for Technology's Impact on Real Estate

Back in 1963 when servers were people who delivered your order in a restaurant, and about five years before I wrote the original first edition of this Guide, I founded my first company, Data Realty Corporation. We quickly became the dominant income property brokerage force in New England with 20 agents doing nothing but listing and selling various types of income properties. In addition to wheeling around town with my first car phone—a huge Motorola that took up half the trunk and a big chunk of space in front of the dashboard—I used an old IBM keypunch and sorter and the funny looking cards with holes punched in them to match buyers with sellers.

In 1968, I described my vision for a future commercial broker who would use all-in-one "videophones" for communicating with clients, sending documents, and viewing three-dimensional presentations in an article I wrote titled "The Computer—A Powerful Aid for Selling Income Property," published by what was then the commercial division of the National Association of Realtors® (now The CCIM Institute).

I described the office of the future as follows:

Mr. Broker then pushes the buttons on his videophone. This links him directly to the central computer, which takes five seconds to scan all the properties available in the location desired. A printed sheet then comes out of the side of the phone with the names of four properties that fit his needs. Each of these properties is analyzed as to how it will affect Mr. Investor's tax and growth picture.

By pushing a separate button on the phone, Mr. Broker then activates a videotape which projects over a small screen next to the phone. The investor is able to sit in the comfort of the Realtor's office and view the exterior, lobby, sample rental units, boiler room and neighborhood of the four properties already selected and analyzed. If he wants to fly out and see the property in person, the instrument on Mr. Broker's desk can even make his reservations and print the airline tickets on the spot!

—John M. Peckham, III "The Computer—A Powerful Aid for Selling Income Property" CID Letter, May 1968

The only thing I missed was selecting the seat on the flight and printing the boarding pass! I continued: "Technology is ready for us—But are we ready for it? The resounding answer is no."

Today the answer would be—absolutely—for those who embrace it. And for those who don't? Get out of the way because today we are ready and we're rockin' and rollin'!

Tech Tools Evolving

Since then commercial real estate has evolved into an industry that thrives on the capabilities technology has to offer. Today, commercial real estate professionals are using technology to lower expenses, trim hours from their workdays, and spend more time with clients and run circles around the Stone Age competition.

And the tools we have today actually level the playing field in a meaningful way, allowing those who use them (even newcomers) to gain a significant competitive advantage. Technology can now give you the power to eliminate significant overhead, reach out to a much broader market, and provide exceptional client service. The predictions I made in 1968 weren't voodoo as some suggested then. The implications of technology today are simply the precursor of what's to come. Today, we are standing at a door marked awesome, and the rate of change is so rapid that it would be hard for anyone (including me) to foresee the complete extent of the incredible changes that will take place over the next few years.

An Eye Opening Experience

Many years ago, when the Internet was brand new to the industry, I listed a 13,000-square-foot retail property located in New Bedford, Massachusetts, net leased on a long-term basis to Walgreen's and the National Bank of Fairhaven.

I posted the property on the CCIM listserv (more on listservs later in this chapter), which at the time was in its infancy and only had 92 brokers subscribed. Within three hours I had eight responses from brokers who had potential buyers for the property. Three days later, after several e-mails and faxes, one of the buyers flew up from Florida to view the property and signed a contract. The selling price: $2.6 million.

I whistled and muttered something like, "Wow, this is powerful stuff!" It was quickly obvious that e-mail marketing would offer a greatly expanded market and incredible speed. With listservs, I could contact a much larger pool of buyers, and the speed with which negotiations could be conducted shrunk to hours rather than weeks.

A Marketing Plan Evolves

Shortly after that, I conducted the first annual "Selling in CyberSpace" 6-hour seminar at the Federal Reserve Bank in Boston. A few days after the presentation two young brokers called me and asked my advice.

They had an appointment coming up to convince the owner of a very expensive home on Cape Cod to list with them instead of the owner's other two choices: the largest agency on the Cape and a large international firm.

They had other obstacles too. Their firm was brand new. Their office was in Brighton, Massachusetts—over 80 miles from the property—and they looked like teenaged geeks!

They excitedly alternated their comments and questions. "We have a great idea that we think will set us apart from these two big firms. After listening to you the other day, we would like to take some of your ideas and incorporate them into a presentation that we can use to convince the owner to give us the listing."

They told me that they were working on a presentation for the owner that would incorporate all of the powerful ways they could promote the sale of his property using the new cyberspace tools that had recently become available to the industry.

I encouraged them to give it a shot and told them that the worst they could do was learn some lessons in salesmanship.

About a week later they called and told me that they "beat out the big rascals and got the exclusive listing." I was the one who learned a lesson in salesmanship and began to quantify the materials I taught in that seminar into a marketing plan and presentation that could be used to:

1. Market income properties and needs in cyberspace, and
2. Convince sellers (and buyers) to use our services.

Because technology changes so rapidly, what follows here is today's version of this ever-evolving plan. You will want to update and customize it to fit your business and your style. Hopefully these materials will give you a solid base.

Creating Your Marketing Campaign in Cyberspace

My philosophy for marketing in cyberspace is three fold:

1. I will cooperate with any licensed broker in the world to get my sellers property sold at the best price possible.
2. I know that by using the Internet I can quickly and inexpensively reach out to thousands (or tens of thousands) of investors and other brokers who represent investors.
3. I know that a good number of those multitudes I can reach quickly either are a current buyer for my offering or, if a broker, have a buyer who has a customer who currently wants what I have.

There are two basic components you will use to build an effective online marketing campaign—a place for buyers and sellers to go and a process to get them to go there! They are the World Wide Web and e-mail.

Using the World Wide Web to Market Your Property Listings

The web allows you to post the information on your listing in a place that can be viewed by potential buyers. Look at your real estate web site as a worldwide office. Anyone in the world can visit it in seconds.

First you will want to get the information posted and then drive potential buyers and cooperating brokers to that listing.

Remember, however, that if you expect to simply post your listings on the web and have them snapped up by eagerly awaiting buyers, you will be sorely disappointed! Someone once put it this way: "Build a web site and they will NOT come. You will have to drive them to your site." And we'll show you how in this chapter.

The Places You Can Post Your Listings

Post to Your Site. Start by posting your listing to your own (or your company) web site. This can be as easy as posting a short headline that links the visitor to an executive summary.

Here is an example of a simple headline summary of offerings from my personal web site at www.inetworks.com/revest

Note: Please don't get overwhelmed with fears of big costs and time involvement. I have spent less than $800 to set up and maintain this site, but using the methods in this chapter have been instrumental in helping me to sell hundreds of millions of dollars in income property.

$\boxed{\text{SOLD}}$ **WALGREENS FOR SALE** *25 Year Absolute Net Lease*—Vermont. 7.15% cap. Click for details.

$\boxed{\text{SOLD}}$ **WALGREENS FOR SALE** *25 Year Absolute Net Lease*—Connecticut. 7.15% cap. Click for details.

■ **LAS VEGAS LAND** Estate assemblage of 358 prime, undeveloped, commercial acres within the Golden Triangle Development Area of Las Vegas/North Las Vegas, Nevada USA.

■ **AIRPORT** located in Vermont. Price $850,000 includes terminal, hangers and all associated equipment. Top-notch ski resort destination. Surrounded by exceptional airport condominium community and spectacular golf course.

■ **MILLIONS OF TONS OF TALC FOR SALE** Acquire an unmined proven talc deposit located on approximately 500 acres in southern Vermont. Click for details.

$\boxed{\text{SOLD}}$ **HIGH LEVERAGE $8 MILLION NET LEASE PACKAGE**—92% non recourse financing assumable!

$\boxed{\text{SOLD}}$ **GOVERNMENT GUARANTEED LEASE**—Hawaii. 11% cap.

$\boxed{\text{SOLD}}$ **DOWNTOWN BOSTON RETAIL/OFFICE BUILDINGS FOR SALE**—HUGE UPSIDE! Click for details.

SOLD **WALGREENS FOR SALE**—Net Lease—8.75% cap. Click for details.

SOLD **PRIME APARTMENT LAND IN SOUTHERN NEW HAMPSHIRE**—30 acres zoned for 61 apartments.

SOLD **WALGREENS FOR SALE** *20 Year Net Lease*—$750,903. Cash required. Click for details.

SOLD **WALGREENS FOR SALE** *20 Year Net Lease*—$750,595. Cash required. Click for details.

SOLD **WALGREENS FOR SALE** *20 Year Net Lease*—$685,731. Cash required. Click for details.

SOLD **56 APARTMENTS FOR SALE—PLUS LAND FOR 200 MORE!** Click for details.

SOLD **$29 MILLION NET LEASED DEAL—ONLY 6.1% CASH DOWN.**

SOLD **WALGREENS FOR SALE** *20 Year Net Lease*—$1,093,000. Cash required. Click for details.

SOLD **THE ONLY 5 ACRES FOR DEVELOPMENT ON HISTORIC PLYMOUTH HARBOR** For sale—Marina ++++ Potential. Click for details.

SOLD **WALGREENS FOR SALE** *20 Year Net Lease*—$659,150. Cash required. Click for details.

SOLD **WALGREENS FOR SALE** *20 Year Net Lease*—$448,500. Cash required.

SOLD **WALGREENS FOR SALE** *20 Year Net Lease*—$428,200. Cash required. Click for details.

SOLD **WALGREENS FOR SALE** *20 Year Net Lease*—$464,000. Cash required. Click for details.

SOLD **$30 MILLION INSTITUTIONAL GRADE NET LEASE FOR SALE**—9% Cap. Click for further details.

Notice that this web page intersperses the *For Sale* offerings with the *Sold* offerings. This helps to give a sense of urgency to those that remain available.

The visitor can simply click on an offering and view an executive summary of that offering. Here's an example of that style of summary:

$30 MILLION INSTITUTIONAL GRADE NET LEASE FOR SALE

Location: This property is situated in a solid New England office park location supported by a very strong office market.

Description: This 160,000 square foot office building consists of fully built-out first-class office space.

Land: The building is located on approximately 12.5 acres of land in a prime office park.

Lease: Leased to Bell Atlantic (NYNEX/New England Tel and Tel) (S&P AA). The lease commenced September 30, 1987. The annual rent is $1,615,000 until April 1, 1998 and then $2,720,000 until March 31, 2008. The lease is a bond type lease with ALL expenses, including roof and structure, paid by the tenant.

Extra Land: There is an additional parcel of approximately 2 acres of commercially zoned land included in this offering. Ownership indicates that a 40,000 square foot building can be constructed on this parcel.

Price: $30,222,000 (9.0% cap on 4/98 rent).

Contact: John M. Peckham III
Peckham Boston Advisors
Four Longfellow Place, Suite 2003
Boston, MA 02114
Phone 617-523-4441 Fax 617-523-5555
E-mail: bostonjack@earthlink.net
Web: http://www.inetworks.com/revest/

All information is from sources we deem reliable and is submitted subject to errors, omissions, prior sale, lease, withdrawal without notice, or change in price and conditions. While we do not doubt its accuracy, no representation thereof is made.

You can get as fancy as you wish, with virtual tours, verbal narratives, and all the latest bells and whistles, but I have found that a straightforward recitation of the summary facts often works better because it puts me quickly in touch with more prospects.

Posting to Other Sites. There are a significant number of sites on the web that will allow you to post your offering so that investors and other brokers are able to see its availability. Posting your offering to these web sites in addition to your own will help you sell your offering more effectively. For simplicity's sake, we will discuss two categories of commercial investment property web sites: affinity and open.

- Affinity Sites

   First you will want to post to your *affinity sites,* where you are entitled to post properties because of your relationship with the organization sponsoring the site. CCIM NET (www.ccimnet.com) is an example of this type of site.

- Open Sites

   But you say, "I'm not a member of CCIM or any member group that has a place to post listings!" Then you will want to post to one or more of the web sites that welcome posts from any practitioner, regardless of affiliation. These sites specialize in disseminating information on commercial investment properties for sale or lease. There is no charge to post your offering to most of them. (Some may be free but provide enhancement options for a fee. Also keep in mind that the Internet is a moving target, and many of the hosts of Internet service sites are realizing that they have to feed their families so more and more are charging for their services.)

   An example of one of the major commercial investment sites is currently LoopNet (http://www.loopnet.com). The Real Estate CyberSpace Society (www.REcyber.com) tracks information regarding the various open sites and maintains a database of this information.

Now that you have a listing summary on the web you are ready to drive potential buyers to your listings.

How to Use E-Mail to Reach a Wide Network of Potential Buyers

Almost without exception, real estate cyber pros agree that e-mail is a highly effective tool for marketing your listings. When you use the power of listservs, it allows you to communicate directly to hundreds, even thousands, of pre-selected real estate specialists and investors. It is the most powerful means of getting your listings onto the desktops of thousands of prospects quickly and inexpensively.

E-Mail Is Your $10,000 Promotion for Peanuts

Sometimes I get the feeling that real estate folks can pinch pennies with the best of them. Maybe it's because we have become so enamored with leverage in real estate that we expect to leverage everything around us! It's like that with e-mail. Today, real estate pros are using e-mail to reach buyers, sellers, and prospects for their services—inexpensively, quickly, and effectively.

Here are a few reasons why e-mail is so effective:

1. You can send thousands of messages at little or no cost. You can send your message to one person or ten thousand—the cost is virtually the same in either case. The flat monthly fee you pay your Internet service provider normally includes all the e-mail you want to send at no extra cost.
2. You can target your audience. For example, when I list a net leased property or shopping center for sale, I prepare a brief message (a lot like a classified ad but with a little more of the human touch). I then select my target list so that there is a significant probability that the recipients of my message are real estate pros who will be a buyer—or have a buyer for that product.
3. The response is virtually instantaneous. I have sent messages out on investment properties and received as many as 50 responses from interested parties in less than 2 hours—and 100 or more within 24 hours. I tell my sellers that I can get them instant gratification to their offering!
4. E-mail gets read—and by the right people. If you compose your subject line like you would an effective classified ad headline you will reach the right people. The beauty of e-mail is that you bring your messages right to your targeted audience's desk, and the recipient can respond easily with a single click of the mouse—and at no cost to him or her. You push your message right in front of their faces!
5. Negotiations are quicker. You and your buyer can communicate instantaneously, back and forth, speeding up the process. You can e-mail letters of intent and contract drafts, making them easy to edit and return.

Magnifying the Power of E-mail By Using Listservs

The year after I discovered the power of e-mail listservs I closed more sales as a one-person office than I did in a year with 15 salespeople in the pre-Internet era. And I did it in 20 percent of my working time. I can thank e-mail for those results.

The trick is the strategic use of listservs—electronic mailing lists. The way it works is simple: You send one e-mail to the right listserv, and your message is distributed to thousands of commercial brokers and investors.

What is a Listserv?

A listserv is nothing more than a managed list of e-mail addresses of people (in this case investors or commercial brokers) who have opted in to join an online forum or discussion on a topic of mutual interest. When you send a single message to a listserv, it is rapidly disseminated to the hundreds, thousands, or tens of thousands of individuals who have registered with the listserv. Thus, you can reach hundreds or thousands of targeted recipients with one message. And an important thing to know is that you are reaching these multitudes *without* spamming. That's because the recipients of your mail on the listservs have subscribed to receive e-mail on that subject. These are the ultimate opt-in recipients!

Although it doesn't cost to use listservs (they are free as of this writing), you must subscribe using a simple process. This is a quick and easy process, and once registered you will be free to use the listserv at will. (It is not necessary, but it is a pretty good idea to set up filters in your e-mail software so that it will automatically file the big bunches of e-mail messages you will be receiving as a subscriber to a folder.)

Listserv Tips. If you plan to register to several active lists you may not wish to receive the volume of mail that can be generated from the lists. Here are some suggestions to help maintain your mental stability:

1. It's a good idea to obtain one of those extra e-mail addresses your ISP normally offers and use that e-mail address to manage your e-mail from the listservs.
2. Set up "filters" or "rules" so that incoming listserv messages are directed to appropriate folders in your e-mail filing set up. (See "Help" on your e-mail software.)

3. Some listservs allow you to choose to receive your messages in a "digest" format. Rather than receiving dozens of individual e-mails you will receive a digest of all those individual messages compiled into one e-mail message.

4. If you intend primarily to use the broadcast function to *send* messages you may want to use the "receive no e-mail" option offered by some listservs. If you select this option, you can still review and receive all of the messages on the listserv web site.

5. If you select the "no e-mail" option it's a good idea to browse the incoming messages at the list's archive and read new messages to get the flavor of the discussions, offerings, and general demeanor of the group. This will help you to select the appropriate groups for your outgoing messages.

6. Remember that if you opt to receive the listserv mail, you don't have to read them, and can delete them whenever you like. This is the only inconvenience that accompanies the power opened up to you from being able to send your message to tens of thousands of recipients.

"Members Only" Listservs

Members Only real estate listservs are just what the name implies. Only members of the organization sponsoring the listserv can use it to send broadcast e-mail. These Member Only listservs are maintained by franchises, networks, companies, and other membership organizations. For example, the Real Estate CyberSpace Society (www.REcyber.com) maintains a Members Only listserv for the dissemination of information on commercial properties for sale and property needs.

"Open To All" Listservs

Open to All real estate listservs require no organization membership and are maintained by the list originator—almost always at no cost to the user. You will need to subscribe (*register*) to become a member of the list and, in turn, send and receive e-mail through the listserv.

There are thousands of real estate listservs, and the trick is to be sure you have identified and are using the most effective listservs targeting those who want to buy the type of listing you are marketing.

Listservs in Action

In courses conducted by the Real Estate CyberSpace Society, we take one of the student's active income property listings and post it at around 11:00 AM on some listservs. At 2:30 PM we check it again and, without exception, we find responses from more than 50 potential buyers for the property (or brokers representing those buyers). In three hours, we have ferreted out as many buyers as we could locate in three weeks (maybe three months—maybe never) without the Internet.

Here's an example of an e-mail promotion for a property from an actual seminar in Ohio:

Subject: OHIO ESTATE SALE—208 APARTMENTS!

I'm here in Columbus with the CCIMs from the great state of Ohio doing the Society's one day RECS designation seminar, "Selling in CyberSpace."

John Aubry CCIM (about to become: John Aubry CCIM, RECS) is here with me and has a substantial apartment complex to sell.

John represents the trustees of a deceased manufacturing executive's estate who want to sell the estate's 208 unit, 10 building apartment complex, located on 14.76 acres of attractive landscaped grounds with every amenity imaginable.

This gem is over 95% rented and offered for only $4,950,000.

John said that he will show you how your buyer can create a huge increase in value with a discrete upgrade. Please get back to me post haste. John has promised to get all of the details back to you pronto!

This e-mail message went out at 9:42 A.M. Within 15 minutes we had 14 responses. And by the time the seminar adjourned at 4:00 P.M. we had received 118 responses. Not bad for 15 minutes work!

We have conducted this live exercise over a hundred times in dozens of geographical locations with many types and sizes of property with similar results. And in the majority of cases the property has sold!

As we progress in this chapter, we'll show you more about this process and how you can get similar results.

Listserv Power and Closing Results

Here's another case study, this one from outside the classroom.

Earlier in this chapter you may have noticed a $30 million property posted on my personal web site. Despite the fact that the owner was a friend, every broker from Boston to Biloxi had this open listing. Despite the "competition" I listed this 160,000-square-foot office building for sale. While the rest of the rascals were scurrying around designing brochures and addressing envelopes, I sent an e-mail with the following information about the property to more than 10,000 commercial specialists and investors using several listservs:

Subject:

A few years back I bought a 60 unit Oceanfront Apartment building from the family that owns this prime single tenant property and we became long term friends.

The family now wants to sell their prime free standing single tenant 160,000 SF office building here in the Northeast. The lease is net net net to an institutional grade tenant (tenant is responsible for all costs including roof and structure).

This First Class office building, in a top notch office park, is leased to March 31, 2008 and priced at $30.2 Million to yield 9.0% net net.

Now, here's the kicker—included in the sale price is an additional adjacent parcel of 2 acres (zoned for an additional 40,000 sf office building, according to the owner) which is unencumbered by the lease! And to top this off—the office market here is hotter than a pistol!

Please let me know if this is a fit for one of your investors (1031 or otherwise). Please include your phone and fax numbers.

Also—have a happy holiday season!

Kindest regards

Jack Peckham (signature)

Tom Rochford, a commercial practitioner 3,000 miles away in California, responded, and after the normal period of negotiating and due diligence we completed the $28.75 million sale. I never met Tom or the buyer in person, and, although the property is less than 20 miles from my office, I have never seen the building we sold!

Automating—Using the E-Mail Broadcast Wizard

Because there are literally thousands of real estate broadcast e-lists available to real estate professionals, the trick is to identify the ideal ones that will reach the constituency you need for your message. In addition you want to be sure that the lists you use are not the majority that contain only a handful of users (most less than 10).

Faced with this dilemma, the Real Estate CyberSpace Society developed a significant e-mail aid that makes listservs an even more powerful tool in your hands. The tool is called the E-Mail Broadcast Wizard (the E-Wiz), and it is available to society members without cost.

In developing the E-Wiz, the society found that there were over 3,000 listservs dealing with real estate and selected the lists for inclusion in the E-Wiz by eliminating all lists with fewer than 100 registered users.

They then identified over 50 lists that would be of the most interest to various specialties (e.g., residential specialists or commercial specialists).

Next, they created a short description of what each list is best used for—its fundamental interest (e.g., "For distributing commercial properties for sale or needed" or "For agent networking").

Finally, they obtained an estimate of the actual number of registered users for the list and provided this information at the end of each list description.

When the research was completed they structured the E-Wiz to complete all of the following tasks:

- Register to the lists you wish to use,
- Un-register from lists you have selected but decide you don't want to use at this time,
- Keep track of all subscribed lists, and
- Send your message to any or all of your selected lists—simultaneously with one click.

Using this online tool now makes it very easy for anyone to manage e-marketing. See http://www.recyber.com/broadcast.html for current information on the E-Wiz.

The 3 Steps in a Powerful E-mail Marketing Program

Remember back in Chapter 10 (Advertising) when we talked about callers who wouldn't identify themselves? Well, there are folks like that on the Internet too. For this reason and others, it is a good idea to use a four-step process—protecting your listing information all along the way.

Here are the four steps I use to market a listing using e-mail.

Step 1: Send an E-Mail with General Information. This is an example of an initial e-mail message regarding the property and is designed to reach as many prospective buyers or brokers who may have buyers for this property as possible.

Subject: Walgreens Net Lease for sale. Ideal 5.5M 1031

Make me an offer he says!

This is a solid offering—even more so if you have a 1031 situation.

I have sold 5 Walgreens for this developer. He is a real deal-maker and just called and said that he's ready to rock 'n roll with this brand new offering just completed, occupied and ready for your client.

This Walgreens has 14,490 square feet of net rentable area and carries a lease guaranty from Walgreens Co.

The lease is for 25 years with ten 5-year options. All expenses are paid by the tenant. This is an absolute net lease with no owner responsibility. The net rent is $388,420 per annum payable monthly. The offering is priced at market (7% Cap) at the asking price of $5,548,000.

The Walgreens credit is as good as you can get short of a U.S. Government guarantee! Obviously this prime property is ideal for a 1031 exchange or outright conventional purchase.

Just drop me a note: mailto:recyber@earthlink.net and I'll get the details back to you pronto!

Kindest regards,
Jack

John M. "Jack" Peckham III CCIM, CIPS, RECS
Peckham Boston Advisors
mailto: REcyber@earthlink.net
Web: www.inetworks.com/revest/

Step 2: Respond with Some Additional Information. This message brought 182 responses within 48 hours. The main chore at this point is to narrow the field by providing additional information (but, of course, saving all of the responses in your "Net Lease Buyer" database).

Remember to protect yourself if you do not have an exclusive listing by not providing sufficient information to allow an "end around" attempt to bypass you as the broker.

If you do have an exclusive listing, you can be a bit freer in identifying the property. In any event you should include a "confidentiality agreement" attached to your response and insist on not releasing any further data until that has been signed and returned to you. This serves two purposes: It weeds out the lookers, and it helps to protect you from nefarious netizens.

A Note on Confidentiality Agreements. Because circumstances and state laws vary widely, I'd suggest that you get examples of confidentiality or non-circumvent agreements by searching on either of those terms using Google or your favorite Internet search engine. Then have your attorney review the form you will be using to be sure that you are protected.

Hello—

Good to hear from you! The information on the Walgreens net lease offered for sale is attached.

As I'm sure you know, Walgreens is a top notch credit. You may obtain the latest financial information on Walgreens as filed with the SEC at:

http://www.sec.gov/Archives/edgar/data/104207/000010420703000005/may0310q.htm

You can check out Walgreens corporate and investor news at:

http://biz.yahoo.com/n/W/WAG.html

You can also view tons of Walgreens corporate information at:

http://www.walgreens.com/about/default.jhtml

The lease is the typical new triple net Walgreen format. The property is offered free and clear, and the Walgreen credit is readily financeable on very favorable terms.

(cont.)

Once I receive the attached confidentiality agreement I will be pleased to discuss a letter of intent outlining your terms of sale with the owner and will be happy to work with you on this offering.

Information regarding the Peckham Boston Advisory Company is at:

http://www.inetworks.com/revest/

I look forward to the prospect of closing this transaction with you!

Kindest Regards,

Jack Peckham

John M. "Jack" Peckham III CCIM, CIPS, RECS

Peckham Boston Advisors

Four Longfellow Place, Suite 2003

Boston, MA 02114

Phone 617 523 4441 Fax 888 555 5555

mailto: REcyber@earthlink.net

Web: www.inetworks.com/revest/

Notice that in responding, in addition to the executive summary on the property, we have provided links to several documents.

a. The latest (at the time) SEC report answering any question anyone could ask about Walgreens. (Just a few years ago this information would have cost you $60 per report on CompuServe. Now it is free, thanks to the U.S. government.) In addition, think of the paper, ink, and postage you save with this one link!

b. The latest news stories on Walgreens.

c. The Walgreens corporate web site.

Also learn to use your e-mail software (Outlook, Eudora, etc.) so you can set up form messages and rules (filters) to automate this process. An excellent source on how to use these tools is located in the upper right of the menu bar labeled "help."

The attachment to the e-mail looked like this:

PECKHAM BOSTON ADVISORS
Four Longfellow Place, Suite 2003
Boston, Ma. 02114
Telephone: 617-523-4441   Fax: 617-555-5555
E-mail: REcyber@earthlink.net
Web: http://www.inetworks.com/revest/

WALGREENS
25 YEAR ABSOLUTE NET LEASE
7% CAP

EXECUTIVE SUMMARY

LOCATION: New England

IMPROVEMENTS: Single story freestanding retail building completed and occupied in 2003. Constructed of masonry concrete block over structural steel frame, with a Carlisle glass storefront and decorative brick facade on the remaining three sides. Property consists of 14,490 square feet of net rentable area, 100% leased with lease guaranty from Walgreens Co.

LEASE ABSTRACT:

TERM: 25 years commencing 2003.

OPTION: Ten 5-year options

EXPENSES: All paid by tenant. This is an absolute net lease with no owner responsibility for any expenses.

RENT: $388,420 per annum payable monthly.

NET OPERATING INCOME: $388,420

PRICE: $5,548,000   Cap 7.00

Contact: John M. Peckham III   617-523-4441

Information contained herein is from sources deemed reliable, however no representations are warranted. Offering is subject to change in price or withdrawal without notice.

Step 3: Follow Up on the Most Promising Leads. What may start out as an overwhelming response will slowly dwindle to a more manageable number. As the prospect list dwindles, you will find that the quality of the remaining leads will improve until you are dealing with a healthy group of motivated buyers.

Once you have received the potential buyer's signed confidentiality agreement you can then provide all of the property-specific information, such as address and detailed lease terms.

Remember to retain all of your original responses to an initial e-mailing in a specially marked e-mail address book folder. In the event you are well down the road with a deal and it falls apart or if in the process the price or terms become more favorable, you have a ready-made prospect list to get back to with the "good news."

In effect the Internet marketing plan brings the prospects to your doorstep. All of the other techniques discussed in this manual then come into play to help you bring the parties together and close the transaction.

So there you have it. Your listings are posted at your web site and you have conducted a "push" e-mail campaign to ferret out the buyers. You may ask, "This is all well and good, however, how will this help me get listings?" We'll address this shortly. But first let's look at one more online source of buyers (and sellers).

A Huge Online Source of Buyers, Sellers, and Tenants

We've been talking about buyer resources that are virtually free; however, there are additional sources such as the powerful online program called "Real Buyer Direct." Although it's not free, this program is sold at a very modest price and is made available at a majorly discounted price (currently $45 for 12 months unlimited service to members of the Real Estate CyberSpace Society—somewhat more to non-members). More information is at http://www.REcyber.com/real_buyer/rb_info.cfm.

What Is Real Buyer Direct?

The Real Buyer Direct real estate buyers' database is a searchable national database of more than 7,000 institutional and investment property buyers, including their detailed investment criteria. Each lead provides the appropriate contact person, address, phone and fax number, e-mail address, type of property sought, preferred investment size, geographical preference, minimum square footage (if applicable), and minimum number of units (if applicable). In most cases, notes pertaining to the company are included that contain valuable information about acquisition desires and plans.

What Can Real Buyer Direct Do for You?

You can search for specific buyers by desired property type, investment size, geographical preferences, square footage and number of units (if applicable), and you can group buyers accordingly. Using Real Buyer Direct you will be able to present your property to the most qualified and interested buyers in the country in minutes. In addition, the database may be used to locate potential sellers.

What Makes Real Buyer Direct Unique?

Real Buyer Direct is not only a compilation of the nation's leading buyers of commercial and investment real estate and businesses, it's also an intricately designed system allowing you to locate, through a simple online search box, just the right buyers for your property. This system, designed by brokers for brokers, will produce active buyers whose specific buying criteria match your property or listing.

What Criteria Are Searchable in Real Buyer Direct?

There are hundreds of buyers' preferences for all the "regular" type investments—multifamily, retail, industrial, plus land in many categories—all searchable by size and location. And the criteria are in the buyers' words describing their specific needs. Plus there are multiple buyers for hundreds of special category properties—no matter how obscure that type is. Got a listing on a correctional facility? Shazam! Your search delivers multiple buyers with contact information, including web sites. How about a golf driving range? A loan company? A hospital? A hotel (17 types to pick from—or pick all)? Raw land (43 categories)? A racetrack? A resort or recreational property? RV parks? A theater? Timberland?

That's the power of Real Buyer Direct. No matter what type of real estate or business you have to sell, you can find multiple buyers in the Real Buyer Direct database 24 hours a day. And they do all the research and keep the Real Buyer Direct database up-to-date for you.

How Do You Use Real Buyer Direct? It's a very simple point-and-click process. By entering your property type, price, and location from the filter select options, Real Buyer Direct will pin point specific buyers, sorting and producing only those buyers whose specific buying criteria match your property. Through this unique selection and grouping process, you are able to contact the right buyers for your offering in mass.

The Real Buyer Direct research staff updates the database on a daily basis, providing you with access to the very latest contact information. The system can produce multiple buyers for the same property, which helps to ensure a rapid sale at market price for your property.

Information is power, and this on-demand list of multiple targeted buyers can give you the upper hand in the competitive commercial real estate world.

Getting Properties for Your Buyer on the Internet

"This is all swell," you say, "but what if I have no listings and a great buyer comes along and wants a property when my listing well is dry? Show me how to use this cyberspace stuff to get me a deal then!"

Once you get rolling with these techniques, the potential sellers will see you on the Internet. They will have read some of your PR (see Chapter 10). They will have seen the many promotions you have done on the Internet. Maybe you will use Real Buyer Direct to locate the owner of the type of property you need and turn him into a seller using the same basic techniques discussed in Chapters 2 and 3. And then, for the fastest results of all, you simply let the right group of owners and brokers know what you need using listservs!

Getting Sellers—A Short Case Study

A few years ago an attorney/friend (we'll call him Tom) called from Honolulu. His client, a family trust, had agreed to sell the land it owned free and clear on Waikiki for $7 million. The land had been leased for many years to a world-famous hotel who was the buyer in this transaction.

Because most of the beneficiaries of the trust now lived in the Northeast, the family wanted to acquire three hotels or motels in the New England area as replacement properties. And to add a little extra pressure on me, Tom and the trustee in charge wanted to discuss my "hotel inventory" at a meeting at the Logan International Hyatt Hotel in 10 days! *You should know that my knowledge about hotels doesn't go much beyond checking in.*

Here is the e-mail that brought in so much product:

Subject: IMMEDIATE 1031 NEED—2 OR 3 MIDRANGE FLAGGED HOTELS—EAST COAST

Last Thursday I closed on a 60 unit property in New Hampshire for a long term client from Honolulu (my 3rd closing with them recently). Now they have an immediate 1031 need that I hope you can help me with.

They have just escrowed Seven Million in cash from the sale of land in Hawaii and have asked me to arrange to buy 2–3 mid-range full-service flagged hotels for them. For tax purposes we prefer to buy all cash or with modest financing. Musts are: Mid Range/Full Service/Flagged/East Coast—Maine to Florida. Northeast—especially New England—would be preferred but not required—all other things equal.

Please let me know if you can help me to fill this requirement. Executive summary will help and can be e-mailed or faxed to me at 617 523 5555. My client will be in Boston on March 17th to review your submission with me and to begin the acquisition process.

I look forward to working with you on this immediate 1031 need.

Kindest Regards,

Jack

/ /

John M. "Jack" Peckham III CCIM, CIPS, RECS
Peckham Boston Advisors
(Founded 1963—Our 43rd Year)
Four Longfellow Place, Suite 2003
Boston, MA 02114
Phone 617 523 4441 Fax 617 523 5555
mailto: admin@REcyber.com
Web: www.inetworks.com/revest/

/ /

By using a few listservs I was able to uncover 25 hotel properties for sale from brokers around New England in the desired area. After discussing the pros and cons of the 10 closest matches with the listing brokers, I narrowed the field down to five for the family to consider at the upcoming meeting.

We closed on three of the recommended hotels within 90 days. Ten days before we met at Logan I didn't know hotels from Adam. Isn't the Internet wonderful?

How to Develop a Custom Presentation Template

Earlier I mentioned that the Internet can be a powerful tool in helping you obtain listings on income property or enlisting the assistance of fellow brokers to obtain a property matching a specific need. Having already discussed reaching out to fellow brokers, now let's talk about nailing down listings.

You may remember the two young brokers I mentioned at the beginning of this chapter. They rolled up their sleeves and obtained an exclusive listing against what appeared to be insurmountable odds.

Shortly after they told me how they took the detail of the marketing plan taught in the Society's "Selling in CyberSpace" course they attended and converted it into a listing presentation, I rolled up my sleeves and developed the "Cyber Presentation Template" so that seminar attendees could easily develop an effective presentation without having to reinvent the wheel.

You can pick and choose from sections of the template presented here to suit your personal or company business style and the nature of the properties or services you wish to market. Many Real Estate CyberSpace Society members customize their own versions of the following template as an add-on to their conventional listing presentation or as a section of their web sites.

You can modify and present this template to use with sellers, buyers, or prospects for other real estate services, such as property management and appraisals.

If you are not yet a member of the Real Estate CyberSpace Society, you will also want to modify the last paragraph, which refers to membership in the society. Even better, why not join the Society and use it as is?

About Our Cyberspace Capabilities

In addition to our traditional marketing procedures outlined here, we will provide extensive and significant coverage with our special Internet marketing program. Naturally, we will provide whatever level of confidentiality you require in connection with this program. Specifically, we will:

(Insert For Sellers)

1. Put the appropriate information regarding your property on our company web site and on several affinity and other major web sites. This affords us the opportunity to reach out to the tens of millions of Internet users, many of whom may be prospects for your type of property.
2. Conduct extensive prospect casting that will point prospects to our office and your property on our web site. Our prospect casting campaign consists of many highly effective elements including:
   a. E-mail announcements to a broad range of recipients.
   b. Extensive use of listservs, which reach thousands of brokers and buyers instantaneously.
   c. Posting of information regarding your offering on our affinity web sites.
   d. Posting of information regarding your offering on other real estate web sites.

(Insert For Buyers)

1. Put the appropriate information regarding your real estate needs on our company web site and on several affinity and other major web sites. This affords us the opportunity to reach out to the tens of millions of Internet users, many of whom may be prospects for your type of property.
2. Conduct extensive prospect casting that will point prospects to your needs on our web site. Our prospect casting campaign consists of many highly effective elements including:
   a. E-mail announcements to a broad range of recipients.
   b. Extensive use of listservs, which reach thousands of brokers and sellers instantaneously.
   c. Posting of information regarding your needs on our affinity web sites.
   d. Posting of information regarding your needs on other real estate web sites.

(Insert For Prospective Clients for Services)

1. Put the appropriate information regarding your real estate needs on our company web site and on several affinity and other major web sites. This affords us the opportunity to reach out to the tens of millions of Internet users, many of whom may contribute to the achievement of your real estate goal.
2. Gather extensive information that may contribute to the achievement of your real estate goal. Our information gathering efforts consist of many highly effective elements including:
   a. E-mail announcements to a broad range of recipients.
   b. Extensive use of listservs, which reach thousands of other real estate professionals instantaneously.
   c. Posting of information regarding your information needs on our affinity web sites.
   d. Posting of information regarding your information needs on other real estate web sites.

As members of the Real Estate CyberSpace Society, holding the Real Estate Cyber-Space Specialist (RECS) professional designation, we are able to bring all of today's technological resources, combined with our existing local, national, and international networking structures, to bear on obtaining the best solution to your real estate needs.

I look forward to being of service.

Kindest Regards,

Your Name, RECS

Use Cyber Marketing to Sell Anything—Including Yourself

Let's talk a bit about using cyberspace tools to sell YOURSELF! I have sold a lot of unique properties on the Internet, but if we ever meet I don't want you to be disappointed. First, I'm not even close to 6 feet tall. I'm not a young Whiz kid (for you CCIMs, my PIN #359 tells that story!). I've been on Medicare for seven years and always thought that Franklin D. Roosevelt was a communist until I turned 65 and discovered that he was a pretty smart guy!

I'm half deaf. I can't type (except painfully slowly). I don't own a car. I don't have a secretary, and I don't have any salespeople now. I'm really kind of shy. And I'm certainly not a natural born salesman.

I used to drink, smoke, and think impure thoughts (often simultaneously), but

I got too old for all of that craziness. Now, when I'm not selling real estate, I like to watch cement harden and go to bed early.

I share this with you to help you understand why I am in complete awe of the power of cyberspace and what we can do using the Internet to network, sell, and lease lots of real estate—and *to sell ourselves* while saving a ton of our valuable time!

With these space-age tools available, you don't need to limit your horizons based on any lack of technical or real estate knowledge. For example, over the past few years, using these tools, I have sold a hydroelectric dam and, as mentioned earlier, several hotels. What I know about hotels might fill a thimble (like how to make these newfangled keys work). What I know about hydroelectric dams wouldn't cover the head of a pin!

Tools to Supercharge Your Visibility

Remember in Chapter 10 when we discussed advertising and using press releases to build awareness of your listings and yourself? The Internet also pumps up your ability to build your visibility. Here are two ways to supercharge your image using the web.

Use Signature Files to Build Image

Every time you send an e-mail with your "signature file" (sig file) at the end you build your visibility. You may have noticed in the e-mail examples throughout this chapter that each e-mail sent ends with a sig file—or sign-off statement.

Here's my brokerage sig file:

_/
John M. "Jack" Peckham III CCIM, CIPS, RECS
Peckham Boston Advisors
(Founded 1963—Our 43rd Year)
Four Longfellow Place, Suite 2003
Boston, MA 02114
Phone 617 523 4441 Fax 617 523 5555
mailto: society@earthlink.net
Web: www.inetworks.com/revest/
_/

Here's my Society sig file:

_/

John M. "Jack" Peckham III, CCIM, CIPS, RECS
Real Estate CyberSpace Society "The Society That Means Business"
Four Longfellow Place, Suite 2003, Boston, MA 02114
Phone: 617 523 4441 Fax: 617 523 5555
mailto: society@earthlink.net
Web: www.REcyber.com
Fifth Annual Virtual Convention Info: www.REcyber.com/preconvention
There is a Chapter Near YOU! See:
http://www.REcyber.com/societychapters/index.cfm
_/

Here's my Real Estate CyberSpace Radio sig file:

_/

John M. Peckham III, Editor/Host
Real Estate CyberSpace Radio (RECR)
Four Longfellow Place, Suite 2003
Boston, MA 02114
Phone 617 523 4441 Fax 617 523 5555
mailto: radio@REcyber.com
or mailto: newscenter@earthlink.net
Web: RECR: www.REcyber.com/masters/audio.html
_/

Notice that each sig file is selling something different. With just one click, I can automate and customize how I build my visibility. Imagine how your visibility will grow when you send just one message a week using the E-Broadcast Wizard to 40,000 commercial real estate pros and investors. If you need help setting up a few sig files, just click on "Help" in the upper righthand corner of most e-mail programs (Outlook or Eudora, for example).

Build a Following with a Monthly Customer E-Newsletter

The very best way to build visibility is to stay in touch with your constituency every month, and the best way to do that is with an e-newsletter that contains valuable information.

Some Background: Many years ago, when I was writing my column for the *Boston Sunday Herald,* I began writing and mailing (now we call it snail mail) a newsletter to my customers, prospective customers, and "centers of influence" (lawyers, accountants, bankers, etc.).

This newsletter was responsible for millions of dollars in sales over the years.

To produce a promotional newsletter, you can either write it yourself or subscribe to a service that will prepare the newsletter content and layout for you and allow you to personalize it and send it to your list.

During that time, I collaborated with a publisher and authored a bulk real estate newsletter that was marketed and distributed by Harcourt Brace Jovanovich (the largest publisher in the world at the time). Real estate professionals purchased these newsletters in bulk (over 200,000 per month at the time) and imprinted their names and contact information on them, put them in envelopes, stamped and mailed them to their clients and centers of influence. Many subscribers spent thousands—even tens of thousands—of dollars each year to distribute these business building letters to their constituents.

Why? Because they worked!

How to Use Cyberspace Tools to Handle Your Newsletter

Years later, as I began to appreciate the power of e-mail, I designed an e-newsletter called Real Estate CyberTips for a similar group of customers and centers of influence. But this time I didn't have to pay for any printing. I didn't need to fold the newsletters and stuff them into envelopes, and I didn't have to lug them to the post office and pay a ton of money for postage. All because it was an e-mail newsletter.

The ease and success of the CyberTips e-newsletter led me to replicate the system I developed years ago for members of the Real Estate CyberSpace Society so that they could send a personalized e-newsletter to their clients without having to write it every month. The big difference is that it doesn't cost them a penny. It is included with their society membership.

As an additional service, the "Real Estate CyberTips" Program helps the members broaden their reach and strengthen their image as cyber-savvy real estate professionals. The program allows members to:

1. Send a professionally prepared promotional e-newsletter to their clients and centers of influence (lawyers, bankers, press, accountants, title companies, etc.) that they can automatically customize.
2. Publish their own newspaper column in minutes.
3. Carry a traffic building feature on their web site.

Now that you can send an e-newsletter at very little expense, the only choice you have is whether to write it yourself or use a service. There are many services that you can use, ranging in price from about $150 to over $500 a year depending on the bells and whistles you want. Or you can use the free e-newsletter as a member of the Real Estate CyberSpace Society.

Building an E-Mail Client, Press, and Center of Influence List

It's one thing to have an e-newsletter. It's another to get it into the right hands. To do so, you will need to be sure that your client, press and centers of influence e-mail list is in order and ready to use. You can start small and build that list. The process is really quite simple:

1. Ask all of your current and previous contacts for their e-mail addresses. Get on the phone or have your assistant call former customers and accountants, bankers, lawyers, press, title companies—any center of influence who is in a position to refer business to you.
2. Add to your list from the pass-along subscribers who contact you.

Enjoy the Rewards of Cyberspace Marketing

You can enjoy all of the very significant marketing rewards that will come from using all of the new technology available to you today. Real estate professionals who combine the sound basic techniques contained in the other charts of this guide with today's e-tools are reporting major increases in productivity along with significant savings of time. You will be able to use that extra time to close more sales while enjoying more free time!

CHAPTER 15

How to Make a Final Presentation That Clinches the Sale

No matter how well you have listed and financed the property; no matter how professionally your operating statement has been prepared and your prospect has been qualified; no matter how brilliantly you have shown the property and answered your prospect's questions and objections—he is not going to buy the property until he understands *how* it will benefit him—and how *much* it will benefit him.

You can be a human computer, but if you cannot put the whole picture into perspective for the buyer in terms that he understands, your efforts will have been in vain. If you have prepared yourself well, however, and have shown your prospect what the investment will do for him, you can make the sale—and many more.

In leading up to this crucial point, your initial conversations with your prospect will have been extremely important. The confidence you inspire while qualifying him; the professional manner in which you select the proper investments for him; the thorough inspection you conduct of the premises; the knowledgeable manner in which you explain the benefits of income property investment; and the thorough way you answer his questions and objections—these should have all prepared your prospect for the moment when you will summarize your conclusions and make your final recommendations. All of the preceding chapters have prepared you for this moment.

How to Dramatize What the Property Will Do for Your Prospect

I have no sympathy for the broker or salesperson who thinks that throwing a batch of facts and figures at a prospect on attractive letterhead is going to make the sale. I also have no sympathy for the salesperson who thinks that the prospect is going to buy any property "out of the sky." Sales don't just happen in any phase of real estate—they are *created.* The prospect doesn't just up and buy. The salesperson creates the desire to buy by showing his prospect what he stands to gain by buying. In this section, you will learn how to do just that—to sum up what your prospect will gain by acquiring the property you are proposing.

The Peckham Boston Analysis: A Powerful Wrap-Up

In Chapter 7, you learned to convert "seller's net before financing" to a more accurate net operating income, by using lines 1 to 5 of the Peckham Boston Analysis sheet. You continued on lines 6 through 11, by showing your prospect what the property would do for him on the offered terms.

In Chapter 7, you learned how to use the analysis sheet (lines 12 to 22) to demonstrate to your prospect how much "net cash flow after taxes" he would derive from the property after all income tax considerations.

In Chapter 4, you learned how to use lines 23 to 35 of the Analysis Sheet, to show your prospect how he could expect to handle a purchase-money mortgage that requires refinancing to pay off a *balloon* balance.

Now you are ready to consolidate these three sections into one compact folder that contains a complete analysis of the benefits he will derive from owning the property.

Consider the background of this case in point: Let's set the scene. You have listed a modern 24-unit apartment building in Yourtown, a suburban community just north of Yourcity, Yourstate. The owner has given you certain facts and figures that are shown consolidated on the operating statement reproduced in the illustration on pages 334–335.

The problem: No offers. After two months of disappointing activity you decide to dig a little deeper, so that you can make an intelligent presentation to a new prospect. Before approaching him with your presentation, you meet with Mr. Owner and explain that, although his property is most attractive and you have submitted it to 14 very logical buyers, you haven't had a nibble.

The owner's motivation: Mr. Owner explains that he is anxious to move to the West Coast to live with his son, and that he will cooperate in any way. Together you start to analyze the operating statement. He points out that he has not had any vacancy loss since the property was completed two years ago, and that he has had negligible turnover. He also makes it clear that his rents are well below comparable rentals. He rides you around to show you other similar properties in the area.

Income and expense: You determine that his rents could be upgraded substantially, but that at fair market value he could expect about 3 percent rental loss due to vacancies and rental commissions. He continues by verifying his other expense figures with a notable exception: His expenses are expected to increase over the next 12 months.

In addition, he finally agrees that a new owner either should obtain professional management at 5 percent of rents collected, or if he doesn't, should be compensated for managing the property himself.

ORIGINAL OPERATING STATEMENT

THE PECKHAM BOSTON COMPANY

Four Longfellow Place
Boston, Massachusetts 02114
617-555-1212

DATA #311YT

LOCATION: Well-Located in Yourtown, Massachusetts
TYPE: Modern brick apartment building containing 24 units

ASSESSMENT: $ 900,000   TAX RATE $40   2006
TOTAL ANNUAL INCOME: $ 207,360

RENT ROLL:

12 Two-bedroom apartments	$800
12 One-bedroom apartments	$640 (All apartments are under lease)
Laundry income:	$540 per annum

ESTIMATED EXPENSES:

Taxes	$ 36,000
Heat	28,000
Electric	9,500
Water & sewer	6,000
Janitor	13,500
Insurance	6,000
Total	$ 99,000

NET BEFORE FINANCING: $ 108,360
FINANCING:

First mortgage (existing)	$ 500,000	Interest 6% Term 20 yrs.
Second mortgage (proposed)	$ 325,000	Interest 7% No principal. Term 10 yrs.

FINANCE EXPENSES:

First mortgage interest	$ 30,000
First mortgage principal	$ 13,000
Second mortgage interest	$ 22,750
Total	$ 65,750

NET INCOME:	$ 42,610	
PRINCIPAL SAVINGS:	$ 13,000	
TOTAL YIELD:	$ 55,610	
PRICE:	$1,350,000	CASH DOWN: $525,000

Notes: (1) Modern electric kitchens. (2) Ceramic tile baths. (3) Forced hot water heat by oil supplied by owner. (4) Adequate parking. (5) Tenants pay own utilities. (6) Sliding glass doors to balconies. (7) All apartments are air-conditioned. (8) Beamed ceiling dinettes. (9) Low competitive rents.

Price and financing: The owner agrees that his original asking price of $1,350,000 was a bit high, and authorizes you to sell it at $1,250,000. He wants a $425,000 cash down payment, and will take back the balance on a purchase-money mortgage at 7 percent interest, no principal for ten years, as originally proposed. You point out that his existing first mortgage of $500,000 is assumable at a favorable long-term rate. The lower price, coupled with the favorable financing, should spark some immediate action.

How you should respond: The owner gives you a 90-day exclusive on the property on the new terms, but tells you he wants it sold as soon as possible.

You return to your office, roll up your sleeves and prepare an analysis worksheet for your prospect. You have already determined that he is in the 40 percent tax bracket. You make an appointment, take him through the property, and return with him to your office. You then produce a blue folder. On the front you have entered the following notations:

THE PECKHAM BOSTON COMPANY

INCOME ANALYSIS WORKSHEET

ADDRESS 10 Main Street

Yourtown, Mass.

DATA # 311YT

DATE 8/12/—

Prepared for William Investor

by Jack Peckham

Four Longfellow Place
Boston, Massachusetts 02114
617-523-4441

Inside of this folder is stapled your original operating statement. You turn to page 2 of your Analysis Worksheet which looks like this:

INCOME ANALYSIS

1. Seller's net before financing		$108,360	
2. Rent stabilization	+	14,400	
3. V & R allowance	–	11,088	
4. Expense adjustment	–	17,922	
5. Net operating income		93,750	93,750

FINANCING

6. Interest (total)		$52,750	
7. Principal (total)		13,000	
8. Total		65,750	– 65,750
9. Cash flow before taxes			= 28,000
10. Cash down payment		425,000	
11. % return on equity		6.6%	

You proceed to explain: "Bill, I have reviewed this solid property backward and forward. Yesterday I spent four hours with the owner so that I could present an accurate analysis of what this property will do for you."

State the owner's motivation: "You can see from the original statement that the owner was expecting to receive $1,350,000 from this sale. Yesterday he informed me that he is anxious to move to the West Coast to be with his son and grandchildren. He authorized me to reduce the price to effect a quick sale for him."

Then talk net income: "Here is an analysis of what the property should do for you based on his new price. Notice that on our original statement the owner computed his net income before financing, before a vacancy and repair allowance, and before an allowance for management. We have made certain adjustments as a result of yesterday's meeting, and now conclude that a realistic net operating income for this property will be $93,750. This represents the amount that this property should earn before financing and before the return on your investment."

"Here's how we arrived at that figure. First, we adjusted the rents to market value by studying comparable rents in the area (line 2). Then we determined that you will have to set aside a vacancy allowance ($7,096) and an allowance for repairs ($3,992), totaling $11,088 (line 3)."

Explain the expense calculations: "We have substantially adjusted the expenses shown in the owner's original figures, raising the total expenses by $17,922. This figure was arrived at after carefully analyzing the owner's operation and finding that the expenses would be expected to increase by $9,336 due to an anticipated real estate tax increase and increased utility costs, and an additional $8,586 for professional management. After all of these adjustments, we project a net operating income $93,750 as shown on line 5."

Explain the financing: "The owner needs $425,000 down, but has agreed to take back the balance over the existing $500,000 first mortgage. This mortgage is assumable, and the seller is willing to put the property under agreement subject to your assuming the mortgage at 6 percent on a 20-year direct reduction basis."

"Look at lines 6 to 9 for a minute, Bill. These lines show you how much the financing will cost. And line 9 indicates that the property will produce a cash flow before taxes of $28,000 after the cost of your financing. Remember that this figure is after we have made all of the adjustments above, including the cost of professional management."

Highlight the yield: "Lines 10 and 11 show you that this represents a 6.6 percent cash return on your equity; however, I want to give you the whole picture because this is only a small part of the overall benefits you will derive from this property."

Bill Investor finally interrupts: "But, I'll have to pay taxes on that, so that my return won't really be 6.6 percent—will it?"

You proceed, "Bill, you're right, your return won't be 6.6 percent—it will be closer to thirty percent!"

He says, "I don't believe you yet, but go ahead. I'm intrigued."

Now hit home with depreciation benefits: "Bill, you observed that income taxes would have some impact on your ownership of this property. Strangely enough, the cash flow from this property will go untaxed in your first year of ownership. Look at lines 12 to 18 on the Analysis Sheet."

TAX ANALYSIS

Depreciable Improvements $1,150,000   Straight-Line .03636%

Depreciation: 27.5 Years

12. Net operating income (line 5)	$93,750
13. Less interest (line 6)	– 52,750
14. Less depreciation	– 41,814
15. Taxable income/or (tax loss)	<814>
16. Cash flow before taxes (line 9)	$28,000
17. Less estimated tax (line 15 × tax bracket)	<814>
18. Net cash flow after taxes	= 28,000

Note: If a tax lost exists on line 15, any loss must be carried forward and zero tax will be entered on line 17.

"The assessment on this property has a very high ratio of building to land value, which means simply that you should be able to depreciate $1,150,000. Using straight line depreciation, the deduction is $41,814. This of course, does not mean that the property is losing money. This is merely a *paper* deduction allowable under the income tax structure of this country. Now, Bill, there are many ins and outs of taxation, and I would recommend that when we finish with this analysis that we sit down with your accountant and go over this section of the analysis. I'm sure that he will agree that this investment will produce significant depreciation benefits."

PRINCIPAL SAVINGS ANALYSIS

Secondary Due Date __10 Years__ (SDD)

19. Fair market value now		$1,350,000
20. Annual growth 6% × years	×	1.6
21. FMV at SDD	=	2,160,000
22. Estimated loan/FMV%	×	70%
23. Estimated new first mtg. @ SDD	=	1,512,000
24. Total existing mtg. bal. @ SDD	−	647,500
25. (Surplus) or Bal. required	=	864,500
New first mortgage (line 27)		
26. Amount _$647,500_ Debt. serv.		$55,685
27. Secondary amount _None_ Debt. serv.	+	
(If necessary)(line 25)		
28. Total debt service	=	55,685
29. Debt service now (line 8)		65,750
30. Debt service after SDD (line 31)		55,685
31. Cash flow before taxes (increase) or decrease)		$10,065

Tell how the balloon mortgage will be handled: Bill Investor says, "I think I see. Is there anything else we should go over before I call my accountant?"

You continue, "Yes, Bill, remember that the seller is taking back a purchase-money mortgage of $325,000 at 7 percent interest for ten years, and that when this comes due you must refinance your first mortgage in order to pay off this loan. Of course, without his taking back this mortgage, the down payment would not be $425,000, but $750,000. Look at lines 19 through 31.

"Here, I have projected your position in order to estimate where you might stand in ten years when this loan comes due."

Appreciation and amortization are the keys: "Property values in this area have increased at a rate of over 8 percent in the past few years. Naturally we can't guarantee that appreciation will continue at this rate, but we certainly expect nothing less in the next ten years. However, I am projecting a lower 6 percent growth rate, which shows that this property could be worth $2,160,000 when refinancing time rolls around. Your potential loan should be around 70 percent of that fair market value, or approximately $1,512,000. The balances on your existing financing will be about $647,500."

"At that point, you can refinance your first mortgage to $647,500 and pay off both loans. At current rates and terms your total financing costs will drop $10,065 (line 31), which of course will increase your cash flow before taxes."

"Of course, if you refinanced to the maximum estimated new loan amount of $1,512,000, you would put $864,500 in cash in your pocket. If you do this, it will be *tax free!*"

Use the return after-taxes as your clincher: "Bill, we're almost finished, but I want to show you what this property should do for you, *after taxes,* over the ten-year term! Look at lines 32 through 35."

YOUR TEN-YEAR RESULT		
32. Net cash flow after taxes		$280,000
33. Total amortization	+	177,500
34. Total growth @ _____%	+	810,000
35. Total equity return $1,267,500	Averages 29.8% Annually	

"This building will give you approximately $280,000 to spend after taxes. This is based on your first year's net cash flow after taxes from line 16."

How the Analysis Worksheet Sells the Property and the Broker

On the back page of the Analysis Worksheet, you have entered the terms of your seller's offering plus a summary containing your reasons for recommending the purchase of the property as shown on page 341.

The enclosed computations are based on the following terms:

Price $1,250,000

Cash   425,000

First mortgage   500,000.00

Interest   6

Term   20-year D.R.

Purchase money mortgage   325,000.00

Interest   7%

Principal   0

Term   10 years

Other terms:

Other Notes

Broker recommends acquisition of this solid 24-unit Apartment Building for the following reasons:

1. Current rentals are well below surrounding competition.

2. Investment provides depreciation-sheltered income, plus excellent equity growth through mortgage amortization and expected area growth.

Note

The information on this Income Analysis Worksheet is intended as an EXAMPLE ONLY, to demonstrate estimated net cash flow after taxes, percentage returns, possible income tax consequences, and growth potential. All figures and percentages shown in this analysis are estimates. All information, allocations, and projections shown here, while based upon information supplied by the owner or from other sources deemed to be reliable, are not, in any way, warranted by The Peckham Boston Company. Tax bracket computations are assumed to be applied against the last dollars of taxable income. This is a simplification in most cases; however, the results projected will give a reasonable indication of possible tax savings. Independent tax counsel should be obtained concerning all income tax considerations involved.

Then sum up dramatically like this: "In addition, your mortgages will be reduced by $177,500, increasing your equity correspondingly (line 33)."

"On top of this, Bill, the increasing value of your property because of economic growth could amount to another $810,000. Your total equity return should be somewhere around $1,267,500 (line 35)."

"Remember we observed that your return would not be 6.6 percent, but significantly higher. $1,267,500 represents a 298 percent ten-year equity return, or 29.8 percent per year after taxes."

Bill Investor says, "Let me have your phone. We'll go see my accountant right now!"

Bill Investor now has in his hands a complete and accurate summary of what the property will do for him. He has the results of your research ready to hand to his accountant.

If Bill has dealt with less knowledgeable brokers in the past, he is probably used to hearing a sales pitch on what a great opportunity this property is, and getting a statement based on "owner's net"—not much more. He may also have a few notes on some scrap paper or on the back of an envelope.

Bill has probably never witnessed such professionalism as you've shown him. Is it any wonder that from this day on, you are Bill's real estate pro? Believe me, if he has been hopping around from office to office before, and getting the kind of skimpy information that's traditional, he is now your client. And as long as you continue to render professional service, he will remain your client.

The most important thing you have done is show Bill that you care—you care enough to show him the property in financial depth.

Following is a reproduction of the Analysis Worksheet, with a capsule summary of how to put it to use.

(Front Page of Worksheet)

REALTOR®

THE PECKHAM BOSTON COMPANY

INCOME ANALYSIS WORKSHEET

ADDRESS _____   DATA # _____

_____   DATE _____

Prepared for _____

by _____ , Investment Broker

Four Longfellow Place
Boston, Massachusetts 02114
617-523-4441

(Inside Page 1 of Worksheet)

INCOME ANALYSIS

1. Seller's net before financing _____
2. Rent stabilization _____
3. V & R allowance _____
4. Expense adjustment _____
5. Net operating income _____ _____

FINANCING

6. Interest (total) _____
7. Principal (total) _____
8. Total _____ − _____
9. Cash flow before taxes = _____
10. Cash down payment _____
11. % return on equity

TAX ANALYSIS

Depreciable Improvements _____   Straight-Line

Depreciation _____   ____%

Useful Life _____

12. Net operating income (line 5) _____
13. Less interest (line 6) − _____
14. Less depreciation − _____
15. Taxable income/or tax loss = _____

Cash flow after taxes

16. Cash flow before taxes (line 9) _____
17. Less estimated tax (line 15 × tax bracket) − _____
18. Net cash flow after taxes = _____

(Inside Page 2 of Worksheet)

PRINCIPAL SAVINGS ANALYSIS

Secondary Due Date _____ (SDD)

19. FMV now   _____

20. Annual growth   % ×   years   × 1. _____

21. FMV at SDD   = _____

22. Estimated loan/FMV%   × _____

23. Estimated new first mtg. @ SDD   = _____

24. Total existing mtg. bal. @ SDD   – _____

25. Surplus or Bal. required   = _____

New first mortgage (line 24)   _____

26. Amount _____ Debt. serv.   _____

27. Secondary amount ___ Debt. serv. + _____

   (If necessary) (line 25)

28. Total debt service   = _____

29. Debt service now (line 8)   _____

30. Debt service after SDD (line 28)   _____

31. Cash flow before taxes (increase/
    or decrease)   _____

YOUR TEN-YEAR RESULT

32. Net cash flow after taxes   _____

33. Total amortization   + _____

34. Total growth @ _____%   + _____

35. Total equity return _____   Averages ____ % Annually

(Back Page of Worksheet)

The enclosed computations are based on the following terms:

Price   _____

Cash   _____

First mortgage   _____

Interest   _____

Term   _____

Purchase money mortgage   _____

Interest   _____

Principal   _____

Term   _____

Other terms: _____

_____

_____

Other Notes

Note

The information on this Income Analysis Worksheet is intended as an EXAMPLE ONLY, to demonstrate estimated net cash flow after taxes, percentage returns, possible income tax consequences, and growth potential. All figures and percentages shown in this analysis are estimates. All information, allocations, and projections shown here, while based upon information supplied by the owner or from other sources deemed to be reliable, are not, in any way, warranted by The Peckham Boston Company. Tax bracket computations are assumed to be applied against the last dollars of taxable income. This is a simplification in most cases; however, the results projected will give a reasonable indication of possible tax savings. Independent tax counsel should be obtained concerning all income tax considerations involved.

A Line-By-Line Summary of the Income Analysis Worksheet

Line   1. From "seller's operating statement."

2. Adjustment for sub-market rentals.

3. Contingency allowance for vacancies and repairs.

4. Adjustment for high or low expenses (include management).

5. Represents net operating income before debt service.

6. Total interest cost on all financing.

7. Total amortization this year on all financing.

8. Total debt service.

9. Represents cash flow before taxes after all expenses.

10. Down payment required.

11. Line 9 ÷ down payment.

12. Same as line 5.

13. Same as line 6.

14. Purchase price less land value × annual depreciation factor.

15. Line 12 less line 13 less line 14.

16. Same as line 9.

17. Line 15 × tax bracket (note that if a tax loss occurs on line 15 this loss must be carried forward and will not be deducted on line 17).

18. Line 9 less line 20.

19. Purchase price.

20. Annual growth factor times years to SDD.

21. Line 22 × line 23.

22. Percentage loan expected at SDD.

23. Line 24 × line 25.

24. Total mortgage balances at SDD (present balances less amortization).

25. Surplus—amount of surplus if mortgage in line 23 is obtained. Balance required—amount of additional financing or cash required.

26. Enter amount shown in line 23 or line 24 (whichever is less). Debt service = annual payments for interest and principal.

27. Secondary financing required if line 25 shows a balance required. Debt service = interest at commercial rates (10%, for example).

28. Line 26 plus line 27.

29. Line 8.

30. Same as line 28.

31. Amount present cash flow before taxes (line 9) is increased or decreased as a result of new financing.

32. Line 18 × 10 (years).

33. Total debt reduction over ten-year period.

34. Estimated growth of equity due to area growth.

35. Total of lines 32, 33, and 34.

Helpful Hints

The following hints should be helpful in using the Analysis Worksheet to its greatest advantage:

1. When you have completed the worksheet, fold it on the dotted lines at the left and staple the corresponding broker's operating statement in at the top.

2. Once the operating statement is attached, fold the worksheet along the dotted lines in the center, thus creating a four-page presentation with the owner's operating statement enclosed.

3. Remember to explain your conclusions in terms your prospect can understand.

4. Remember to keep a copy for your files, so that you can answer any questions your prospect or his accountant may have.

5. Practice with this form. Once you have used it a few times on actual properties you will find that each section falls easily into place and that it is easy to use.

The Analysis Worksheet will earn you the respect of your prospects and their tax advisers. It will also earn you the satisfaction of a job well done—and many tens of thousands of commission dollars!

CHAPTER 16

How to Keep the Ball Rolling and Put These Profitable Techniques Into Action Now

You are now adequately prepared to matriculate into the most important school of brokerage ever conducted—the "school of hard knocks." The material contained in this Guide has focused on the *practical* aspects of income brokerage. Combining this practical information with experience in the field will help you develop a career that is rewarding in dollars, and in the satisfaction of an important service well done.

You may ask, "Where do I go from here?" The answer depends greatly on your present position.

If you are conducting a successful residential office now, and are ready to expand your operations to include income property brokerage, you have two choices: (1) "go it alone" and assign one of your top-notch people to this specialty, or (2) develop a cooperative alliance with one of the income property specialists in your area.

How to Get Into Income Property Brokerage—Step by Step

If you are located in an urban area where a heavy concentration of income property exists, consider establishing an income property division within your own firm. Don't go overboard with this operation. Develop it slowly at first. Assign one of your up and coming "go-getters" the collateral duty of developing a portfolio of listings and a good solid list of local investors.

The salesperson can start with smaller properties (four- to eight-family dwellings) and small store blocks. Let her sharpen her abilities while still maintaining her income from single-family sales. In time, when she is successful in developing her department into a successful operation that is paying its way, then assign more people to her so that she can develop this specialty within the office. Have her take every course available on the subject and read every book that investors read, and follow local real estate trends. Make sure that she understands how to apply the techniques in this Guide, and that she expands her knowledge and understanding of income brokerage by applying these techniques in the field. Have her use the 20-week timetable set forth in this chapter to guide her in getting started.

How to Use These Techniques In Other Areas of Selling

If your geographic area is concentrated enough to sustain a separate department, and if you have chosen the right broker, you and that broker will earn many commissions that otherwise would have been overlooked. If, on the other hand, your office is not located in an area heavily dotted with income property, you can still profit from the contents of this Guide. Have all of your salespeople study it from cover to cover. There are many techniques that are equally applicable to all forms of brokerage. Some of them, such as the listing methods in Chapters 2 and 3, the financing techniques in Chapter 4, the advertising tips in Chapter 10, and the qualifying systems in Chapter 9, are methods of producing sales that may easily and profitably be adopted by the residential salesperson.

By studying these methods she will not only boost her residential production, but will also be in a position to spot a potential income property sale.

Keep in mind too, that even an occasional income property sale can bring a commission equal to *several* residential sales, so that even in an area with a comparatively low concentration of income properties, it will prove to be a very profitable sideline.

How to Form a Cooperative Alliance with a "Specialist"

This is the age of specialization, and in many areas of real estate there are brokerage houses that do nothing but negotiate the sale of income property. You can profit from the information in this Guide with a minimum of effort on your part. Simply call one of the specialists in your area, and work out an arrangement whereby you will be paid a prearranged percentage of the commission received on a sale resulting from your sources.

For example, a while back a suburban broker called our office and explained that he had been dealing with an investor who wanted to invest in a larger-type apartment house. The broker had exhausted his leads and asked if we would try to find his investor a property that would meet his requirements. Ten weeks later we sent the broker a check for $15,000 for just picking up the phone!

The specialists, who are usually located in the city, depend upon the suburban broker to provide them with potential investors and leads on income property listings in the suburbs.

The specialists usually recommend that you explore all of your own leads first. If you have done this without results, keep in mind that all is not lost. Many of the specialists will assign a salesperson to your lead. She will do the lion's share of the work, applying her day-to-day knowledge of the field, and when successful in consummating a sale, will pay you a pre-agreed percentage of the commission received.

If you do not have a large residential office and are, in effect, a *one-man show,* you can still earn your share of the big commissions in this field.

You can easily begin your program now, using as a guide the following 20-week timetable, which provides a step-by-step program to help you get started quickly and easily.

You can also profit from the cooperative alliance with the specialist. She will welcome your leads as outlined in the preceding paragraphs. Additionally, if you have solid sales ability, remember that the larger income offices are always looking for qualified salespeople to participate in their brokerage operations.

Your 20-Week Timetable—A Road Map to Success

Here's a down-to-earth schedule for getting started in this fascinating and lucrative specialty. By adhering to this timetable, you can gradually ease into income brokerage activity without interfering with your normal routine. You can use this schedule as flexibly as you like, spending an occasional weekend on your self-training, or you can devote an afternoon a week. Others within your office or in your area may also be interested in pursuing this training schedule. By all means, meet together regularly and discuss the techniques you are preparing to apply. Practice them together; then put them to use on an individual basis and compare notes on your results.

Plan to start next week. Keep this Guide close at hand during the next few months. Refer to the various chapters whenever you need help. If you follow this proposed schedule, you will learn and profit by putting these techniques into action.

Week 1—Survey Your Area

During your first week, survey your area and inventory the types of income property available. Don't be dismayed if the countryside is not dotted with apartment houses or office buildings. Even the smallest towns have some income property—small store blocks, a sprinkling of three-family type houses, single-tenant commercial buildings.

If your area is not crowded with income property, there is still a great opportunity for financial reward. You will probably be the first real estate person in your area to show any proficiency in this specialty. Let people know of your pending activity in this field. If there is an abundance of income properties, there are probably already a few brokers who handle them, but if your area is like most, there is much potential business. Don't let competition worry you. Armed with the information contained in this Guide, you can quickly become a valued competitor in your area. If you apply these techniques, you will quickly be several giant steps ahead of the competition anyway!

Use Chapter 1 as a guide during this first week. It will help you spot potential listings.

Weeks 2, 3, and 4—Gather Your Listing Leads

During these three weeks, let everyone know that you are looking for income properties to sell. After you have completed your survey, start with the 12 listing leads given in Chapter 2 and devote some time to each of them.

When you're getting started, lead 10 (blitzing) should be very productive. Go back out and make a list of all the prospective buildings you can spot. Write down the address and a brief description of each. During these three weeks, you should be able to put together a sizable list of buildings, some of which you will soon add to your listing portfolio.

The first half of Chapter 2 will give you dozens of helpful techniques. Put them to use during weeks 2, 3, and 4.

Weeks 5 and 6—Locate the Owners of Your Leads

During the next two weeks, spend your spare time tracking down the owners of the properties you have itemized. The last portion of Chapter 2 gives you five time-saving shortcuts to locating the owner.

Weeks 7 and 8—Contact the Owners to Find Which of Them Will Consider Selling

Spend the next two weeks calling the owners of the properties you have itemized. By using the techniques set forth in the first half of Chapter 3, you should be successful in interesting a percentage of them in the possibility of selling their properties.

Weeks 9, 10, and 11—Meet with the Owners Who Will Sell, and Gather the Property Data

During the next three weeks, using the methods in the last portion of Chapter 3 as a guide, meet with all of the owners who have indicated that they would consider selling and gather the information you need to prepare an operating statement. Chapters 4 and 5 will also help you in pricing the property at the action level and in financing it properly.

Weeks 12 and 13—Prepare Your Operating Statements

During the next two weeks, take the property information you have gathered on your listing sheet and transfer it to a neatly typed operating statement. Keep in mind that at first a few callbacks to the owners may be necessary to fill in some missing or overlooked items of information. Chapter 6 will be helpful to you as you prepare your operating statements.

Week 14—Advertise Your Best Listing

In week 14, select the most salable property you have available, and place a small ad in the local paper. Use Chapter 10 as a guide in preparing your ad. You will find that it's a good idea to have at least two or three listings prepared, in addition to the one you advertise. Then, if the caller shows no interest in the advertised property, you can still sit down with your prospect and discuss your other offerings.

Remember to record the caller's vital statistics, so that you can get back to her if you don't have the right property. You are building your prospect files this week!

Weeks 15 and 16—Qualify Your Prospects and Show Your Listings

During the next two weeks, you should be face to face with real live prospects. Use the practical guidelines given in Chapter 9 to help you qualify them. Chapter 11 gives you some strategies for showing the property, and Chapter 12 will prepare you to answer your prospects' questions and objections.

Weeks 17 and 18—Prepare Income Analysis Sheets for Your Most Promising Prospects

Once you have shown your listings to several prospects, prepare an income analysis work sheet showing just what the property will do for them. Work these out on an individual basis, and prepare them only for your most promising prospects. Chapter 15 gives you a step-by-step guide which will make these important weeks easy.

Weeks 19 and 20—Close the Sale with Your Income Analysis Sheet

During the next two weeks, sit down with your most promising prospects (the ones who have shown a genuine interest in the property they have seen), and go over your analysis sheet step by step. Show them how much profit the property provides for them.

If you have used the techniques in this Guide, you should be close to a sale. Don't be dismayed, however, if your first presentation doesn't result in a sale. Your batting average will improve considerably with time and practice.

Remember that this timetable is flexible. The following illustration will give you an idea of some of the minimum goals you should set for yourself during this 20-week schedule.

Your 20-Week Timetable			
Week	*Your activity during this period*	*Your minimum goal during this period*	*Your Silent Partner Chapter #*
1	Survey your area.	Inventory the types of income property available.	1
2, 3, and 4	Gather your listing leads.	Assemble 30 addresses and descriptions of potential listings.	2
5 and 6	Locate the owners of your leads.	Track down and list the names, addresses, and telephone numbers of the owners. Find at least 20 owners.	2
7 and 8	Contact the owners to find which of them will consider selling.	Convince at least 4 or 5 owners to sit down and discuss the prospects of a sale with you.	3
9, 10, and 11	Meet with the owners who will consider selling, and gather the property data.	Of the 4 or 5 leads from weeks 7 and 8, you should come away with the property data you need on at least 2 or 3 buildings.	3, 4, & 5
12 and 13	Prepare your operating statements.	Smooth out your property information and prepare operating statements on at least 2 or 3 buildings.	6
14	Advertise your best listing.	To receive at least 15 to 20 telephone calls and to make appointments to sit down with 8 to 10 investors.	10
15 and 16	Qualify your prospects and show your listings.	Qualify 8 to 10 investors and show your listings at least 5 to 6 times.	9, 11, & 12
17 and 18	Prepare income analysis sheets for your most promising prospects.	Prepare at least 3 individualized income analysis sheets.	15
19 and 20	Close the sale with your income analysis sheet.	To make at least 3 complete income analysis presentations.	15

Stick to this timetable, and refer regularly to your "silent guide" chapters for any assistance you need. If you find that you have not reached the minimum suggested goals for any particular step, extend the time period allocated for that step until you have reached that goal. By using this flexible and practical timetable, you will progress gradually in an orderly and systematic manner.

If you lean toward specializing full time in income property sales, it will pay you to investigate the active income property offices. These firms are usually made up of anywhere from 5 to 20 salespeople who are working together in a cooperative effort. They share each other's listings and knowledge, providing a large variety of listings and constant activity.

How an Income Office Operates

Listing Procedures

Each salesperson in the larger firms turns his listings in to the listing department, where they are edited, typed, and distributed to all of the salespeople. One person operating alone might be able to obtain and process ten new listings each month. If 20 percent of all listings obtained are really "salable," he has a very small portfolio to choose from. On the other hand, fifteen salespeople generating ten listings per month results in 150 new listings each month, of which (using the same 20 percent figure) approximately 30 can be classified as being salable. Each salesperson then has increased his portfolio fifteen fold, and has much more to offer his clients.

How Advertising and its Responses are Handled

Usually the office pays for and creates all of the advertising. The calls that come in on ads are distributed to the salespeople on a "round robin" basis. Each salesperson receives his fair share of the calls coming in.

The office secretary normally answers the incoming calls, and refers ad inquiries to the salespeople in the office. If a salesperson is out of the office or busy when his turn comes up, that call is referred to a salesperson who can take the call. The salesperson who misses his turn in this manner is assigned an extra caller when he returns and is available to receive calls.

How a Salesperson Acquires and Services Prospects

After affiliating with an income office and completing the training, the new salesperson accumulates a portfolio of prospects who want to invest their funds in real estate. The office will then provide the sales rep with a list of additional leads. The leads' down payment capabilities generally range from $20,000 to $1,000,000 and over. Their objectives, locational preferences and other desires vary greatly. By combining the many listings available with the prospects developed and provided by the office, the salesperson is able to get started quickly and effectively.

The larger offices generally have a well-trained staff to relieve the salesperson of unnecessary administrative functions. A typical large office is usually coordinated by the *president* or *general manager.* This person may be the owner and he is charged with the fiscal operations, and the authority and responsibility for the overall operation. The *sales manager* is responsible for coordinating the training and sales efforts of the company. The *listing department manager* is responsible for maintaining the proper volume of listings and for the editing, updating, and distribution of the listings and information concerning the listings. The *secretarial staff* is responsible for typing, filing, maintaining equipment, maintaining computerized and online databases, receiving visiting investors, and routing incoming phone calls. Usually two or three efficient secretaries can handle all of these functions effectively and have time left over for additional tasks that may come up.

The office should be geared to assisting the salespeople at each stage of negotiating the terms of a sale. There is usually a well-appointed conference room where the sales manager can sit down with the salesperson and principals involved to ready a transaction for a meeting between the principals and their lawyers.

How Commissions Are Split In Large-Income Offices

Many income offices operate on a 50/50 commission split. Fifty percent of the commission received is retained by the office to cover advertising, wages, supplies, computers, Internet connectivity, equipment, telephones, legal and accounting costs, rents, and profit. The other 50 percent is paid to the salespeople. If one of the salespeople listed the property, he usually receives anywhere from 10 to 25 percent of the commission. The selling salesperson receives the balance of the non-office 50 percent, which can range from 25 percent to 40 percent, depending on the lister's share.

It may surprise the residential broker that the lister sometimes receives as much as the selling salesperson. The lifeblood of this business, as you have seen, is listings.

The listing broker is involved with all negotiations. He usually does as much work as the selling broker, and he often does *more!*

Select an Office That Stresses Sales Training

If you decide to join an income property office, be sure to select one that is highly training-oriented. Determine whether weekly sales meetings and training sessions are conducted. The well-equipped office should provide its salespeople with training manuals and continuing sessions devoted to exploring the latest selling and listing techniques. Many offices use this guide to augment their training.

For example, at Peckham Boston we hold two general meetings each week, one on Wednesday morning from 9 to 11, and the second on Thursday afternoon from 3 to 6. These meetings double as training and working sessions.

For example, we conducted a 20-week exchange and taxation seminar. We took one listing at each meeting and analyzed the owner's present income picture after tax considerations. Then all of the salespeople put their heads together and "brainstormed" a solution to the owner's dilemma, proposing various moves he could make to improve his situation.

These meetings proved so productive and valuable that owners scramble to be added to our "waiting list" to have their ownership positions analyzed, and to receive our recommendations.

Things to Consider if You Decide to Join a Specialist

If you decide to join an income property firm, use the same amount of caution you did when you gave your spouse the diamond engagement ring. Be sure that you are joining a firm where the goals, ambitions, and ethics are compatible with your own.

When you interview with the firm, ask to meet some of the salespeople. Ask them whether they received a top-notch training program and whether the training continues. Ask them if they consider the firm the best in the area. Ask them if the boss is progressive and well respected in the community. Ask them if he runs the office by the golden rule. Then, before making your decision, call the local real estate board and ask them to name a few of the top income property firms in the area. Be sure that the firm you are considering is among those named. Also talk to anyone involved indirectly with the firm, such as lawyers, bankers, owners—anyone who can give you a solid, unbiased opinion of your potential future there.

Be careful of overly restrictive agreements—make sure that the agreement between you and the firm spells out your respective rights and obligations, but don't sign your natural rights away in your haste to get going. All the highly respected firms that I am familiar with have very fair contracts. If you have investigated a firm carefully, you can usually be sure that its agreement is not a one-way affair. If you're in doubt, have your lawyer look it over first.

Five Qualities That Spell Success

After you have made your decision to enter this exciting field, either on a limited basis or full scale, go at it with enthusiasm. The real estate profession, in itself, is both fascinating and rewarding—and income property brokerage is a phase of it that will stimulate you and improve your abilities every day. It's a practical, down-to-earth business for practical, down-to-earth people. Read what the late Dan MacKenzie of the *New England Real Estate Journal* said about the five qualities that determine the success of a salesperson:

MACKENZIE'S CORNER

Certainly there must be some truth and accuracy in the results of the real estate merchandising surveys made by a number of experts, when their conclusions are all so similar. One of the first axioms established is that there are five qualities that determine the success of a salesperson.

1. Initiative
2. Stability
3. Confidence
4. Enthusiasm
5. Perseverance

Herbert True, Marketing Specialist at Notre Dame University, found that—

44% of all salespeople quit trying to sell after the first call.
24% quit after the second call.

14% quit after the third call.

12% quit after the fourth call.

This means that 94% of all salespeople quit after the fourth call. But, 60% of all sales are made after the fourth call. This survey shows that 94% of all salespeople don't give themselves a chance at 60% of the perspective acceptance.

Stanley Edge, a prominent real estate merchandiser, said that the average home-buyer visits a house four times before buying, and spends eleven months shopping for it.

Dr. Gallup found in his nationwide survey that three out of ten salespeople get 70% of the business—or, to put it another way, seven out of ten salespeople get only 30% of the business. The conclusion? Personal selling in many real estate offices has been undernourished and underdeveloped, and because of this selling anemia, many prospects and potential sales have been lost. Personal selling needs some energetic fuel to give it oomph, to get it off the ground and into orbit!

MacKenzie's words are as true in income brokerage as in residential sales. You have been given the basic tools within these pages to cope successfully with listing and selling income property. Add to these your own five basic qualities, and you'll be off to a flying start:

- Show *initiative* when you take the first step.
- Develop *stability* to overcome some of the initial disappointments of "losing the big one."
- Be the successful salesperson who displays *confidence* in himself and his product when facing his first big prospect.
- Just as the successful salesperson in any field of endeavor requires and must display *enthusiasm,* you too must enter your new specialty with an abundance of this quality.
- Be a success, and prove your *perseverance* by making that fifth and sixth and seventh call. Apply persistent effort to selling income property, and you will be well rewarded financially; you will also have the pleasure of looking forward eagerly to what each new day will bring.

John M. "Jack" Peckham, CCIM, CIPS, RECS, is President of the Peckham Boston Advisory Company in Boston and serves as the Executive Director of the Real Estate CyberSpace Society. He is the author of several books on real estate marketing including this Guide. A columnist for the *Boston Sunday Herald* for nine years, his syndicated columns have appeared in over 100 papers nationwide and are widely distributed at various Internet web portals.

He served as Chairman of the Strategic Planning Committee of the million member National Association of Realtors® (NAR), is a Past President of the Massachusetts Association of Realtors®, and has been honored as its Realtor® of the Year.

Jack loves to sell real estate and has been involved directly in the sale of over a BILLION dollars of income property. Today he sells income property using the methods and tools revealed in this Guide as a one-man shop with no secretary and no sales people. He closed over $40,000,000 in sales in a recent twelve month period—and, thanks to these tools, he did this in 20% of his working time.

The balance of his time he spends directing the affairs of the 10,000 member Real Estate CyberSpace Society (www.REcyber.com). The Society develops tools such as those discussed in this Guide and awards the highly respected RECS (Real Estate CyberSpace Specialist) designation to members based on the current criteria.

CPSIA information can be obtained
at www.ICGtesting.com
Printed in the USA
BVOW11*2101261117
501143BV00008B/109/P